Innovation Management in Robot Society

T0298384

This book introduces cutting-edge issues and thought-provoking concepts on innovation management. It illustrates how robotic developments allow new powerful support functionalities for harnessing workplace innovations and new types of work in enterprises. In particular, low status jobs—heavy, repetitive and dangerous jobs—are disappearing and increasingly replaced by creative and meaningful work. It situates the research within theoretical developments and academic literature in business and management studies on innovation networks and partnerships.

The book then introduces the notion of "friction management," which invites us to re-examine creative tensions and explore how contradictions may spur or restrain change and innovation in this landscape. Innovation and change challenge established patterns, cultures, value systems, interests and network configurations—which creates a variety of frictions. There-fore, a theory of friction management is crucial, particularly in innovation-intensive industries, and can help professionals to understand change and the dynamics of innovation so that they can orchestrate events and learn to distinguish between the creative and negative frictions that can arise and that are important for change and the innovation process. Thus, the goal of friction management is to orchestrate, mobilize and (re)combine key organizational resources to strategically increase innovation capacity and promote dynamic renewal and creativity. It will be of interest to scholars and post-graduates in the areas of innovation management, sociology and business administration.

Kristian Wasen is a Researcher in Management Studies at the University of Gothenburg, Sweden.

Routledge Studies in Technology, Work and Organizations

Edited by David Preece, University of Teeside, UK.

Innovation Management in Robot Society

Kristian Wasen

Routledge
Taylor & Francis Group

NEW YORK AND LONDON

First published 2015
by Routledge
711 Third Avenue, New York, NY 10017
2 Park Square, Milton Park, Abingdon, Oxon OX14 4RN

First issued in paperback 2018

Routledge is an imprint of the Taylor & Francis Group, an informa business

Library of Congress Cataloging-in-Publication Data

Wasen, Kristian.
   Innovation management in robot society / Kristian Wasen.
      pages cm. — (Routledge studies in technology, work and organizations ; 10)
   Includes bibliographical references and index.
   1. Technological innovations—Management.   2. Human-robot interaction.   3. Robotics.   4. Robotics—Social aspects.   I. Title.
   HD45.W374 2015
   658.4'063—dc23   2014044585

ISBN 13: 978-1-138-61722-3 (pbk)
ISBN 13: 978-1-138-79004-9 (hbk)

Typeset in Sabon
by Apex CoVantage, LLC

To my mother

Contents

Acknowledgments

The initial inspiration for this book was an interdisciplinary conference in Oxford, England, on the timely topic "The Value of Work: Exploring Critical Issues." Many thanks to the three anonymous reviewers commissioned by Routledge for their very useful feedback. For commenting on the original book proposal and/or various parts of the manuscript, I would like to especially thank David Preece, Bernd Hofmaier, Jing Cai, Robin Cooper and Aant Elzinga, who spent their valuable time reading various chapters and whose sound criticism and valuable feedback helped improve the content and structure of this book.

Other friends and colleagues have generously provided ideas and encouragement over many years. There are too many to name individually but I am particularly grateful to participants at research seminars and workshops who inspired many interesting discussions and intellectual debates, especially members of the National Institute for Health Innovation and the Health Informatics Group at the University of Auckland. I communicated my initial thoughts to MBA students in the early phase of the book project and these discussions played a central role at lectures and seminars that I gave in the School of Business at the University of Aberdeen. These research and teaching programs in New Zealand and the UK—as well as my co-workers in the SMEC/STS Research Group at the University of Gothenburg—provided environments of academic support and stimulating intellectual curiosity.

The book is based on several case studies of organizational change and workplace innovation in various industries and sectors. Acknowledgement is given to all practitioners (respondents). At each local worksite, people were generous with their valuable time, for which I am very grateful. The Swedish Research Council for Health, Working Life and Welfare (FORTE) has provided financial support and backed my research on socio-robot organizations in working life.

1 Powerful Robot Laborers in the 21st Century

Robotic applications have radically transformed industrial manufacturing by allowing the sustainable mass production of standardized goods on assembly lines. The prevalence of robotics technology, however, is no longer limited to applications in industrial manufacturing. During the last decade, the proliferation of robotics technology in society has taken place (and, indeed, gained momentum) in agriculture and in almost every other industry—both in private and public sectors. Sectors such as finance (e.g., automated stock trading), transportation (e.g., self-steering vehicles and automation of underground metro systems), space exploration (e.g., robots on the moon), environment (e.g., robots used in oil platform recovery and underwater sanitation), energy (e.g., robots remotely controlled in hazardous events at damaged nuclear sites), commodities (e.g., underground mining), construction (e.g., teams of robots working at building sites), online gambling (e.g., virtual poker robots competing alongside human poker players), etc., represent additional examples of domains and sectors where virtual and physical "artificial robot workers" are being introduced and deployed in society.

By the term "robot society," we mean a new work culture in society, where robotic technology applications are available in almost all sectors and industries. Society applies the growing body of robot labor to boring, repetitive, heavy and dangerous work in standardized ways, and this powerful labor form is an important economic factor. Radical shifts are taking place in working life in the wake of swift technological change. This book addresses how several occupational groups in different industries and sectors (both private and public) are adjusting to work alongside a growing "army of artificial robot laborers," an emerging powerful source of economic labor in business and society. In the robot economy, robotic laborers work non-stop, untiringly and efficiently. The robot's superior functionality and ability to perform many tasks simultaneously are the distinguishing traits of artificial robot labor that can interact with social systems in new ways. Together, the new human-robot partnership appears to create a stronger and more powerful platform compared with prior manual work forms, as robotic functionality and social systems transcend some of the shortcomings of each of their elements. Robotic innovations also challenge traditional occupational structures, bring about new asymmetrical power relations and provoke workplace changes. Altogether, these case studies and examples suggest a robotic era, what we in this book summarize in the notion of a "robot society."

We are at a tipping-point, and developments in robotics will most likely have radical implications for change, innovation and competition in a growing number of work domains and businesses in the years to come. Advancements in robotics technology in working life even exist in some scientific jobs and R&D projects (see, e.g., automated DNA sequencing)—both at universities and at private research institutes. In modern global financial markets, fully automated robotic stock trading systems (so-called "high-frequency trading") are used on a daily basis. In automobile and transportation industries, we find a growing number of applications where robotic functions are capable of replacing human drivers or pilots. Driverless cars are already being developed and even tested on our roads. There are many more examples of applied robotics across the world.

Technological change in business and society thus involves physical and virtual robot labor, which is creating economic growth and the sustainable production of goods and services. Service robotics represents one the most quickly changing, innovative and creative sectors of the economy and symbolizes new and emergent domains for robotics technology. These new arrangements also represent radical changes for occupational groups in organizational practices and redefine the zones of innovation where new forms of creative and innovative work emerge. Indeed, it is the author's belief that organizational changes underpinning robotic innovations are fundamental processes essential to better understanding the powerful transformations in working life.

Despite extraordinary breakthroughs in robotics and automation systems over the last decades, we still know very little about how these technologies affect everyday professional work in various institutions. This book fills this gap in that it provides relevant empirical evidence from real-life applications of robotics in workplaces and provides a number of detailed and contextualized accounts of the mundane day-to-day tasks in practices of innovation that create economic worth across five different industries and study settings. This book aims to provide a novel perspective on the implications of modern robotics in workplace contexts. It is based on a critical analysis of the innovation management literature and in-depth case studies of organizational change and innovation.

In this book, we will show that these technological changes represent a new organizational challenge that is redefining the nature of the economic worker and which, in turn, is disrupting traditional power relationships. Whilst a few institutional domains are already strongly robotized, other areas are just beginning to see the dawn of new uses of robotics. In these emerging areas, it is important to highlight the social choices and decisions that shape and reconfigure workplaces locally in new and unexpected ways. Just like computers in the prior decades were dispersed and put to use in an increasing number of worksites, even recently more and more aggressively across various businesses, now, by the same token, "artificial robot workers" (Wasen, 2013) are beginning to be put to use in a growing number of segments of the economy.

This book explores the second wave of robotics after industrial robotics. It highlights an important topic that is gaining increased strategic significance in the production of modern products and services. The outcomes of this research advance our knowledge about how humans and robots collaborate and how robots allow humans to pursue more challenging and innovative work. Extensive workplace studies and in-depth interviews that are based on an ethnographic approach can contribute new insights into value creation through new forms of socio-robotic organization in key application areas.

This book not only contributes to the existing scholarship on change and innovation management but also aims to advance the study of *socio-robot work organizations* (SRWO) in the service industries (see, e.g., Barrett *et al.*, 2011; Jamie, 2013; Wasen, 2005b, 2010; Weiss *et al.*, 2011). The analysis adopts a bottom-up approach to understanding innovation work, particularly, in small-scale enterprises and production settings. Aside from gaining a better and more nuanced insight into major technological transformations and the interrelation of these with wider business trends and political/economic developments in society at large, the aim of the book is also to stimulate conversation and debate on current rationales, strategies and business practices governing workplace change, competition and innovation in working life.

INNOVATION STUDIES

Joseph Schumpeter has addressed the paradoxical nature of innovation in his seminal work *The Theory of Economic Development*, in which he elaborates on the contradiction that while innovations bring about business opportunities, they may also profoundly disrupt the economy, where one dominant logic or value system is replaced by another. He draws on this important insight in his formulation of a definition of innovation, which, apart from the opening of novel markets and the launch of new goods, also includes organizational issues such as new forms of production and "the carrying out of a new organization of any industry" (Schumpeter, 1934: 66). Innovation involves the recombination of resources and a disruptive force of "creative destruction," where deeply held cultural (or industrial) assumptions are challenged and where recombination eventually substitutes markets for products and abolishes older innovations (ibid., 1934).

Schumpeter's legacy is visible in most of the current research on innovation. In Christensen's (2003) conceptual expansion, for example, the notion "disruptive innovation" replaces the earlier notion of "disruptive technology" (Christensen, 1997), representing a shift in terminology from technology to innovation. This conceptual development suggests that novel technologies do not necessarily disrupt markets or industries, but rather, that it is the underlying business models enabled by new technologies (and by other innovations) that profoundly disrupt markets and institutions.

Indeed, more recent work on innovation has reconnected with Schumpeter's early ideas of innovation as a collective accomplishment involving many different players, which together may recombine their ideas into new products, processes and service offerings. Following Schumpeter, while current innovation management (hereafter IM) research has been influenced by such broad-sweeping ideas and macro-scale explanations in political science and economics, more recent work has reassessed the role of disruption and understands it to also be the impact and mechanism behind creative destruction on the organizational level of innovation. IM scholars have shifted focus back to the role of organizational dynamics in innovation practices.

"Combinatorics" is a term used in economic sociology, management science and STS (Science, Technology, Society) research (Stark, 2009). It captures the productive outcome of clashes that may provoke disruptive innovation. Studies on combinatorics look at the creative recombination of knowledge as well as how such rearrangements are either contested or reinforced in social systems. Combinatorics highlights that humans and their interpretative and analytical skills are deeply involved in innovation processes and that such processes are fundamentally enmeshed in both individual and collective activities.

Recent research by Berggren *et al.* (2011) addresses some of the critical dilemmas facing international technology-based firms in different industries. Berggren and colleagues explain the paradoxes of the knowledge management subject and develop new theories on innovation and networking. They also explain the integration of multilevel technological knowledge and the role of real-world complexity (e.g., "computational complexity"). Technology is only one of many more elements of the more widely defined social system that we understand organizational innovation practices to be.

Innovation studies is a multifaceted topic, and the innovation phenomenon in science and society may take the form of a new piece of equipment or a novel way of accomplishing work, or may entail radically different models to collaborate within and beyond organizational contexts. This research monograph scrutinizes organizational innovation, that is, how robotic innovations are adopted and used to generate new forms of work practices that create social benefits and economic value. Thus, the focus here is on organizational innovations that unite, or merge, technological and socio-robotic elements of novelty. Just because an innovation has been launched does not mean that the process of innovation stops.

WHY DO TECHNOLOGIES HAVE TO BE ARRANGED AND INNOVATIONS MANAGED?

There is a wide consensus that the generation of breakthrough innovations is absolutely necessary for the survival of organizations in an increasingly competitive global market. Carneiro (2000: 92) summarizes innovation broadly as the "search for, and the discovery, experimentation, and development of new technologies, new products and/or services, new production processes, and new organizational structures." Most simply, innovations represent something new. Innovations involve a conduit processual change (O'Sullivan and Dooley, 2008) of some sort that adds value to a given system (Wang and Kafouros, 2009). In the business context, innovation used to be understood as "[the] specific tool of entrepreneurs, the means by which they exploit change as an opportunity for a different business or a different service. It is capable of being presented as a discipline, capable of being learned, capable of being practiced." (Drucker, 1985: viii) However, innovation clearly goes beyond entrepreneurial activities and is thus a much broader concept. This is reflected in the following definition of innovation as "the application of practical tools and techniques that make changes, large and small, to products, processes, and services that results in the introduction of something new for the organization that adds value to customers and contributes to the knowledge store of the organization" (O'Sullivan and Dooley, 2008: 5). It follows that innovation can also be seen as the explanatory concept for the commercialization of new products and services, which in turn provides central incentives and opportunities for international trade (Kafouros *et al.*, 2009).

The noun innovation steams from the Latin words *innovare* and *innovationem* and refers to the process of renewing something. Innovation is a commonly used term in contemporary language and is not merely confined to scientific work and business terminology. It is attributed different meanings depending on subject matter and the context of usage. Péres-Bustamante (1999: 10) makes a distinction between innovations and inventions: "The invention is the discovery that may result in a product/service launched onto the market or a new production process. Precisely, the first introduction of a product or service to the market or the first commercial use of a production process, regardless of their novelty to the market, are innovations." Of course, there are instances where we may find scientific ideas that are true paradigm innovations, but that may not be commercially exploited in a market place, but still may have a great impact in business and society.

From the viewpoint of business studies and organizational theory, innovations are founded on social processes where practitioners in social systems identify and define problems and create new knowledge to creatively solve them. More recently, innovation has been defined by Tidd et al. as "a process of turning opportunity into new ideas and putting these into widely used practice" (2009: 16). In their taxonomy, they distinguish between four dimensions of change: process innovation, position innovation, paradigm innovation and product innovation (Bessant and Tidd, 2007). We are primarily concerned with process and paradigm innovations, where the former refers to new arrangements for delivering and producing products and services, while the latter refers to innovations that challenge traditional assumptions and myths about the mechanisms of organizations.

Bessant and Tidd (2007) see shifts in business logics as representing a form of innovation, and they refer to changes in long-held business and professional assumptions as cases of "paradigm innovation" that may challenge a dominant modus operandi. Vedin (1994) maintains that innovations do not need to be material property but can consist of breakthrough ideas. Thus, an innovation may also be a creative idea or concept that is brought to the marketplace and to the economy (on "conceptual innovation," see Vedin, 2007, 2014). Van de Ven's definition has been adopted by many scholars in the business studies literature, and it is particularly relevant here because it includes both the abovementioned meanings and establishes innovation as the social process of ". . . the development and implementation of new ideas by people who over time engage in transactions with others in an institutional context" (Van de Ven, 1986: 591). This definition is useful because it embraces the institutional and networking context that surrounds the creation of innovations. Another conceptualization of innovation is provided by Nonaka and Takeuchi (1995), who see it as the art of deviating from something already known. Thus, innovation is a social process that can be facilitated by linking together individuals with different backgrounds and preferences. Andriopoulos and Dawson (2009: 33) stress the processual dimension of innovation and argue that there is no clear-cut distinction between the three interrelated concepts of change, creativity and innovation.

In the management literature, there are many distinctions between different forms of innovation. Innovations are usually classified as either incremental or radical (see, e.g., Carneiro, 2000; Dewar and Dutton, 1986; Swanson and Ramiller, 2004). Research elaborating on the distinction between radical and incremental innovations is relevant for conceptualizing breakthrough innovations (Brettel and Cleven, 2011). In the IM literature, a "breakthrough innovation" (Rice *et al.*, 1998) represents a change that has a large impact on businesses and markets in society, and such innovations are sometimes referred to as radical innovations. Coccia (2006), in this context, refers to an innovation's intensity and sets out different levels of innovation intensity ranging from "light" to "revolutionary." Innovating, that is, the process of creating breakthrough innovations, in conjunction with the development of new knowledge and skills, has been described by many notable authors in the business and management literature over the past two decades as representing the most important future source of competitive advantage (see, e.g., Bartlett and Ghoshal, 1999).

Indeed, perhaps the most common distinction in the IM literature is that between incremental and radical innovations. Incremental innovations are seen as minor but important improvements and changes applied to existing products, services or processes. Radical innovations are more disruptive and subversive than incremental ones and may lead to great opportunities and benefits, but they are also more risky. Péres-Bustamante (1999) draws on a sports analogy to introduce a similar division between defensive versus offensive innovations. Defensive innovations are focused on defending an organization's position and market shares against its competitors. Offensive innovations, in contrast, are preventive measures to secure and explore new opportunities. These offensive innovations can eliminate potential competitors in the marketplace, for example, through a new product, service or business model. There is an element of risk attached to these innovations because they can make previously successful innovations redundant. Thus, the diverse and unpredictable effects innovations can have in the marketplace make them more complex to study (Carneiro, 2000). Boisot (1998) notes that many radical innovations are anchored in groundbreaking work by outsiders, such as entrepreneurs and small-scale enterprises.

Innovation today also involves dealing with an extended and rapidly advancing scientific frontier that fragments markets across the globe, political uncertainties, regulatory instabilities and a set of competitors who are increasingly coming from unexpected directions. Innovation management increasingly involves bringing together different people and the knowledge they carry through building and running effective internal and external networks (Bessant and Phillips, 2013). Bessant and Phillips have presented one of the most recent distinctions on innovation practices, in which a distinction is made between "innovation capability" and "innovation networks," where the former refers to innovative capabilities and processes of generating and combining knowledge (cf. the discussion on combinatorics earlier in the chapter), and the latter refers to the significance of developing new dynamic capabilities linked to the management of network arrangements (i.e., the capability of managing innovation and the various managerial actions of harnessing innovation).

Obviously, it is not viable to summarize and discuss the broad diversity of taxonomies and forms innovation can take. Given that this book focuses on the social dimensions of innovation management, we decide to focus on the significance of studying and analyzing innovation networks and partnerships. Because technology does not innovate, the chapter instead draws attention to the significance of wider professional networks and partnerships that shape present and future processes and practices of innovation. Thus, in the next section, we will explore what innovation networks mean and why these are important to acknowledge in IM research. These are the theories discussed in this book, and they are broadened with novel concepts.

WHY NETWORK INNOVATION AND PARTNERSHIPS?

Early studies and pioneering work in the IM field were largely preoccupied with research and development (R&D) activities, and IM has therefore partly been equated or reduced to R&D management in prior generations of scholarship on innovation. However, IM is no longer seen to be limited to well-defined R&D projects but also extends to activities in the wider societal and industrial landscape. More recent generations of IM studies have adopted a broader approach informed by other disciplines, such as change management and organizational theory, to focus on science and technology (S&T) as well as partnerships and network collaboration between organizations (Tidd, 1997). It is now possible to maintain that the emphasis on multicultural factors is increasingly vital to making sense of how firms are able to cope with turbulent market conditions in a globalized world. In recent years, scholars have discussed the effects of higher volatility and uncertainty in the global marketplace. For innovation management, this means new challenges where focus is placed on adaptability, acceleration and speed (Bessant *et al.*, 2005, Tidd *et al.*, 2009). Responsiveness, swiftness to change, and flexibility have become the new fashionable words, and being able to "speed up" innovation, in particular, is considered key for business enterprises to maintain a competitive edge in the industry.

In turbulent times, radical innovations should, at least in theory, primarily be encouraged because they can potentially yield the highest returns on investment (Vedin, 1994). That the demand of products in the marketplace can rapidly subvert this also means that assurance of steady earnings generated by incremental innovations is no longer granted. If not for a turbulent and volatile market, such earnings would otherwise be fairly easy to calculate and thus assess in terms of a business exposure to risk (Vedin, 1994). Thus, in today's digital economy, firms operate increasingly in a dynamic, complex and chaotic environment in which the flow of resources in the international global marketplace is highly unpredictable. As we will see, chaos will not necessarily lead to negative outcomes. From an innovation theory perspective, chaos can trigger change for innovation. Biemans (1992), similarly to Morgan, sees a link between chaos theory and the nonlinear development of innovations. An adequate level of chaos, Biemans observes, can contribute to the discovery of new innovative patterns and the introduction of new views, a process wherein human creativity and chaos in the environment interplay in a dynamic fashion. Morgan (1997) also elaborates on the relationship between radical and incremental innovations and notes that within nonlinear complex systems, incremental innovations may serve as catalysts for radical innovations, where small but crucial changes, implemented at the right time, can initiate major changes in organizations. In theory, if a system such as an organization or a network has a high degree of inherent complexity and instability in its modus operandi, it increases the likelihood of change. Moreover, due to the internal complexity in nonlinear systems, "random disturbances can produce unpredictable events and relationships that reverberate throughout a system, creating novel patterns of change" (Morgan, 1997: 262).

Traditionally, the process involving the development of innovations (both material and immaterial) has either been locally situated within a specific country, where the innovation has met certain national needs, or developed in a centralized corporate location for a global market (Bartlett and Ghoshal, 1999). However, the new global situation in which the technological environment is changing at an accelerating rate also practically requires that organizations must find new ways to speed up the development of innovations. In the future, it will be increasingly difficult for companies to make revenues solely by producing established physical goods and services. Instead, in the longer term, the emphasis on value creation will increasingly be transferred to innovations and innovative activities to strengthen the continuing competitiveness of the firm, in which knowledge and development is promoted.

Following this progression of the field from an early focus on R&D management to later developments that stress the emergent character of innovation as well as the collective (social) aspects implies that IM now includes wider issues such as networking and partnerships. One of the present challenges in the management of innovation is how to pursue local and global networking. This progression also means that a greater emphasis has been placed on the firm's own "core competencies" as well as the firm's ability to track down matching competencies that it does not itself have (Leonard-Barton, 1998; Prahalad and Hamel, 1990). Such networking across "dynamic capabilities" (Teece and Pisano, 1994) within this turbulent and challenging landscape, in turn, entails the challenge of allowing a wide range of actors and partners involved to collaborate productively and efficiently across professional, organizational and cultural boundaries.

This book, however, maintains that the majority of IM research has largely neglected aspects of politico-cultural practices (e.g., the multicultural forms of innovation), specifically how creative tensions and social frictions arise when professional, organizational and cultural boundaries are crossed. Because innovations include a wide range of actors with complementary competencies, tensions will erupt despite all the best efforts among managements to smooth them out. An increasing number of innovation arrangements are embedded in a complex web of relationships and global networks (both formal and informal). Therefore, we need to better understand heterogeneity and multiplicity as well as the positive and negative tensions that emerge. Doing so will allow us not only to theorize the impeding sources of organizational innovation (for example, the stably reinforced and obstructing "lock-ins" that innovations sometimes challenge) but also recognize spheres of expert activity, or interaction zones between humans and robots, where management should focus its efforts.

Tensions, however, can also be beneficial to innovation, and this book advances the argument that social and cultural-cognitive frictions may be supportive and productive and may enable dynamic and complex innovation processes. In acknowledging the role of creative tensions and social frictions, innovation management requires balancing between change and continuity, tension and relief, long-term prospects and short-term benefits, and internal activities and external networking, among others. Lindholm (1990) argues that it is possible to identify two contrary forces in both organizations and in nature. The first force is sluggish and acts to maintain the status quo, while the other acts on adoption, change and development. In biological terms, preservation stands in contrast to evolution. Both forces, of course, complement each other and play important roles, but in different ways. Tardiness is necessary so that a system (biological, social or technological) will not fall apart, and innovation and change are necessary so that the system will not stagnate and solidify. Organizational change and innovation management are therefore complex phenomena and also often represent a contradictory multilevel endeavor.

Organizational innovation specifically focuses on the complex balancing acts that influence processes of innovation (i.e., how to organize and innovative work and orchestrate technologies) rather than the objects or outcomes of innovation work as such. Thus, the emphasis here is not on innovation networks as material and objectified properties, which the popularized terms "knowledge infrastructure," "virtual networking" or "knowledge networks," for example, may suggest. Rather, the emphasis is on the unfolding multilevel and multi-paradoxical processes by which organizational innovations are envisaged, enhanced, personalized, locally optimized and productively utilized. Creating such innovation fundamentally depends on complementary expertise and different competencies among network members in working life.

As we will see in the next chapters, it is difficult to straightforwardly arrange, develop and orchestrate organizational innovations. Thus, robotic technologies and workplace innovations are not so easily "managed" and orchestrated. Socio-economic and technical dimensions are intertwined in organizational innovation processes, and development of new robotics technology, for example, depends on the contributions of small groups of professionals as well as powerful actors in the socio-economic regulatory domain. It was noted earlier in this chapter that conventional models of innovation partnerships and business networks generally have been reluctant to take into account the *professional tensions* and *social frictions* that drive change and creativity. Hence, we have seen an increase of theories on the discipline of innovation management that assume homogeneity and steadiness rather than heterogeneity and volatility. Innovation networks and partnerships are characteristically simply seen to be formal contexts that allow the exchange of business transactions, but their significance to organizational innovation and creativity is much broader.

While innovation management is an established field of knowledge, what is new about this research monograph is the focus on robotics technology and what it means for innovative processes in the workplace and the emergence of new jobs and new types of work. As we can see from the case illustrations, many groundbreaking robotics innovations and organizational changes require that many professionals and a multitude of firms and public organizations be involved. Each of the professionals and enterprises that participate and contribute often have something unique to offer, which stresses the importance of friction, variance and heterogeneity in networks. In particular, the book demonstrates the significance of bottom-up change and radical workplace innovations. As such, the book aims to fill an important gap in studies on innovation and creativity and the literature on network theory in management research. Having situated the research and offered an indication of the focal analytical themes explored and empirical issues addressed in this monograph, the next sections will provide a rationale for the research studies, followed by an outline of the book and an overview of each of the chapters.

TODAY, ROBOTS ARE NOT INNOVATORS!

Despite sophisticated robotics technology, innovation management is a laborious process that demands social involvement, creative input and complementary expertise and knowledge. Once we realize that robots are not "innovators" today and that the change dynamics profoundly include important socio-political aspects in innovation management that extend beyond this technology, it becomes clear that the focus of any analysis must be placed on those influential social and cultural systems that either promote or obstruct innovation processes. Some of the more prescriptive views in management theory assume innovation to be quite a linear and unidirectional process, and they often conceptualize innovation as a "top-down" practice that is seen to have a definitive and distinguishable "end point" within organizational contexts. From this perspective, data and information flow along predefined hierarchical channels in a "top-down" manner. In contrast, some scholars have dismantled "top-down" innovation strategies to change and innovation and have re-conceptualized innovation and change management as an open-ended, unpredictable and non-deterministic endeavor. In Dawson's (1994) processual-contextual framework on change, the social uptake of technology and the development of innovation are seen to be complex, nonlinear, and multifaceted processes. Because different worldviews, perspectives and interests co-exist, change and innovation will typically be negotiated in social sensemaking events.

Dawson's (1994) study of technological adoption at an Australian laundry firm illustrates how change, creativity and organizational innovation are inseparable. This firm identified the need to modernize its operations to remain competitive and to secure its commercial future in the industry. Members of this firm pursued new innovative combinations and experimentation to cope with technological challenges and dysfunctions, but they managed to find solutions because of high user participation. The case study findings thus illustrate how this Australian firm managed to successfully employ new advanced technology in a new organizational arrangement that resulted in increased productivity. However, this success was not to be attributed to technology alone: "It was not simply the technology that determined innovations in the system's design and new forms of work organization, but it was the interplay between the context in which change was taking place, the generation of new ideas that were realizable, the politics of negotiating acceptable change routes, and the characteristics of the available technology . . ." (Andriopoulos and Dawson, 2009: 33). This argument nicely summarizes the three main elements of Dawson's (1994) processual framework on change, which includes the context, substance and politics of change. This case study also illustrates that innovative work often necessitates the creation of new local solutions (e.g., new ideas and optimizations adapted to local circumstances).

Similarly, in STS research and in STI studies (Science, Technology and Innovation), scholars have adopted critical sociological approaches to reflexively dismantle notions of technological determinism and have placed emphasis on the combination of strategic choices and intricate power politics that come into play in the design of technology. They therefore stress the social construction dimension of technology and how social systems actively shape and reshape technological circumstances (see e.g., Bijker and Law, 1992; MacKenzie and Wajcman, 1985). Löwstedt (1985) critically assesses the treatment of technology in management studies, especially those approaches adopted by the contingency school in organizational theory, and argues that the interaction between cultural and social factors and how these shape work organization should be highlighted more in frameworks on technology. Critically oriented approaches on technological change are particularly useful in that they also provide a frame of reference for comprehending reluctance to and potentially blocking forces against the adoption and use of technology and for exploring potential conflicts and competing strategic choices in the process of innovation and change.

The culture and politics of change and innovation are two key dimensions that are often missing in mainstream studies on innovation management. These concepts, however, may explain forces that hinder or enable change. For example, Andriopoulos and Dawson (2009: 268) argue that "strong cultures *per se* are not necessarily conductive to generating and complementing ideas in organizations; rather, what is required is strong cultures that foster innovation-enhancing norms and at the same time promote the social cohesion necessary for turning ideas into product innovations." This suggests that it is not enough to just generate ideas; innovation ultimately relies on the integration of creative ideas so that they gain the necessary collective approval and support within a social system to be implemented into day-to-day affairs.

Zuboff (1988), in studies of adoption and usage of information technology and automation in workplaces in the U.S., notes both how individual choices actively shape and reconfigure organizational arrangement and channel change and development in certain directions and how occupational, economic and socio-political elements are brought together in unforeseen ways both at micro- and macro-levels. The key role these socio-political elements play has amply been summarized by Fleck *et al.*, who conducted empirical studies on robotics and automation applications in British workplaces:

> Our historical analyses of the actual development process shows that while the dreams and philosophies of the promoters of technologies may inspire the initial form of a technology, as soon as it is adopted and implemented within industry it becomes subject to a much wider range of forces. These include the objectives and strategies of industrial managers and practitioners, the social and productive conditions within the organisation, and the practices and relationships between groups of labour, all of which take place within the context of constant shifts in economic and political conditions in society at large. These forces in the implementation process act upon the offerings of promoters and designers. This interaction serves to reconstitute technologies and produce new 'states-of-the-art' solutions, which are then again modified in response to the industrial conditions they meet.
>
> (Fleck *et al.*, 1989: 23)

From this vantage point, innovations are seen to be historically vibrant processes that unfold across interlinked events and are directly and/or indirectly shaped by situated actors in the contested terrain of workplace transformation and the politics and culture of technological and organizational change. Moreover, these approaches highlight how management and workers tactfully and tactically use (e.g., control and manipulate) technology to achieve desired business goals as well as to accomplish their own ends and promote certain arrangements to protect their own interests. Preece (1995) notes that technological adoption and use are constrained by contextual factors and are influenced within a social system's politico-cultural system:

> The success (however it may be defined) of the new technology adoption process therefore depends upon the appropriateness and quality of the non-technological changes which go hand in hand with the technical changes, and upon the social economic and organizational contexts into which that technology is in due course introduced.
>
> (Preece, 1995: 235)

From this viewpoint, professionals and managers are never completely informed and perfectly rational, but organizational members strive to do their best to seek out new optimizations in order to innovatively and creatively solve their practical dilemmas and cope with industry-specific challenges and organizational predicaments. It is imperative to understand cultural norms and restrictions placed on actors (power-holders). Thus, the narrative is much more multifaceted than firms simply implementing well-defined solutions (e.g., technological platforms) in their workplaces. Robots must be "up-dated," and the new ideas calls for local solutions and changes in production processes (optimizations) and organizational arrangement, which is a complex, fluid and locally situated process of innovation captured in Fleck's (1991) term "innofusion."

In this chapter, attention has been directed at a selective range of literature in the management science domain to situate the research. However, space limitations preclude the viability of treating all the aspects on the link among technological change, creativity and innovation with the detail they indeed merit. We have noted how innovation networks and IM scholarship are interconnected with other fields in social science, such as organizational theory and related theories on change processes in organizations and technology-rich workplace domains (for an overview on critical approaches to change and technology studies, see Preece *et al.*, 2000). Students who want to grasp some of the most taxing IM challenges will benefit from acquainting themselves with more critically oriented sociological analyses in fields related to IM research.

The book reviews various work characteristics related to technologically artificial economic laborers (i.e., robots), and it elucidates the association with current methods and creative practices (e.g., digital optimizations) as well as some of the management trends and fads. The book seeks to unmask the hype of some simplified models in the IM field, or at least nuance these models. Some of these theories draw on rather familiar notions in management theory, while other theoretical discussions develop complementary ways of seeing and exploring ideas that are relatively "fresh" (i.e., unconventional) and that will likely generate more questions than definitive answers or "prescriptive solutions" as managerial advice. While entrepreneurial activities are often interchanged with new technology in popular debates, and while innovation is sometimes synonymously used with technological change, it is argued that robotics technology is not simply about technological innovation. As we noted in the discussion of radical innovation, technology is often a product that has been facilitated or inspired by organizational innovations.

While robots certainly provide important supportive functions and productive outcomes, today's robots are not "innovators" in the true sense of the word; rather, the popular phrase "to innovate" is (still, at least) a significantly distinctive trait of human activity, creativity and ingenuity. However, the argument in this book suggests that the idea of a single isolated human innovator also needs to be challenged. Most of the recent technological developments and spectacular advancements have become increasingly complex and difficult to "manage" in the sense that they rely on the combination of a variety of domains of expertise and specialized knowledge, and it is often necessary to integrate a multitude of different sub-components in high-tech innovations. The power of "innovating" is therefore largely rendered possible because of the emerging properties of a social interaction that is situated in network collaboration, where complementary resources and activities are brought together to jointly create something that each of the network participants could not create by themselves. Thus, modern innovation management is understood as a complex organizational and socio-cultural undertaking.

This book provides empirically informed accounts of parallel and multilevel partnership and network processes that enable professionals to create new combinations and interpretations that fuel innovative optimization and the creative tweaking of robotics technology and work processes. To identify what is missing from the mainstream debate on robotics technology and its social and organizational implications in the workplace, it is essential to understand what is taking place on the micro-level of institutional change when professionals pursue analytic and creative discovery work in the teaching hospitals, medical faculties, retirement villages, milk production farms and administrative library offices of academic institutions. The subsequent chapters in the book will demonstrate how this can be done by drawing on recent examples of innovations in robotics. The central insights and lessons learned from empirical case studies inform current scholarship on the management of change and innovation.

New and emerging developments in robotics have been studied by the author in several different sectors. The case studies draw on original research findings, interviews and on-site observations from several workplace studies in research projects undertaken by the author between 2004 and 2014. Based on original, field-based research that used ethnographic approaches (the research methodology adopted in a series of case studies to explore work practices and is described elsewhere; see Wasen, 2010) to understand changes in everyday work, this book offers a unique insight and analysis of new emerging forms of innovation work. Thus, this research monograph highlights the processes and practices of change and innovation in several industries and sectors. The empirical part of the book offers a detailed socially scientific analysis of processes of robotization, that is, how robotics technology is creatively put to use in day-to-day practice. All these workplace studies have helped to suggest the notions outlined in this book, and also served to anchor these notions concretely in the real-world contexts of robotics. By drawing on original case study material, this monograph highlights a wide range of key areas for robotization in business and society. These cases demonstrate how goods and service production is accomplished innovatively in novel arrangements.

OVERVIEW OF CHAPTERS

To appreciate the diverse nature of innovation practices and processes in working life, it is necessary at the outset to outline the implications of formal as well as informal arrangements of innovation networks and partnerships. Chapter 2 discusses the key characteristics of innovation networks. It begins by introducing a micro-level perspective on inter-organizational networking and change, and the remainder of the chapter aims to dismantle some popular network theories and models. We also focus on the prescriptive and critical management literature on Communities of Practice (COP) in this chapter. Unlike mainstream conceptions of business networks, COP highlights informal networking, where joint participation and social interactions aim to accelerate professional learning, change and the generation of new ideas.

Next, in Chapter 3, attention is turned to the social forces and cultural dimensions of innovation networks and networking, and the discussion presents an alternative structure for thinking about creative tensions and frictions in the management of change and innovation. A new concept is introduced, namely "network friction," not as a distinct, narrow definition but rather as a useful analytical perspective to account for the varied scope of action potentials that are derived from institutional variety, professional frictions and creative tensions. Inspired by the maxim *unity in diversity*, this chapter nuances network theory by reinstating the value of epistemic tensions and cultural diversity as well as the role of asymmetrical power relations. Thus, this chapter summarizes the theoretical discussion and sets the stage for the subsequent chapters that aim to explore the implications of robotics technology and new forms of work.

The empirical material in Chapters 4, 5, 6 and 7 presents the primary case study data on robotics applications and includes empirically rich accounts of robotic innovation and new ways of work. The reader is introduced to concise case descriptions of real-life robotization processes in both public and private sectors. The cases illustrate that automation and robotics innovation have no definitive "end-point" but unfold in both new and unexpected ways.

In Chapter 8, attention is turned to the managerial implications of robotics innovation and how the nature of professional work is changing. The discussion presents a structure and conceptual apparatus for thinking about the paradoxical nature of technological and social change and further develops the theoretical issues related primarily, but not exclusively, to the notion of friction. This chapter establishes a bridge from the preceding meta-theoretical discussions and abstract arguments about the paradoxical nature of variety and unity, or tension and harmony, in innovation networks to a specific review of the role of network friction and its implications for change and innovation. The notion of friction management invites us to examine creative tensions and how contradictions may spur as well as restrain innovation in this new landscape.

In the concluding chapter that follows, the main themes and points of the book are recapitulated and summarized. Workplace change is a dynamic pursuit and, at times, a contested terrain, and the radical transformation of work forms in light of technological and institutional change suggests new partnerships and interactive forms of work between humans and robots. Additional examples of robotics are provided, and we see how robotics technology is already used in nearly every industry. We also see how it is further developed and adapted to new domains of work, allowing the conclusion that we already live in a "robot society."

2 Innovation Networks and Partnerships

The societal transition toward global, changeable, fluid and temporal partnerships signals a reconsideration of the strategic elements of innovation management. This chapter addresses the following two questions: How can firms channel their activities beyond conventional institutional boundaries to harness the capabilities of innovation networks and business partnerships? And what are the contrary forces and tensions that typically evolve over time in inter-organizational networks? The first question primarily concerns corporate strategy; the second, culture and political will. This chapter begins by introducing a micro-level perspective on inter-organizational networking and change, and the remainder of the chapter aims to dismantle some popular network theories and models.

UNDERSTANDING PARTNERSHIPS: NETWORKS AND NETWORKING

The management of change, innovation and technology increasingly relies on joint partnerships. Innovation partnerships consist of multiple "actors" ("network partners") where one of the goals is to counter the totality of the shortcomings of each actor. Thus, partners come together because they bring unique and often complementary abilities and resources to a partnership, and they jointly pursue collaboration to harness and drive innovative activities that can fulfill anticipated business outcomes. Most simply, a network is understood to be a metaphor that describes an interconnected structure (think, for example, of how a spider's web is organized). The term "network" commonly illustrates various structural properties (a "hybrid network" sometimes suggests the mixture of various shifting properties). Hence, a network comprises a set of nodes (e.g., actors and resources) and links that join them. In this sense, networks show the relation among a number of factors and/or elements to each other (e.g., network relations in support structures for academic entrepreneurship; see Bourelos *et al.*, 2012). By contrast, the term "networking" highlights the dynamic processes and "emergent properties" of a network (Bessant and Phillips, 2013; Wasen and

Lodaya, 2012). In modern network theory, increased attention is drawn to the ambiguity and inherently unstable ("nonlinear") properties in network structures. By bringing together a variety of individuals and professional groups, business networks are not only multidimensional but also multi-faceted arrangements where desirable and undesirable states co-exist, e.g., they simultaneously involve both trust and distrust/mistrust (Dirks *et al.*, 2009), as well as both collaboration and competition. Recent research has also observed significant changes in the global business environment that call into question some of the old assumptions of mainstream approaches both within and outside the network management field. There is a growing recognition that in many instances, networking events cannot be fully "controlled," "managed" or predicted and that the very outcomes (e.g., costs and benefits) that network interactions generate cannot be known by actors *ex ante*. In such unstable conditions, it therefore becomes imperative for institutions to develop a capacity to rapidly adapt and to aptly change. Modern enterprises must increasingly cope with highly uncertain and volatile conditions, which are increasingly complex. Such conditions are complex because uncertainties emerge in both the local and the global business environment, where seemingly ambiguous forces and unpredictable patterns (economic, political, social, etc.) evolve.

The unpredictable patterns and circumstances are in themselves shaped by speedy international "hyper-transformations." As a case in point, consider the avalanche-like increase in the global supply of highly educated people—or even people with a doctoral degree—around the globe. This significant change is reflected not only in a massive increase in the percentage of technical schools and universities but also in the rapidly growing numbers of knowledge-intensive firms and research institutions pursuing advanced development and groundbreaking innovations. In times of increased change and radical shifts in innovation and customer requirements, organizations need to realign their traditional business strategies to become more interconnected and less hierarchical. Less hierarchical organization increases the capacity of institutions to better and more efficiently adapt to rapidly changing environments. Thus, firms start to look beyond old boundaries and conventional forms of business organization to becoming increasingly nimble, innovative and receptive to change. As Dawson notes, no company is an island:

> The importance of developing a network of relations within organizations, across departmental and operational divisions or sites, . . . signal the emergence of collaborative organizational networks. . . . It is not simply about developing networks based on mutual trust and reciprocity, but also about maintaining and managing change within a less clearly defined unit of operation. As a result, the successful management of change will, in future, require negotiation and consultation beyond the company in which change is taking place. It is change within the

collaborative network of organizations which will pose new challenges for management and will ultimately shape the development of competitive strategies for companies operating in the global market place.

(Dawson, 1994: 167)

Clearly, the traditional hierarchical logic of work organization that relies on a top-down "conquer and rule mentality" has proved to be too inflexible, uncompetitive and slow to mobilize for change. Hence, organizations increasingly chose to participate in less hierarchical forms of work organization instead, and by engaging with various stakeholders in novel distributed partnership arrangements, they hope to become increasingly responsive in a rapidly shifting environment. Inter-organizational networks not only help reduce business risks and lower transaction and production costs in R&D but also accelerate innovation and the speed of the product to market. Organizational activities comprise intertwined structures and processes that represent both inputs and outputs from social and technological systems. While innovation still very much relies on human capacities, these complex innovative achievements also rely on well-functioning infrastructures and technological tools that interconnect people (Wasen, 2013). As social and technological change is accelerating, in order to attain or maintain competitive advantages, firms are increasingly required to find new and more efficient ways of facilitating networking. Channeling development from the bottom up rather than from the top down entails the encouragement of cultural diversity, which, in turn, can foster innovative stimulation and can provide complementary solutions and new arrangements.

As we will see, the terms network and networking are imperative for understanding modern innovations. Innovation partnerships play an increasingly important role in our "knowledge economy" and underlie many of the changes that are currently taking place in industry and society. Such partnerships fundamentally signal a reconsideration of old hierarchical structures toward the adoption of more tactful, flexible and vigilant forms of collaborative arrangements, as well as the adoption of advanced technological solutions that allow network participation to evolve in new directions. In particular, the terms "network" and "networked business" have become increasingly prevalent in industrial-economic contexts. Nohria and Eccles (1993) describe three factors that contribute to this popularity. First, prosperous regions, such as Silicon Valley in the United States and Modena in Italy, put the spotlight on small dynamic entrepreneurial companies that were able to innovate and cooperate successfully in inter-organizational networks. Second, the ongoing evolution of computer technology and the Internet have enabled organizations to be more tightly integrated through technological networks. Third, the network concept has fascinated scholars and caught their attention as an attractive research subject in the academic world. It should come as no surprise then that the network concept has captured the imagination of scholars in virtually every discipline (see, e.g., Barnes, 1954, 1979; Borgatti *et al.*, 2009; Easley and Kleinberg, 2010; Watts, 2004), and although it is used in very different contexts, the "network" term and its various theoretical constructs appear in scientific areas such as computer science, biology, chemistry and engineering. It is important to be aware, however, that despite all the great efforts and scholarly accomplishments that have been made during the last few decades, there is a danger looming in the use of the network concept, as network approaches are not all-encompassing frameworks that can be used to describe everything.

That said, the idea of a network remains a cornerstone of modern management inquiry and innovation management. It would not be an exaggeration to state that the term networking has once again re-emerged as a popular term for understanding change and innovation. Yet the very idea of a *network* is not "new" (see, e.g., Barnes, 1954; Marshall, 1919), and even by the 1930s, researchers systematically looked at informal network relationships within and between organizations (Nohria and Eccels, 1993). The next section explores how the notion of a network evolved in early sociological accounts. It was in the field of sociology that social scientists first embarked on studies to grasp how the complex ties between individuals and society dramatically changed in the midst of the Industrial Revolution.

NETWORKS AND SOCIAL NETWORKING—A CONCEPTUAL BACKGROUND

The first academic contribution in this stream of research was provided by Georg Simmel (1858–1918), a sociologist who is considered to be one of the first scholars to acknowledge social structures in terms of relational properties situated in a wider changing societal environment. Most simply, relationships between two persons are actually different from interactions between three persons—because coalitions ("two persons against one") emerge between three persons. Thus, individuals' dynamic (altering) positions in networked relationships and the pattern of such relations were found to be important and to result from varying forces imposed by different social circles. For Simmel, modern life in cities unfolded as part of the "fluid" interrelatedness of social actors. In the beginning of the twentieth century, Simmel noted that:

> Economic, personal and intellectual relations in the city (which are its ideal reflection) grow in a geometrical progression as soon as, for the first time, a certain limit has been passed. Every dynamic extension becomes a preparation not only for a similar extension but rather for a larger one, and from every thread which is spun out of it there continue, growing as out of themselves, an endless number of others. . . . For the metropolis it is decisive that its inner life is extended in a wave-like

motion over a broader national or international area. . . . The most significant aspect of the metropolis lies in this functional magnitude beyond its actual physical boundaries and this effectiveness reacts upon the latter and gives to it life, weight, importance and responsibility.

(Simmel, 1903/2002: 17)

The understanding of interrelatedness and triads (i.e., a "web of group affiliations") was also used by Simmel in his analysis of the significant rural-urban transformation (which continues today). This massive shift in society occurred as increasingly larger numbers of migrants moved from the countryside, or from small villages, to big cities and industrial districts to obtain employment in factories. This urbanization in the wake of the Industrial Revolution also contributed to the gradual decline of feudalism. At that time, Simmel's (1903/2002) sociological work was many sided and reflected an ambivalent relationship to freedom and individuality. He noted that life in a metropolis in the beginning of the twentieth century was characterized by a more materialistic lifestyle where "calculability," "antipathy," "hardness" and "distantiation" were symptoms of this more profound societal change. He also observed, among other things, that while rural life in small towns and the countryside provided a "smoothly flowing rhythm" and depended more on emotional relations, life in big cities conversely "[signified] a purely matter-of-fact attitude in the treatment of persons and things in which a formal justice is often combined with an unrelenting hardness. The purely intellectualistic person is indifferent to all things personal" (Simmel, 1903/2002: 12).

Ferdinand Tönnies (1855–1936), a sociologist, also observed the pervasive rearrangements in modern urban life that gradually materialized in the wake of industrialization. In Tönnies' (1955/1987) sociological investigation of the changing fabric of modern life in the Western world, his accounts illustrated how the Industrial Revolution implied not only a dramatic shift in the movement of labor to big cities, in addition to an accelerated rate of mechanization, bureaucratization, rationalization and division of work, but also an erratic rural-urban transformation and cataclysmic changes that disrupted many traditional expressions of human co-existence.

Tönnies introduced and elaborated on the conceptual pair *Gemeinschaft* and *Gesellschaft*, terms in the English language that translate to *community* and *society*. While "Gemeinschaft" largely concerned cooperation and mutual aid, "Gesellschaft" privileged rivalry and fierce competition. In pre-industrial societies, "Gemeinschaft" was the dominant logic—love, friendship and social proximity underpinned many family-oriented ties. In industrial societies, "Gesellschaft" came to dominate, and social relations seemed to become merely instrumental means that served to fulfill individual interests. However, Tönnies argued that group solidarity, which commonly signified kinship in groups and social harmony in earlier feudalistic societies, was largely being replaced by "impersonal" and cool relationships.

Thus, he largely emphasized how new developments constrained social life. Has solidarity largely disappeared in modern society? The EU (2011: 12), for example, indicates that "solidarity has to be the principle in bridging the geographic divide"; thus, the principle of solidarity still exists.

While George Simmel and Ferdinand Tönnies had rather different views on the shifting character of interrelated human relationships, they also addressed similar notions to make sense of fast-paced societal changes. Simmel wanted to explain why individuals, despite an ever-increasing division of labor—which practically meant a higher degree of interpersonal reliance (albeit also impersonal relationships) as people increasingly had to depend on the complementary work and actions of others—could still maintain a sense of originality and personality (individuality). To understand this tension, Simmel elaborated the meanings of conceptual pairs such as difference versus conformism, particularistic versus universalistic, change versus continuity, and so forth. In the increasing number of contractual relations, the "rational" human would seem to appreciate more self-centeredness and self-realization, but this form of life could also mean separation in the traditional sphere of social life. Yet Simmel suggested that increased freedom and individuality might bring about positive and productive effects in society that could contribute to the common good. This essential idea is also reflected in contemporary discourses on innovation studies, and it may refer to what we today, in largely positive terms, commonly understand as the "spirit of entrepreneurship." Simmel noted, ". . . within feudal systems there was [no] room . . . for the spirit of individual enterprise and private energy. The same restrictions that prevented the emergence of conceptions of a higher social union also prevented, at the lower level, the actualization of individual freedom" (Simmel, 1971: 270). Thus, for Simmel, freedom in the metropolis encouraged "individual enterprise."

Indeed, it is currently widely accepted that innovative activities involve "individual enterprise." It is also assumed that a high degree of individual independence and freedom represents a situation in which individuals are given free hands to fully express their drive for creativity, entrepreneurship and serendipity. Notions such as "individual free thinking," "human ingenuity" and the idea of a "sole inventor" are still applicable for understanding some of the intrinsic dynamics that come to play in the modern emergence of innovation. However, innovative work is becoming increasingly networked, complex and versatile, and such characteristic notions are perhaps becoming less powerful variables in our network society. This is not to downgrade individual contributions to this knowledge, but in a rapidly changing environment in which the majority of successful inventions essentially are products of collective undertakings rather than singular ones, the focus unavoidably also needs to shift to professional partnerships that are situated in large-scale networking projects and efforts under conditions of high uncertainty (Boisot *et al.*, 2011). Innovation partnerships often entail new types of network arrangements to make the previously impossible

possible. Thus, modern innovation partnerships increasingly yield multifaceted, collective ("multi-individual") and massive collaborative practices that ultimately thrive on the inherent tension between collaboration and competition in business and society.

In the beginning of the twenty-first century, network theory represented a steadily growing interdisciplinary field that incorporated contributions from the disciplines of economics and sociology, including network theory's offshoot in the study of work organization and ICT systems (e.g., information systems, organizational learning, leadership, marketing). The intention here is not to describe and map out all the various network perspectives in the analysis of work organization. Given that this chapter focuses on explicit (formal) partnership efforts and social activities of developing and driving innovation, the next sections focus on some key elements that we suggest are useful for analyzing inter-organizational innovation.

THE MEANING OF NETWORK—THEORETICAL CONCERNS AND CONCEPTUAL ADVANCES

Different views on inter-organizational networks and partnerships exist. Network research on organizations may typically focus on social (individual) ties, intra-organizational ties or inter-organizational ties in terms of formal or informal relationships. Powell and Smith-Doerr (1994) suggest that network analysis in management theory and organizational analysis roughly can be separated into two specific meanings and streams of thought. One meaning, in particular, concerns an "analytic perspective" that views the degree to which relationships are embedded in institutional structures. This perspective emphasizes how different organizational entities are integrated and interrelated. The other meaning of a network is related to the "logics of organizing": it emphasizes that a network is as much about processes as it is about structure. The elaboration that the network (or "net-working") metaphor has undergone in earlier management studies may therefore vary depending on the accentuation given to either of these meanings.

Cook and Emerson (1978) provide another useful distinction that, most simply, assumes that a network consists of groups of two or more intersected relationships. The term "network," or simply "net," is usually associated with patterns or structures within an organization and sometimes has a normative connotation attached to it. For example, organizations that are structured as networks are considered to be "better" suited to gain competitive advantages than organizations with conventional hierarchical formations because of their "better fit" to their dynamic and complex competitive environment (Nohria and Eccels, 1993).

A network can also refer to various situations in the market, meaning that the term reflects a broad and abstract concept. The sensibility to various situational circumstances is still undeveloped in current network theory. Nohria and Eccels (1993) argue that the metaphorical structure-like interpretation of networks is based on inadequate knowledge and understanding of emerging, real-life empirical phenomena. Possibly, because the network metaphor is somewhat abstract, the term 'network' has lost some of its meaning and usefulness. In the sections that follow, we more closely explore the distinction between different forms and models of inter-organizational networks. Unfortunately, space limitations do not allow for further elaboration of the essential stream of thought known as social network theory.

One seminal contribution is, nonetheless, mentioned here. In the 1960s and 1970s, scholars in sociology and anthropology aimed to examine personal networks, that is, the idea that social structures constitute a network phenomenon. Granovetter and colleagues, for example, looked beyond individuals to distinguish their roles and connections between persons. Some types of connections were found to be more important for social actors than others. Thus, Granovetter and colleagues found that to whom a person is connected truly matters, not least because some connections more effectively enable access to various resources (e.g., sources of news). In Granovetter's (1973) work, it was argued that weak social ties (e.g., mere loose associations) might provide a better source to acquire novel information from. Thus, for social actors to be able to find valuable information or novel insights, group members of a small association may have to look beyond the association's own (limited) sphere and extend the search to also include wider spheres and other associates and friends (weak ties). This idea is captured in what Granovetter has termed "the strength of weak ties," and it has influenced managerial theories (for a summary of social network analysis, see Freeman, 2004).

It is important to be aware that a distinction exists between personal and organizational networks, even if they interact dynamically. Organizational networks are more explicitly established and durable, and they do not stop existing when individuals are replaced (Gustavsen and Hofmaier, 1997)—a feature that makes them more powerful and stable than more fluid, individual-based personal networks. One advantage of individual networks, however, is their quantitative potential and superiority in terms of the number of links that connect actors to each other. Personal relationships (e.g., one individual knows another individual, who, in turn, knows another, and so forth) are often interlinked in chain formations, and these formations can often outnumber the formal links of more conventional business partnerships. Yet these forms of networks are not mutually exclusive; rather, they are mutually dependent. In the author's opinion, it may be fruitful to regard both of these networks (personal and organizational) as two complementary lenses that allow different interpretations and explanations. What characterizes inter-organizational networks and networking, in contrast to personal networks and networking? In the following sections, we focus on inter-organizational networks, but it is important to keep in mind that inter-organizational networks are deeply entrenched and that they co-exist with fluid personal networks.

Based on our understanding thus far, a business network may be explained in a very simplified way as a group of nodes and a group of ties that are structured in two or more interconnected relationships (Brass *et al.*, 2004). Inter-organizational networks are based on the principle in which interconnected relationships are organized in complex patterns between different units and subsidiaries, thereby allowing organizations to interact dynamically and to adapt over time. Lomi and Grandi (1997) found that in such inter-organizational networking, mutually dependent relationships emerge, which partly explains why organizational networks hold together. Wikström and Normann (1994) argue that such organizational structures can be considered to be dynamic systems whose intrinsic elements interact with each other.

Although structures and processes may co-exist in various models, the approaches to networking that focus on structure tend to overlook the emerging and evolving characteristics of networking as such. Gustavsen *et al.* (1996: 11) address the tension between structure and process and note that while "the evolutionary element is sometimes a part of studies of, e.g., industrial regions and enterprise networks," they nevertheless continue "the majority of contributions (such as Piore and Sabel, 1984) [that] describe structural properties of network formations and their environmental context rather than the network-generating processes." What makes these systems or emerging networks extremely complex is thus not only the number of relationships but also the degree of unpredictably in the interactions that occur among their various elements and actors. Theories on self-organization appreciate complexity and highlight the emergence of new patterns and formations that are not necessarily based on external conditions but that are also inherent in the dynamics of networks. Thus, the process of self-organization relates to the ways that (semi-)autonomous entities seemingly interact with each other (cf. Murphy, 1998).

However, some inter-organizational perspectives may highlight regulation rather than self-organization and autonomy. Such formal connections typically involve inter-organizational collaboration, joint ventures, strategic alliances, strategic networks and Mergers and Acquisitions (M&As). While some approaches appreciate closely and formally linked business relationships, other perspectives stress more loosely linked connections between actors who have divergent interests and objectives. Instead of primarily relying on formal information systems to manage the flow of information among the actors within a network, some networks rely on personal relationships and informal channels of communication between the various actors and co-workers (Bartlett and Ghoshal, 1999).

Indeed, network analysis has gained increased popularity in a number of fields in business and organizational studies, including innovation management, stakeholder relations, entrepreneurial activities, leadership and power, knowledge exploration and skills utilization. In the scholarly context, networking is sometimes associated with social activities ranging from various forms of cooperation to innovative work and regional development. Strategic alliances and partnerships, joint ventures, social networks, personal networks and technological R&D collaborations are all typical examples of notions that can be related to the general and widespread idea of networks (Ebers, 1997; Lütz, 1997; Ring, 1997). Lomi and Grandi (1997) address a very legitimate issue: namely, by what means can network concepts serve as useful tools for analyzing inter-organizational relationships. Håkansson *et al.* (2009), for example, set out to describe the complex characteristics of network relationships by using the analogy of a rainforest. A rainforest is an appropriate image of a business network, as Håkansson and colleagues argue, because it stresses not only symbiosis among plants and animals but also systemic interdependence and collaboration. In other words, one part of the rainforest system affects its other parts.

Biemans (1992) proposes a classification of inter-organizational networks based on three different factors: (1) the partners involved; (2) the network complexity, such as the number of actors involved; and (3) the type of environment in which interactive relationships between actors unfold. Biemans (1992) further argues that a fundamental prerequisite for organizations to fully exploit the potential of external networks is to first allow internal networks within the organization to function and interact well. The notion of a network is typically related to the distinction between personal and organizational networks. Nohria and Eccels (1993) note that all organizations are based in one way or another on network relationships (personal and organizational); the network metaphor is ubiquitous, and using the term "network organization" would therefore be a tautology (i.e., a "cake on cake" reasoning). Ring provides a very broad definition of inter-organizational networks, which represent:

> Co-operative efforts among business firms, governmental bodies or organizations, persons, or other entities that are interconnected in various ways. These connections permit them to be seen clearly apart from the environment in which they are embedded. . . . More so than in other forms of collaborations designed to facilitate economic exchanges, networks are also infused with social exchanges.
>
> (Ring, 1997: 115)

These are but a few examples of how network and networking phenomena have been theorized. Although there is a broad consensus about the imperative role of networks in business, management scholars have clearly disagreed about how to conceptualize and understand various forms of networks (Ebers, 1997; Lutz, 1997; Nohria and Eccels, 1993; Provan *et al.*, 2007). Regarding the term "partnership," definitions and vocabulary are, arguably, equally vague, which has contributed to the lack of definitional clarity and conceptual uniformity. Partnership here refers to a regulated legal relation that usually involves close collaboration and joint responsibilities and rights. However, despite the multiple uses of the terms "networks" and "partnerships" and the existence of a variety of useful and informative distinctions and taxonomies on networking and innovation partnerships, a unifying, clear-cut understanding of what network and networking activities actually are does not exist. Such a definition depends on which level of analysis one focuses on. Because networks are multifaceted, debates about what distinguishes network phenomena (and their limits) still endure.

The meaning of the term "network" is thus rather elusive; the various definitions attached to it contribute to its lack of conceptual clarity. The risk of using such a broad term, of course, is that it may be used everywhere to explain everything universally, thereby causing it to lose its usefulness. However, the purpose here is not to resolve any disputes regarding the conceptualization of the term *per se* but instead to provide a nuanced treatment that aims to extend and contrast, as well as reconcile, some perspectives regarding innovation networks and partnerships in the management literature. Indeed, it is outside the scope of this chapter to further explore the various traditions and approaches on networks and networking, but for the following discussion, a condensed discussion is provided to further address the two questions raised in the introductory section: (1) How do organizations channel their business activities beyond conventional managerial, professional and cultural boundaries to promote innovation? (2) What are the contrary forces (e.g., tensions and controversies) that typically evolve over time in such network partnerships? The primary focus of the rest of the chapter then is to discuss the relevant attributes of social activities that span traditional boundaries in inter-organizational networks. The next section elaborates on the strategic dimension of networking and briefly reviews the industrial network approach.

STRATEGIC NETWORK PARTNERSHIP

"There are two key questions mainstream management researchers have traditionally addressed in their studies of firms' behavior. First, in what direction should a firm channel its activities? And second, how should a firm be organized? The first is a question of strategy, the second of organization design" (Tsoukas, 1996: 94). These two basic questions that Tsoukas addresses are indeed two matters that many strategy-oriented studies adopting a network approach seek to address. Strategies concern how organizations channel their business activities and, in contrast to tactical moves, how organizations address more long-term thinking in networks. Important strategic elements include, but are not limited to, how certain resource configurations are set up and how actors are grouped in anticipation of change in the wake of societal and financial transformations. Strategy work is not to be considered a onetime "fix" or an isolated "exercise" but rather an uninterrupted "work-in-progress" endeavor because inter-organizational networks are situated in dynamic business environments that transform more or less abruptly. Strategy work considers the more enduring effects of volatile market conditions and modifications in resource reconfigurations, for example, changes that may drastically redraw the entire map of a competitive landscape because of the introduction of new production processes, technologies or types of competitors. Strategy work is essentially also a collective achievement. It can be considered a communicative "sensemaking" event that acknowledges an evaluation of the past ("what has happened"), the present ("where are we now") and the desired future state (e.g., "where do we really want to go"). One "side effect" of such collective sensemaking is social coherence, which binds a management team together and gives them a common sense of purpose (Targama and Wasen, 2012; Wasen, 2005a).

Biemans (1992) is another organizational scholar who stresses the importance of strategies in networks and who notes that every firm needs to analyze, design and evaluate their cooperation profile strategically. Biemans also stresses the change and dynamic property of strategies. If an organization, for example, loses certain skills and knowledge assets, this may seriously affect and weaken the organization's strategic position in the network. Axelsson and Agndal (2012) state that strategy is an essential component for the successful functioning of networks and that inter-organizational networking, in turn, is an essential ingredient of strategic development. They note that firms may seem to exploit random chances that emerge and that success is less about exploiting coincidences and more about correct timing—i.e., a firm's ability to be in the right place at the right time and to address the right problems. Agndal and Axelsson (2012) also argue that networking (i.e., the process) does not primarily presuppose an organizational network (i.e., structure) *per se*; rather, it refers to the multitude of interactions that take place among different actors. Indeed, firms may be involved in several different networks simultaneously, as they supply their services or products to several distinct industrial sectors. The idea of business networks is defined in this context as "a set of two or more connected business relationships, in which each exchange relation is between business firms that are conceptualized as collective actors" (Johanson *et al.*, 1994: 2). Strategic networks involve memberships and alliances (Chetty and Agndal, 2008; Gulati *et al.*, 2000; Jarillo, 1988).

A classic tension in organizational studies and management theory exists between agency and structure (Borgatti and Foster, 2003). Easton (1992), however, interestingly chooses to go beyond this distinction, and instead of reiterating an antiquated dichotomy, he chooses to structure the network approach into four distinctive metaphors: (1) networks as relationships, (2) networks as structures, (3) networks as processes and (4) networks as positions. A common factor for all of these assumptions in the industrial network approach is that networks are not fixed but that they constantly change. A network relationship is not given automatically, and therefore, it involves both uncertainties and opportunities. Although actors tend to seek long-term relationships, rapid reconfigurations in actor networks occur from time to time, and these dramatic changes can have profound effects on factors such as trust and confidence among actors.

Håkansson and Waluszewski (2002) differentiate heavy networks from light networks, where the latter have less inertia (i.e., a reduced mass of the network structure) and thus have a tendency to be easier to influence than the former. However, it is important to remember, as Lütz (1997) notes, that inter-organizational networks are composed of independent, yet inter-dependent, actors who often have varying (and sometimes even conflicting) interests and needs. What is interesting about inter-organizational collaboration networks is that they combine elements of both flexibility and stability in unique ways (Castells, 2000). Savage (1996) also suggests that trust in inter-organizational networks may allow organizations to more quickly make correct predictions and to respond more flexibly to new business opportunities; both of these developments are considered to be decisive factors in the face of increasingly challenging global competition.

Indeed, networks and networking have received increasingly more scholarly attention over the last few decades. Prior to this development, discussions regarding the organization of economic activities focused on either a market or a hierarchical perspective. Coordination is typically hierarchically organized in production and manufacturing facilities, for example, and these types of businesses are therefore treated as bureaucracies. Sales departments, in contrast to production facilities, are often self-organized (less hierarchical), and consequently, they run as more or less autonomous divisional units that are adapted to the firm's market situation. While relationships are "businesslike" and impersonal in both these domains, it follows from the above distinctions that they are more likely to be distinctively formal and multilayered in hierarchies. This also affects how the dissemination of information is organized. In bureaucracies, it is often extremely restricted and under concentrated control and supervision, whereas the opposite holds true for markets (i.e., information dissemination is typically not under centralized management) (Boisot, 1998).

The market form, which, in Weber's (1952/1968) vocabulary, can be understood as an ideal type for organizations, assumes a collection of actors—individuals and organizations who assume the roles of buyers and sellers. An important underlying assumption in the market context is that these actors are independent of each other and that they actively strive to maximize their own gains (i.e., actors are assumed to act rationally in the marketplace). Relationships that govern the exchange of goods and information between actors are assumed to follow this logic of rationality, and the parties are not expected to develop more lasting and permanent relationships with other actors because they primarily seek short-term gains. In this sense, the market perspective is considered to be almost a "non-organization" (see, e.g., Easton and Håkansson, 1996; Lundgren and Snehota, 1998). The opposite approach is the archetype of all organizations, namely, the hierarchical pyramid structure of organizations, which directly contrasts the previous notion of the "non-organization." Prior to the increased popularity of the market approach, the hierarchical model provided the dominant theoretical conceptualization in both sociology and organization theory. In contrast to the non-organization, a hierarchy establishes relationships involving economical activities that are more strictly regulated and that exist over a longer time period.

Powell (1990) discusses the established dichotomy between hierarchies and markets and notes that this dichotomy is inadequate for describing the emerging characteristics of flexible, information-driven enterprises. The market logic is primarily concerned with competition, whereas bureaucracy and hierarchy are concerned with authority and obedience. Networks, in contrast, primarily focus on negotiation and collaboration. The early hypothesis suggested that networks existed between hierarchies and markets (Thorelli, 1986: 37), but both Powell *et al.* (1996) and Fukuyama (1999) have argued that because the network model of economic organization primarily centers on purposeful cooperation over time, it is therefore distinctively different from both market logics and hierarchical forms. For example, corporate alliances and similar business forms offer viable alternative forms of organizing in the domain "between markets and hierarchies" (Powell, 1990). As Powell suggests, networks also entail more long-term and dispersed connections than markets but more reciprocal and democratic engagements than hierarchies.

When scholars in the 1970s aimed to examine real-life business transactions and relationships in the international marketplace, they encountered considerable anomalies that could not be fully explained by market and hierarchical approaches (Easton and Håkansson, 1996; Lundgren and Snehota, 1998). Encountering such anomalies motivated the formation of new approaches. An example of such an approach is the so-called industrial network perspective. The dominant methodological approach adopted in the industrial network tradition also differed in that it adopted an inductive and descriptive approach to elucidate how buyers and sellers relate to one another in practice. Some leading scholars in this tradition distinguish the industrial network approach from other mainstream research because the former is "less quantitative and more qualitative, less deductive and more inductive, less theory testing and more theory developing, less specifically oriented to marketing management and more holistic, less prescriptive and more descriptive" (Johanson and Mattson, 1993: 24).

Because of this research methodology, connections and relationships have become particularly accentuated in studies of internationalization and distribution processes within industrial markets. Actors have become the focal study object, and from a methodological perspective, the main analytical object ("actor") is typically determined by individuals, so cases in the industrial network approach therefore typically include multiple field studies that include in-depth interviews with practitioners. Interestingly, in his research study on Swedish companies, Håkansson (1989) found exchanges with relatively small customer bases. It turned out that the ten largest customers accounted for approximately 70 percent of the sales (cf. the so-called famous 80–20 rule; see, e.g., Mulhern, 1999), and relationships were established over a longer period of time. Thus, researchers have reached the conclusion that business relationships must be seen in a larger context. For example, both Johanson *et al.* (1994) and Vahlne *et al.* (1998) note that a company's network of relationships is situated in a so-called "embedded context" involving not only customers but also suppliers and partners, and so forth. The network properties of business markets have also been used to explain marketing efforts initiated by enterprises (Axelsson, 2010; Axelsson and Agndal, 2012). Strategy work needs to be an ongoing concern and needs to be sufficiently flexible because conditions shift rapidly in a competitive global environment. In light of changing circumstances in the surroundings, firms often need to develop and revise collaborative profiles, and thus, they may need to sift through and categorize various types of known competitors that potentially could become cooperators. We see an opportunity to understand these issues by using the terminology provided in the so-called Uppsala-based network theory model, which can be applied as an analytical tool or lens not only for scholars but also for practitioners of strategic planning and decision making.

INDUSTRIAL NETWORK APPROACH

The following retrospect is provided by one of the founding members of the so-called "Uppsala school" who was involved in the early developments that came to be known under the umbrella term the "Industrial Network Approach": "Situated at the main parquet, I was able to be present when the market network concept emerged. I saw all the initial struggling and torments . . . , and I have been sitting there on the main parquet watching the baby grow and become mature. . . . I think of the idea of markets as networks (Johanson, 1995: 7, the author's translation). Thus, this approach assumes that business actors are embedded in complex network relationships, and the framework provides conceptual tools with which to analyze how industrial organizations operate. This scholarly tradition emerged in the 1970s to address "important contemporary problems in society and in business" (Johanson and Mattsson, 1993: 2). Easton (1992: 3) further notes that "the industrial network approach has emerged as a separate and viable paradigm in its own right." It is widely used in the management science field, and it establishes a particular view of industrial markets as networks (Johanson and Mattsson, 1993; Johanson, 1995).

Research in this vein has resulted in several key works, among others, "The Company's Purchasing Behavior" by Håkansson and Wootz in 1975 and another publication entitled, "Business Networking: A New Approach to Competitiveness," first published in 1982. The hallmark of these early publications was that they represented a different approach, which distinguished itself from the traditional view within economic theory that was pervasive in the 1970s. Corporate transformations were not treated as a direct result of rational managerial decisions *per se*. In other words, in the industrial network approach, scholars assumed that relationships do not necessarily presume rational motives among industrial actors. Some of the key concepts and models that have been developed in this school of thought since the 1970s have spread to other disciplines. It is not an overstatement that the Industrial Network Approach has become a cornerstone of contemporary work on networks and networking in the broader scholarly field of business administration and that includes various sub-disciplines, such as international business, marketing and organizational studies (see, e.g., Axelsson and Agndal, 2012; Håkansson and Johanson, 1994; Håkansson and Snehota, 1995).

Academic studies in the early 1970s, for example, sought to understand Swedish corporate development in foreign markets and to determine how these firms handled changes and challenges in the marketplace (Johanson, 1995). One of the early studies involved data analysis of buyer-seller relationships between Swedish businesses and actors in other European countries, such as England, Germany, France and Italy (Håkansson and Snehota, 2000). Indeed, "actors" represent one of three key terms in this scholarly tradition. Similarly, the processes of innovation can be considered to consist of networks of actors, resources and activities that are (inter)connected in various constellations.

In the industrial network approach, actors refer to individuals, groups and separate divisions within an organization, and they sometimes include larger "business units" within a single firm, several organizations or groups of organizations. Actors also adopt a "network horizon"—a particular overview and various perceptions of the network structure. Actors perform activities in their realm of specialty and expertise and control resources in specific domains (Axelsson and Agndal, 2012; Håkansson and Johanson, 1994). Importantly, technology is conceptualized as a resource, not as an actor, in the industrial network approach. In addition to the term "actors," two other terms are essential in a network analysis: activities and resources.

Two different categories of activities are performed by actors. *Transformational activities* utilize and correct resources, whereas *transactional activities* link dispersed transformational activities, thereby creating new constellations of relationships and connections among actors. A "chain of transactions" or an "activity cycle" refers to systems of interconnected activities. Another important distinction is the one between primary and secondary functions (the latter functions are sometimes termed "network functions"). Primary functions reflect interactions within a dyadic relationship. The word "dyadic" is derived from the Greek word *dýo*, which means two, where the adjective form *dyadic* stresses interactions between two individuals (i.e., the smallest possible group formation). Secondary functions, instead, reflect indirect effects of such dyadic relationships (both positive and negative). Hence, secondary functions stress the fact that primary relationships are often indirectly linked to other relationships in networks. In summary, activities are processes performed by actors, and they may facilitate the "linking" of resources (Håkansson, 1987). Resources include physical assets, such as machinery, equipment and technological tools, as well as financial and human assets, such as business expertise, labor and personal relationships and various goodwill assets (Axelsson and Agndal, 2012; Johanson *et al.*, 1994).

Håkansson and Johanson (1994) emphasize various types of links, connections and bonds among the different actors. The links refer to the activities of the various actors. The links also relate to the different types of resources that are interconnected between the different actors. These resources may involve specialist skills that are shared between the various stakeholders in the innovation process. Thus, links refer to the activities among the various actors; by contrast, connections refer to actual resources that are shared and utilized among the actors. Further, bonds refer to interpersonal relationships and evolving identities (Johanson *et al.*, 1994) that join actors, e.g., technical, social, legal, economic, administrative and educational bonds.

A recurring theme in the literature on the industrial network approach is the co-existence of cooperation and competition. While companies can be considered competitors over market shares, individual companies may simultaneously engage in the exchange of activities and resources. Vahlne *et al.* (1998) argue that developing relationships between cooperating actors can provide a platform for future inter-organizational collaboration. However, lasting relationships take time to build. Once such long-term business relationships evolve, they can be considered strategic assets for a company. It seems that this theoretical argument assumes that all relationships are more or less harmonious. However, as the subsequent sections show, relationships within networks might also be harmful, not just for a single company, but also for the entire industry. In some extreme cases, this form of cooperation may even be illegal (see the formation of cartels and corruption). Thus, clearly, not all relationships and business exchanges in the market place are beneficial and good.

A processual approach has been adopted in later work, which more aptly describes various relational qualities in industrial networking activities. One of the more interesting developments, perhaps, is provided by Håkansson and Waluszewski (2001) and Hoholm and Olsen (2012), who address the key role of frictions. These authors argue that friction explains both the stability ("cementation") within a system (a network) and the tensions and forces that affect interacting bodies and their movements and alignments in networks. We will discuss the concept of "social frictions" in greater depth in another section. Clearly, such developments provide novel perspectives. Johansson and Mattson (1993: 3) have stated that "much work is needed before the network approach can be considered a coherent theory." As with any theoretical framework, room remains to further develop generic notions (e.g., actors and resources) of delineated constructs or sub-categories and of changes in the industrial business environment (e.g., new types of networks in the digital ecosystem). Whereas most empirical research adopting the industrial network approach has focused on industrial enterprises, the conceptual tools may also be applicable to other types of businesses, such as digital/virtual service environments, which adopt an industrial logic of networking.

However, it should be noted that key issues such as contested power and the changing politics of cultural tensions have been largely overlooked in various strategy-oriented approaches in contrast to other perspectives in management science (for exceptions, see, e.g., Cook and Gillmore, 1984; Cook and Rice, 2001; Hoholm and Olsen, 2012). In Chapter 1, for example, it was argued that political process analysis is a useful perspective because it brings important issues such as politics and conflict to the fore. Therefore, we relied on institutional-level and community-level approaches to map out some of the key issues that are related to politics and conflicts. However, before we turn to the increasingly prevalent role of uncertainty and multiplicity that seem to characterize modern networks and networking, we will first explore some of the principles and underlying assumptions behind the institutional-cultural approach to networking, an influential network-centric tradition within business and innovation studies.

INSTITUTIONAL STRUCTURES AND CULTURES

We have already explored the typical hallmarks of bureaucracies and markets, and the major difference, somewhat simplified, is that bureaucratic logic represents functional organizational structures, whereas markets represent distributed (divisional) association. But Ouchi (1980) notes that:

> industrial organizations can, in some instances, rely to a great extent on socialization as the principal mechanisms of mediation or control, and this 'clan' form ('clan' conforms to Durkheim's meaning of an organic association which resembles a kin network but may not include blood relations, [. . .]) can be very efficient in mediating transactions between interdependent individuals. Markets, bureaucracies, and clans are therefore three distinct mechanisms which may be present in differing degrees, in any real organization. . . . [Moreover, 'clan'] organizations are typically in technologically advanced or closely integrated

industries, where teamwork is common, technologies change often, and therefore individual performance is highly ambiguous.

(Ouchi 1980: 132)

The cultural dimension of inter-organizational life was seriously discussed and observed in earnest in the midst of the Japanese corporate successes of the 1980s. Little prior research had been conducted on the culture within and beyond inter-organizational networks. Indeed, in a broader sense, inter-organizational routines as well as workplace socialization (e.g., norms on "code of conduct") can be considered key inputs to shaping organizational culture, and as we noted, routines are also hallmarks for bureaucracies. Nevertheless, both "fiefs" (e.g., R&D units) and "clans" (e.g., strategy development units) involve more personal "face-to-face" interactions, and such relationships have become less formal by nature. Coordination mechanisms and professional relationships are still hierarchically shaped in fiefs, whereas in clans, they are more equally distributed (i.e., non-hierarchical), which leaves more room for negotiation and debate (Boisot, 1998).

Burns and Stalkers' (1961) seminal work entitled *The Management of Innovation* most likely represents one of the first studies to systematically explore how organizational structures and logics of management influence innovation outcomes. They found that in stable environmental conditions, mechanistic (hierarchical) systems promote incremental innovations, whereas organic (non-hierarchical and un-bureaucratic) structures are more prone to adapt to swift changes in the environment. Drawing on these findings, it is reasonable to suspect that the organic type of organization also would, at least in theory, instigate more radical change and innovation. This has been discussed in both previous (see, e.g., Harryson, 2001; Wikström and Normann, 1994) and more recent publications (see, e.g., Wasen and Lodaya, 2012), where it is argued that rigid organizational bureaucratic structures are inadequate for innovative work because such structures tend to inhibit, rather than promote, human creativity and initiative. Often, an organization's clear and prioritized processes and goals to maximize its profits in the short-term may suppress, rather than support, radical renewal and the emergence of groundbreaking discoveries and innovations. Accordingly, "clans" and "fiefs" would be more appropriate for innovative activities in which radical innovations are pursued. Are hierarchies actually antiquated forms of organization that should be discarded because they are no longer fit for a "modern" network society? Or is it possible for a large organization to be technology-oriented and innovative and to still be hierarchically structured? Harryson (2001) offers an elaborative approach for tackling what he calls the "organizational dilemma of innovation." He is an advocate of less self-organizing organic units because of their relative superiority in generating radical innovations and inventions. However, strong hierarchical organizations backed with resources and large infrastructures are needed as well to quickly and efficiently realize and commercialize innovations. Harryson therefore claims that various "paradoxical organizational needs of radical innovation" practically entail that:

> Rapid processing of an invention towards innovation may call for insti-tutionalized routines in a rather bureaucratic organization with clear hierarchies. Above all, it seems that large, hierarchical and departmen-talized organizations are desirable for the production-stage. Hence the ideal organization for creative invention seems to be the opposite of the one that yields rapid innovation. Put differently, the organizational needs change from one extreme to another when we move from the upstream stage of the innovation process to the downstream production stage. . . . Radical innovation may call for initial inspiration, which, for example, can be achieved through market linkages or interaction with extracorporate fields of action. However, we have also seen that a deep focus on technology development requires specialization, which often causes isolation from the very same linkages. . . . The organizational dilemma further suggests that creative invention thrives in a small, organic laboratory, whereas rapid production may call for institutional-ized routines in a large, bureaucratic organization.
>
> (2001: 52–3)

The use of formal team-based R&D structures, for example, may be a way to partly circumvent the dilemma described above. However, this assumption seems rather "idealized." R&D teams usually operate under tight deadlines and are most likely more appropriate than the more informal and "casual" COP form for realizing and exploiting innovative opportunities because business teams primarily reward common goals above individual goals (i.e., what occurs when individuals each pursue their own specific interests).

Hamel and Prahalad (1994: 271) also stress the idea of a "symbiotic relationship between big and small" in the management of innovation. They note that the aforementioned types of organizations are needed in the pro-cess of innovation and that efforts should be directed toward fostering effec-tive interaction between them. It is through networks and external sources that human creativity can support innovative activities. The commercial-ization of ideas and knowledge unfolds through a synergistic relationship between internal and external networks (Harryson, 2001). Each partner's specific roles, norms, values, practices and behaviors come to play in tactical and operational activities, thereby influencing the partnership relationship directly and indirectly (Doz and Hamel, 1998).

COMMUNITIES OF PRACTICE

The notion of a "community of practice" (hereafter, "COP") refers to a collection of individuals who interact (in a network) in less constrained ways and on a spontaneous basis in dynamic creative environments in multiple contexts of work. In a study of craft-based learning, Lave and Wenger (1991: 98) broadly define and describe a COP as "[a] system of relationships between people, activities and the world; developing with time, and in relation to other tangential and overlapping communities of practice." Indeed, prior studies on COPs partly fit the type of network logic described above; however, some proponents of COPs (see, e.g., Lave and Wenger, 1991; Wenger, 1998) oppose the characteristic terminology that is being used in network theory, such as network resources, and its preoccupation with network structures. Instead, these proponents talk about the properties of communities akin to terms such as "participation," "a mutual engagement," "a joint enterprise" and "a shared repertoire." The notion of a COP, as Wenger (1998) notes, bears similarities to the notion of "strong ties" in social network theory but more strongly emphasizes the qualitative side—that is, the social practice that comes out of human relationships and interactions rather than the flow of information (in quantitative terms) and the network of relationships *per se*.

Networking is directed toward professional education and training that extends beyond workplace environments and that involves interactions in occupational gatherings (Gherardi *et al.*, 1998; Wenger and Snyder, 2000). For example, COPs are found in contexts involving processes of apprenticeship in handicraft settings and in intellectual exchange between scientists and policy makers or between human resource departments and recruitment agencies. However, COPs also include more business-oriented relationships between buyer and supplier gatherings as well as informal gatherings of sellers and customers. The focus in a COP is not on a specific business deal as such; rather, a COP seeks to facilitate collective learning and professional development. This form of adult learning is contrasted with conventional contexts of learning in schooling and classroom environments and benefits from the fact that participants have shared work experiences and can learn from sharing these experiences among themselves.

Within COPs, know-how is crucial because the unique experiences of individuals are what make them part of a network (Wenger and Snyder, 2000). Thus, the theory of communities of practice (COP theory) concerns organizational learning, a form of "learning and knowing by participation" rather than the formal acquisition of knowing, which draws on shared work experiences and focuses on the transfer of ideas that occurs at work rather than the learning that occurs outside of the work context or across different work practices. In working life, professional information is also transferred through other channels, such as books and formal manuals, but as we will observe, it is not this type of explicit or "codified" information that is emphasized in theories related to COP and "situated learning." Furthermore, the information that is developed through COP participation often challenges and conflicts with the information that is reported in books and manuals.

COPs are primarily meeting points that operate locally because of their reliance on connected face-to-face interactions (in relatively fixed time and space dimensions). However, it is important to note that it is not obstructive for COPs to connect to globally spanning networks through the Internet and other communication channels. Although new socio-technological developments enable new forms of virtual interactions to unfold in the institutional landscape, as Wenger (1998) notes, such developments do not necessarily affect COPs and force them to become digital. By contrast, Skyrme (1999) advances a rather different view, arguing that in addition to the local (spatially defined) COP environment, local networks may simultaneously bridge into the virtual cyberspace. Hence, from this latter perspective, face-to-face interactions and virtual interactions do not necessarily preclude one another but may co-exist in different complex arrangements and fashions that may in turn be altered because of shifting legal requirements, socio-political situations and/or historical developments. In the event that COPs become digital, this development may also be related to the fact that new virtual environments may create unique productive "spin-off effects" for COPs that cannot simply be realized in non-digital environments, also indicating that one type of social environment is replaced with another (perhaps a less transparent and more complex hierarchical environment).

In COP models, it is assumed that trust, shared meaning and mutual understanding must be present for the three different interactional states to function flexibly and effectively (Wenger, 1998). Davenport and Prusak (1997) argue that COPs can efficiently work beyond traditional organizational boundaries because of face-to-face interactions and because COPs allow individuals to meet face-to-face; thus, these venues and environments are more suitable for establishing trust. Furthermore, these authors argue that interpersonal trust, in turn, is the foundation for the successful transfer of ideas in informal professional settings. Relationships and the productive outcomes of such social relationships have been identified as playing a key role in strengthening an organization's innovative capability (Skyrme, 1999). While COPs entail social support structures and camaraderie, relationship building and interactions among community members also yield productive gains. Not surprisingly, much of the focus of prescriptive management models is directed toward "productive" elements of information management. We have observed this (more or less implicit) assumption of "productivity" even in COP theory (see Wenger, 2008), which suggests that an open and participatory approach to social exchange and learning can encourage members to release and facilitate the flow of information between previously demarcated operatives in a more prolific manner. For example, social encounters may facilitate the generation of new ideas and entail more efficient flows of "qualitative information" to ensure the production of innovations (Wenger, 1998). Thus, although a goal with such interactions may be to establish informal social ties and strengthen personal relationships, such interactions also seek to accomplish productive goals—for example, to accelerate social learning through the sharing of professional experiences. A common factor here is that social interaction acts as the engine and the driving force for idea generation within COPs (Bartlett and Ghoshal, 1999).

Although it is implied that informal and productive activities require personal relationships to be established, it is acknowledged that social relationships influence the dynamics of communities. Another more or less explicit assumption surrounding COPs is that productive meetings between individuals will contribute to new "shared" perspectives that allow for "joint approaches" to problem solving. In contrast to other more formal organizational forms, such as hierarchies and markets, COPs are extremely self-organized while simultaneously directed toward self-preservation, similar to other types of organizations. Social cohesiveness is strengthened, and communities renew themselves through iterative processes of knowledge production and "culture building." Despite this social cohesiveness, one must resist the temptation of viewing COPs as rigid and closed systems—that is, social systems that are isolated from the outside world. On the contrary, COPs are open systems and are thus characterized by their preference for interacting with individuals, organizations and other COPs. In different COPs, we find individuals who have the ability to create meaningful business-oriented connections and to coordinate individuals as well as other COPs. In fact, this capability of interconnecting social entities is commonly attributed to entrepreneurial activities, in which it is theorized that entrepreneurs ultimately are skillfully linking different groups holding different "frames of references" (Wenger, 1998).

Wikström and Normann (1994) refer to individuals who are effective in bridging social and professional gaps as "gatekeepers," and in a competitive environment that requires innovative skills, it is important to have individuals who are good at both attracting and connecting innovation workers and some of the most lucrative sources of expertise to their social communities and networks. In fact, Wikström and Normann claim that "knowledge hunters" would be a more appropriate term for individuals who play important roles in organizing modern arrangements of innovative and knowledge-intensive work. Indeed, a gatekeeper's task is extremely complex because it requires interpretation, coordination and gathering different (often conflicting) perspectives and frames of reference held by the various stakeholders involved. Perhaps because of a politically contested terrain, a "knowledge hunter" (i.e., a gatekeeper) may choose to maintain a certain (social) distance from partners in a COP and other actors with whom he or she interacts (Wenger, 1998).

These boundary-spanning entrepreneurs are often required to uphold a broad multidisciplinary knowledge base and must also possess the ability to disseminate and translate professional jargon and professional knowing (and business logics) between different disciplines and organizational domains. If boundary-spanning entrepreneurs are granted excessive power and influence or if collaborative efforts are overly dependent on gatekeepers and their coordination activities in general, then there is an obvious risk that gatekeepers may be blocking rather than propelling further effort; for example, they may become "bottlenecks" in the flow of valuable information between actors (Leonard-Barton, 1998). However, even in these more or less "dysfunctional" situations, it is reasonable to assume the potential emergence of alternative routes for information to travel. When new links become established between individuals, such links will reduce the dependency on gatekeepers and undermine their power base and political influence in COPs.

The types of collaboration in which COP members interact beyond their own community sphere can be characterized by three different states of interaction: "boundary practices," "overlaps" and "peripheries." Boundary practices can be understood as interfaces between two COP environments. These practices often meet halfway to explore the possibility of forming a new and larger COP consisting of two previously smaller COPs, which would then represent the interests of a wider range of participating COP members. A "boundary practice" is a sort of "compromise" in which different COPs literally meet halfway in a new quasi-environment and that is commonly found in R&D settings involving joint efforts among teams. Such types of cross-border collaboration typically engage individuals with different backgrounds. In the academic world, for example, "boundary practices" are represented by COPs that connect scientists from different countries, disciplines and/or research teams but involve collaboration on a more informal basis. Such settings are suitable for creative and innovative tasks because of the ability of multidisciplinary groups to combine different perspectives and negotiate across boundaries (Oborn and Dawson, 2010; Skyrme, 1999). "Overlaps" represent the second form of collaboration between COPs, referring to a tighter merger between COPs. In this formation, interactions among two or more COPs establish a new joint interactional setting. Finally, "peripheries" represent the third form of collaboration and differ from the other two forms by allowing a COP not only to engage with other groups (COPs) but also to interact with multiple players in its surroundings through both active participation and observation. Peripheries allow interactions with actors who would normally not fit into a specific COP context (Wenger, 1998).

What are the typical assumptions behind the models and theories that have been explored thus far? In most culturally oriented network theories, there exists an assumption that each of the institutional forms or archetypes in themselves function as relatively uniform "entities." Therefore, such theories (more or less explicitly) take "mutuality" and "unity" for granted. In other words, such theories presume that each of the discussed archetypes represent both social stability and managerial homogeneity. This assumption, however, implies that most theories do not leave any room to entertain even the slightest possibility that there could exist inherent contradictions, instability, tensions, struggles and other types of dynamic forces that demonstrate variability—not only variability and movements between different archetypes but also movement within each of them. Hierarchical and cultural differences may create frictions that may undermine cooperation. However, the very understanding of the term "culture" rarely reflects variability; in fact, culture is instead viewed as something that is "mutually shared" among its members: "Shared values, shared beliefs, shared meaning, shared understanding, and shared sensemaking are all different ways of describing culture. In talking about culture we are really talking about a process of reality construction that allows people to see and understand particular events, actions, objects, utterances, or situations in distinctive ways" (Morgan, 1997: 138).

A shared language and terminology are in turn regarded as essential to not only forming a shared understanding (i.e., intersubjectivity) of events but also forming routines and habits that enable efficient communication. In addition to the need to create increased awareness of cultural differences and their role in collaborative activities, Doz and Hamel (1998) argue that it is also important to develop an ability to understand another party's situation and work practices. Through such understanding, cultural gaps may be bridged, and relationships may be strengthened. However, what is taken for granted in such claims? In emphasizing the "centrality of mutuality," social cohesion and organizational affinity and clarity, many network theories tend to downplay the forces of multiplicity, irregularity and changeability—that is, all the things that are sometimes perceived as "messy," unstable and unpredictable. This situation indicates how much is actually overlooked in contemporary theorizing. It should be noted that COP theory acknowledges that the negation of meanings occurs between various communities but somehow takes for granted that all members more or less share the same beliefs and values, among other things. Fox (2000) notes that processes of change in a COP can entail the formation of a series of unequal power relations. In their early elaboration on COP, Lave and Wenger encourage more work in this direction and maintain that "the concept of 'community of practice' is left largely as an intuitive notion. . . . In particular unequal relations of power must be included more systematically in our analysis" (1991: 42).

Sometimes different cultures and frames of reference are regarded as "obstacles" or "gaps" that need to be bridged in the pursuit of sharing experiences and spreading information among different knowledge carriers or between entire communities (i.e., professional networks). The exchange of information requires not only ease of access to expertise but also a common value foundation and shared terminology, such as professional jargon. In Scandinavian countries, for example, drawing on the idea of communicative rationality (Habermas, 1987), participative methods such as "democratic dialogues" and "search conferences" (Gustavsen, 1990) have been deployed to not only foster more democratic involvement in enterprises and local communities but also more fundamentally to initiate and support learning processes that allow for the emergence of a common value base and understanding. However, despite good intentions, certain hindering factors may complicate such information sharing in organizational networks and communities. Practitioners may be lacking the opportunity to interact and communicate smoothly or may not be able to share common experiences, and such instances represent examples regarded as "barriers" to the transfer of information between different network groups (Westelius, 2000). Another underlying assumption is that the receiver of information needs to have an understanding of the original individual's frame of reference or may sometimes even adopt the same frame of reference for any transformation to occur in a timely and cost-effective manner. The preoccupation with "smooth" interaction and homogeneity in earlier studies, as reflected in the discussion of the importance of establishing trust among members of the community or social practice, may largely be explained by the empirical contexts in which these studies have been situated and conducted.

The early writings on COPs revolved around empirical studies of craft-based knowing and work (see, e.g., Cook and Yanow, 1993; Lave and Wenger, 1991; Orr, 1996). In such a distinctive workplace context, there typically exists an "expert regime," a hierarchical structure, and it is imperative for "newcomers" to be able to adjust and to absorb and replicate established traditions in the process of cultivation (and, perhaps more importantly, gain established knowledge of a craft in the mode of apprenticeship). While the practice of a craft fundamentally leaves room for individual expression and uniqueness, there is still often an underlying conception of "good craftsmanship" and shared practices and routines. The latter further assume that in the process of apprenticeship, newcomers should strive for linguistic, cognitive, and behavioral uniformity rather than for plurality. In the process of learning techniques that the "masters" of a craft practice, newcomers adopt new skills and are eventually accepted. In essence, by adopting to the pre-existing values, practices and communicative expressions, craftswomen and craftsmen are viewed as legitimate members of the community. Handicraft work represents a relatively stable and uniform context, and the "cultural heredity" therefore supports the continuity and preservation of established norms. Of course, the practices of traditional handicraft work sometimes change erratically; for example, the introduction of competing tools or new methods may generate radical change (for a discussion of such transformation and innovation in handicraft practices, see, e.g., Wasen and Brierley, 2013). It appears that most culturally influenced network studies and theories typically seek to understand the mechanisms that bind members (and practices) together, as in the "let's-glue-it-together" effect. In these theories, various notions appear, such as social "likeness" and tight professional cohesion, as well as homogeneity among members in terms of "sharing" a culture (e.g., beliefs, attitudes and work practices).

Adler and Heckscher (2006) and Engeström (2007) observe that COPs are historically evolving phenomena; however, mainstream COP theory does not provide much information about the retrospective dimension of sense-making and participation in communities of practice. In a highly competitive professional setting that has developed over a long period of time and in which new actors enter (or abandon) professional communities, it would be valuable to more fully understand both the cultural and socio-political elements of change. Moreover, the wider historico-cultural dimension of network processes could also perhaps be emphasized more in future theoretical work on COPs, which could link micro and macro perspectives. Lindholm (1990) rightly argues that cultural and social aspects on various levels should not be understood as isolated phenomena; rather, they constantly influence one another. The lack of recognition of culture and historical developments may also at least partly explain why COP theory generally appears to fail in addressing the socio-political nature of social relationships and assumes a more or less stable and harmonious co-existence and mutual engagement. The notion of a COP is discussed more in detail in Chapter 3.

In summary, the prevailing notions in COP theory are those of social learning, practice and professional relatedness, which extend beyond the formal organization as a unit of analysis. Although these notions focus on different and highly relevant ideas, all of them share the view that social dynamics and participation are key to understanding networking phenomena on a micro-organizational scale. Although there is a wider cultural dimension of networking phenomena, theories rarely (if ever) account for broader institutional, historical and socio-cultural developments that extend beyond local or temporal COP settings but that may still influence the views and experiences of social learning. In contrast, the first theorizing on social networking in sociological research provided an in-depth analysis of societal and cultural change and its influence on social relationships and participation in communities.

This chapter has described some of the early developments of the COP perspective, which centered on the learning in "communities of practice" (Brown and Duguid, 1991), to more recent developments that either altered the COP perspective to a "toolkit" for managers or expanded the COP perspective and shifted its attention to the key roles of power, dominance and contradictions in epistemic cultures. It is evident that the latter more critically oriented approaches provide a useful "lens" through which to make sense of creative tensions in innovation management and provide complementary insights and new conceptual grounds to critique some of the one-dimensional concepts in COP models and related normative "recipe-based" prescriptions for realizing participatory learning, bonding and innovation "success."

SUMMARY AND CONCLUSIONS

In summary, this chapter has delved into a rich wellspring of prior academic literature on networks and networking to address how institutions channel their business activities beyond conventional institutional boundaries to harness the capabilities of innovation partnership. First, the historical significance of "relationality" and social networking was described, notions with their roots in early sociological work. These seminal studies emphasized how social change and technological and organizational developments in the wake of industrialization intensified the contradictions and tensions between individual creativity and social cohesion, as well as the competing forces of competition and collaboration. Second, theoretical approaches related to inter-organizational networks were reviewed. The ideas behind strategic networks and industrial networking were also charted. Finally, drawing on recent conceptual developments in culturally oriented approaches to networking and collaboration, issues such as shared values, mutuality and understanding in networking contexts were highlighted.

One can clearly see that business networking is a complex, multidimensional phenomenon where processes and partnerships are not only shaped by social interactions but also situated in broader cultural and historical circumstances. Business and society continuously transform, and the various streams of thought in management research have accordingly spurred new approaches to address societal and institutional changes. Recent academic work has observed significant changes in the global business environment, which have led scholars to question some of the old assumptions in mainstream management theory regarding stability, predictability and control. Lately, a number of new daunting issues have instead drawn scholarly attention to the uncertainty and inherently unstable properties in network structures. We have noted that networks are multifaceted arrangements because desirable and undesirable states exist side by side in networks, e.g., they simultaneously absorb trust and distrust/mistrust (e.g., Dirks *et al.*, 2009). Drawing on the notions of changeability and variability, the discussions and critiques of mainstream approaches to networks and networking have suggested a different approach.

However, we also need to ask ourselves whether the changing fabric of the business landscape perhaps poses new global challenges to innovation partnerships. The pace of technological change seems to increasingly accelerate each and every year, and as volatility and unpredictability rather than stability and predictability seem to characterize the competitive landscape in many industries and as rapid technological shifts happen overnight, does this acceleration of technological change affect networking and, if so, in what ways? A premise is that network relationships adapt to rapidly occurring changes in the surroundings and become more "temporal," "changeable" and "fluid" by nature. But this premise also challenges the traditional emphasis on tight social couplings in networks. If relationships are becoming more flighty, or "transitory" so to speak, and if partners are shifted more regularly, an outcome of modern networking may be amplified variability in network contexts. Castells (2000: 150) argues that the network form has its own cultural dynamics, where a type of virtual culture and common cultural codes exists: "[And] culture, in this analytical framework, should not be considered as a set of values and beliefs linked to a particular society. What characterizes the development of the informational, global economy is precisely its emergence in very different cultural/national contexts . . . leading to a multicultural framework of references." Indeed, international work in terms of business networking is increasingly "pluralistic" by nature. Clearly, as we have already been able to see, cultural plurality applies to not only private firms but also public organizations and social enterprises.

But it is also evident that there is room to expand the theory and notions related to innovation partnerships, as certain essential elements of innovation partnerships cannot be adequately described by the established frameworks in the mainstream network literature and, in particular, in schools of thought that stress harmony, mutuality and uniformity within the culturally oriented traditions. Stark (2009: 198) argues that many theoretical network constructs lack an appreciation for different situational accounts that display disparity. Stark thus challenges a range of approaches to the analysis of networks for failing to do so: "With few exceptions network analysis typically focuses on the patterns of ties to the exclusion of the diverse accounts of worth that might be operating in these interactions. Rich in the study of structure, network analysis remains impoverished in the study of situations." Contending that although many theories lack an appreciation for situational variety, Stark also questions the myth of "homogeneity" as such; instead, he makes the case for the key role of variety in innovation and creative tensions. It is reasonable to assume that understanding how various "tensions dynamics" work—or rather how they "play out" in various situations—is key to understanding why some institutional practices and innovation partnerships may flourish, whereas others become dysfunctional and, in due course, risk a soft closure or, worse, calamity. In sum, social and cultural tensions inevitably emerge as different social values and organizational interests come together, and they sometimes, but not always, "clash" and conflict. Acknowledging the presence of cultural multiplicity, competing objectives and different powers and business interests in networks, the next chapter provides a multilayered explanation of innovation networks and networking, which demonstrates that no partnership occurs without friction.

3 Social and Cultural Friction as Creative Forces

Drawing on the notion of social and cultural friction, this chapter reevaluates and explores what creative forces are, how conflicts within networks influence social collaboration and how network tensions may be developed or settled. Frictions in social networks can be either productive or unproductive and either detrimental or beneficial. Frictions can be the emergent, messy and unforeseeable forces of powerful opposition and multi-scale contradiction across cultural diversity and interrelatedness. Friction may emerge across all "new scales of organization" (Wasen, 2013: vii)—multi-scale coordination from "nano" and "micro" to "meso" and "macro." This perspective complements the "social network-level" and "community-level" explanations adopted in earlier network theory and further extends political process studies by highlighting "inter-organizational relations."

First, in attempting to dismantle the homogeneity assumption implicit in most theories of epistemic practices, this work argues that it is necessary to broaden the theory by incorporating notions of cultural multiplicity and productive friction. Followed by a discussion of the key idea of productive tensions in community of practice, we provide an appreciative critique that attempts to reassess the understanding of collective (united) forms of innovativeness. A key idea presented in Chapter 3 is that social and cultural-cognitive frictions should be made more relevant to broaden the understanding of collective forms of innovation creation. Analytical, critically oriented contributions have noted the contradictory nature of collective innovativeness and have intriguingly included key dimensions of power and influence in contemporary models. In doing so, critically oriented contributions have moved away from harmonious and heterogeneous assumptions prevalent in mainstream approaches. Finally, conclusions for the development of ordinary and unconventional approaches are provided, and it is argued that the latter have important complementary contributions to offer, particularly with regard to creative tensions and cultural disparities that may trigger change and innovation.

CULTURAL AND SOCIAL DIVERSITY—A FOUNDATION FOR INNOVATION AND CREATIVITY

With regard to radical innovation, change and creativity, it is highly challenging to combine the powerful force of cultural variety and multiethnicity (multiculturalism) together with forces of social cohesion and shared value systems. This important challenge is perhaps best expressed in the maxim "unity in diversity" (in Latin, *in varietate concordia*), a motto that the Catholic Church and the European Union strive to achieve in addition to principles of *subsidiarity, human dignity* and *solidarity* in community life. Any epistemic community whose objective is to foster cultural and epistemic diversity as a backdrop for change and innovativeness must provide access to complementary viewpoints and tolerance for differences to benefit from such.

Contemporary innovation work often involves a complex variety of professions, and in such a context of epistemic diversity, Amin and Roberts describe such work as follows:

> Purposefully organised to unleash creative energy around specific exploratory projects and typically involving coalitions of scientists, product developers, academics, visual and performing artists, advertisers, software developers, consultants, media professionals, or designers. Such coalitions can arise within organizations (e.g., product-development teams within corporations), they can be offsite (e.g., scientific, artistic or academic collaborations formed around specific projects), or they can exist as an inter-organizational network (e.g., business or advertising consultants working closely with clients in different firms).
>
> (Amin and Roberts, 2008: 361)

To date, a variety of approaches on work-based epistemic practices exist, including "communities of practice" (Wenger, 1998), "communities of interaction" (Engeström, 1999), "communities of knowers" (Klein, 2010) or "epistemic communities" (Miller and Fox, 2001). Although all these perspectives share a pivotal interest in epistemic practices and highlight productive outcomes (e.g., learning and innovativeness), different theoretical perspectives ask rather different questions about epistemic practices and communities.

The realization that sustained innovation is a product of the twin forces of change and continuity means that the organizational circumstances that are supposed to allow for creative ideas and knowledge to be innovatively (re)combined and generated in new network arrangements will also, paradoxically, face limits and obstructing forces with respect to what can actually be recombined and regenerated. This contradiction arises because it is not possible to redefine the innovation knowledge landscape without being influenced by pre-existing cultural landscape(s) and prior circumstances and historical developments. In organizational life, pre-existing cultural-cognitive representations and social landscapes are materialized in organizational circumstances such as structural relationships (e.g., asymmetrical power relations and infrastructures) and routines (e.g., peculiar rituals). Social habits make community life possible in the first place, which also means that members draw on prior structures and experiences and restate (and learn from) existing norms and cultural values. We are more or less "trapped" in our common history, personal outlooks and socially shared comfort zones. (For an excellent overview of the influence of pre-existing structures, norms and symbols in institutional life, see Mary Douglas' (1987) seminal work, *How Institutions Think*.)

Although shared norms and values may indeed contribute to stronger links between actors, the opposite theoretical position maintains that weaker links between the various members may be more beneficial in enhancing the innovative capabilities of firms (Herreld, 1998). Some authors argue that professional and cultural differences represent a positive source of productive social friction that may release creative energy in constructive interaction (Leonard-Barton, 1998; Wasen, 2005a). Such researchers emphasize that energy among individuals must be channeled in the proper direction by adopting a "can-do" attitude (e.g., when finding new solutions in the context of innovative work).

Cultural life is continuously changing and remaking itself, and if there were no change and innovation in society, then a culture would eventually tend to die out, similar to biological systems. Indeed, cultural and epistemic diversity is important, not only because it influences the remaking of social practices and human knowledge but also because such diversity restricts the extent to which change and remaking are possible or feasible. The latter meaning takes peculiar forms in institutional life, in which organizational forces such as social friction simultaneously represent both enabling and hindering elements for innovation. While change and continuity are naturally associated, there is often an asymmetrical balance between the two, which means that one force is typically stronger than the other. Clearly, the idea of conformity and coherence and some of the other simplistic formulas that underlie COP theory (see Chapter 2) need to be disentangled because the push for conformity and unity may stand in stark conflict to the drive for social diversity to promote radical change and innovation. Although members may have different orientations and "frames of references" at the outset, as they interact and "live together" to a greater degree, they are more likely to form strong social and cultural ties. The risk with such a strong drive to bridge differences and "standardize" behaviors, terminology and values is that this bridging occurs at the expense of cultural variety, which is key to improvisation and creativity. We will return to this challenging aspect in a later section.

The notion of COPs has gained increased popularity both in the prescriptive business literature and in more critically oriented research addressing issues related to the development of expertise, learning and innovation.

While the prior conceptualization of COP primarily concerns the value of participation and its contribution to socialization and identity construction, there is room for adding additional dimensions to COP theory to understand the social and professional forces that spur change and innovation in professional communities. For example, Brown and Duguid (1991) assert that participation in COPs is a source of change and innovation beyond professional organizations, but again, this work does not acknowledge that a COP or an informal network may be challenged. In other words, a COP may be situated in a contested terrain, and what may have previously been a highly valuable COP for professional (or economic) progress that may have spurred change and innovation in the past can later unexpectedly and rapidly become an outdated COP.

Furthermore, a COP may be challenged because of political processes and peer pressure. For example, Wareing (2014) finds that practitioners may encounter negative reactions to participation in COPs in situations when mentors participate in learning activities in workplace settings. When attempting workplace learning, both a trainee and his/her mentor may encounter rather unenthusiastic responses from associate team members who may be "quite vociferous in their opposition . . . [and] when a clinical environment is utilised for work-based learning friction arises between participation in clinical practice and providing a service" (2014: 46).

Social friction here appears to be primarily a negative rather than positive experience from the perspectives and experiences of fellow staff members in a busy and acute hospital ward. Wareing interprets social friction in this organizational context as resulting from the specific division of labor that establishes how given workplace roles are to be fulfilled on a daily basis. The author further contends that some of the dominant discourses, such as COP theory, disregard the fact that work demands themselves "can actually be a barrier to learning in the workplace, which is a key feature of busy acute hospital wards that rely heavily on support workers to meet the direct care needs of patients who may have multiple long-term conditions." Perhaps social friction is related to the fact that learning and mentoring requires time and effort and affect working conditions in the social system as well as the fact that other team members may need to shoulder a larger part of the work burden when they substitute for a mentor and/or an apprentice.

In theory, it is central for innovative activities not only to have a narrow focus but also to allow irrational and creative behaviors to unfold in interactions among individuals. Such "irrational" actions are not always accepted in business environments and must therefore be legitimized and made consistent with an organization's norms and values with respect to acceptable behaviors. This process is an important prerequisite for the generation of radical innovations and concepts, which can result in potentially high returns over the longer term.

More recently, others studying COPs, such as Amin and Roberts (2008), call for a better understanding of the key differences between various types of situated learning practice. These researchers argue that moving beyond the original notion of COP and adopting a "more heterogeneous lexicon" could provide a better account of the diverse varieties of "knowing in action" in workplace settings. Wenger (1998) provides the following remark, which appears to partly downplay the otherwise common harmonious conception implicit in COP theory:

> Mutual engagement does not entail homogeneity, but it does create relationships among people . . . because the term 'community' is usually a very positive one, I cannot emphasize enough that these interrelations arise out of engagement in practice and not out of an idealized view of what a community should be like. In particular, connotations of peaceful coexistence, mutual support, or interpersonal allegiance are not assumed, though of course they may exist in specific cases. Peace, happiness, and harmony are therefore not necessary properties of a community of practice. Certainly there are plenty of disagreements, tensions, and conflicts among claims processors . . . there are jealousies, gossips, and cliques. Most situations that involve sustained interpersonal engagement generate their fair share of tensions and conflicts. In some communities of practice, conflict and misery can even constitute the core characteristic of a shared practice, as they do in some dysfunctional families. A community of practice is neither a haven of togetherness nor an island of intimacy insulated from political and social relations. Disagreement, challenges, and competition can all be forms of participation. As form of participation, rebellion often reveals a greater commitment than does passive conformity.
>
> (Wenger 1998: 76–7)

Drawing on this line of reasoning, gaps in a COP may emerge not necessarily because of cultural and professional differences among participants *per se* but rather because of interpersonal differences, such as a lack of personal chemistry between individuals, conflicting personal interests, or asymmetrical power relationships. However, the use of terms such as "dysfunctional" and "misery" to contrast with "peaceful co-existence" and "mutual support" becomes rather problematic in that it may suggest that tensions and power represent less harmonious states, which may be unnecessary and potentially damaging. It is reasonable to assume that detrimental conditions and unproductive states will exist in network and community relationships. Such disadvantageous tensions may have been evolving for a number of years. Sometimes these conditions may be sensed in the general "atmosphere," whereas other times, they may be unnoticed. Furthermore, suppressed tensions and conflictual states are not static but actually overlap with contextual changes.

A key idea presented in Chapter 3 is that social and cultural-cognitive frictions should be made more relevant to broaden the understanding of collective forms of innovation creation. Analytical, critically oriented contributions have noted the contradictory nature of collective innovativeness and have intriguingly included key dimensions of power and influence in contemporary models. In doing so, critically oriented contributions have moved away from harmonious and heterogeneous assumptions prevalent in mainstream approaches. In sum, the discussion thus far indicates that COP theory and the political process approach can enrich one another and can be combined to offer a stronger contribution to our understanding of cultural plurality in innovation contexts.

FROM THE MULTIPLICITY OF CULTURES TO THE CULTURE OF MULTIPLICITY

The notion of social and cultural friction may increase managerial awareness of the inherently productive forces that produce tension and that fuel creativity and innovation. Stark (2009: 177–8) observes that "organizational diversity is most likely to yield its fullest evolutionary potential when different organizational principles coexist in an active rivalry within the firm . . . [but] organizational diversity in itself does not make for adaptability. There must be interaction across forms, principles and cultures to generate new solutions."

Cultural variety is believed to have an imperative role in creativity, change and innovation. Different cultural structures and institutional archetypes were discussed in the preceding section on networks and innovation partnerships. While network theories address variance in their different models and dimensions, it becomes clear that "cultural diversity" *per se* is emphasized and understood differently. The sections that follow will therefore address and comment on two different and contrasting approaches to theorizing diversity, beginning with a discussion of the "diversity of cultures" approach, which recognizes that different cultures (and institutions) represent differences themselves but which also assumes that institutional structures and cultures are largely infused with homogeneity and stability. This discussion is then followed by a discussion of an emergent-contextual approach, which highlights that cultures themselves are heterogeneous and highly unstable. Here, cultures are theorized and understood to be emerging, sparkling human products "in the making." The latter approach emphasizes that cultures are recurrently "co-produced" in social encounters and zones of creative tension.

Lutz (1997: 234) writes that "networks do not only have to be established, but one also has to make them work!" So far, however, no one has found an all-encompassing, perfect solution for constructing inter-organizational networks in "the best possible way"; instead, the proper structure and culture of a network seems to depend on the current situations and circumstances in which the network is historically embedded and socially situated (Ebers, 1997). Various cultural values and organizational forms co-exist, and partners safeguard existing power relations and personal interests. The multiplicity of interests that are involved and enrolled can easily lead to problems in the "design" of commonly accepted strategies. Some actors may have incentives to protect certain interests, and one of the most powerful "protection mechanisms" is the protection of market leadership.

SOURCES OF POWER AND INFLUENCE IN PARTNERSHIPS

In relation to Foucault's (1980, 1982) idea that knowledge is intrinsically entangled with power and identity (devised as the dual notion of power/knowledge), we must note the significance of knowledge and information as sources of power and influence in organizations. Power accrues in organizational settings in which some actors manage to gain access to precious expertise and valuable "carriers" of information. Power also manifests in situations in which certain actors are able to direct others' attention to their concerns and particular interests, and by doing so, these actors are in a position either to define the "rules of the game" or to influence decision making in the processes of management and managing. Morgan notes as follows:

> By controlling these key resources a person can systematically influence the definition of organizational situations and can create patterns of dependency . . . if people define situations as real, they are real in their consequences. Many skillful organizational politicians put this dictum into practice on a daily basis by controlling information flows and the knowledge that is made available to different people, thereby influencing their perceptions of situations and hence the ways they act in relation to those situations. These politicians are often known as 'gatekeepers', opening and closing channels of communication and filtering, summarizing, analyzing, and thus shaping knowledge in accordance with a view of the world that favors their interests. . . . Even by the simple process of slowing down or accelerating particular information flows, thus making knowledge available in a timely manner or too late for it to be of use to its recipients, the gatekeeper can wield considerable power.
> (Morgan, 1997: 179)

The exercise of power and influence in organizational settings relies on subtle tactics and procedures that facilitate the protection of interests and the achievement of goals. For instance, information advantage is related to such subtle power strategies and tactics of gaining and maintaining control. Certain individuals, for instance, may deliberately choose to keep interesting or valuable information (of an innovative nature) to themselves, which can in turn lead to imbalances in cooperation efforts (Norton and Smith, 1997). Moreover, it can be difficult to anticipate and correctly assess the contributions of actors sharing such types of significant information because the relevance and importance of information change over time (Doz and Hamel, 1998).

In theory, an optimal situation would entail complete openness and trust between parties, according to which valuable information and ideas flow freely and thereby strengthen the innovative capacity. However, this circumstance rarely, if ever, occurs. Issues such as power struggles and self-interest may stand in conflict with an organization's commitment to transparency and openness. A divergence between different theoretical positions concerns the appropriate degree of transparency in networks and partnerships. The consequence of different perspectives on the degree of openness leads Davenport and Prusak (1997) to advocate a moderate degree of openness, such that information and ideas should be allowed to pass between parties as long as they do not compromise an organization's own key interests. This situation is a fine and delicate balancing act, of course, and must be adapted to specific situations. In any case, complete openness may not always be desirable or viable. Although transparency has become a popular phrase in developed societies, transparency may be unproductive in that it creates information overload and possibly even "knowledge overload." In situations in which too much information and a massive flood of data cause an organization's situational awareness to become "foggy" rather than clear, it also becomes increasingly difficult to anticipate important trends as high-quality information and ideas drown in a flood of inappropriate data and information or irrelevant knowledge. The information exchange perspective addresses how information dynamically flows in network relationships and has attracted a great deal of interest in the academic community. Davenport and Prusak suggest that "as firms become increasingly intertwined with other organizations in collaborative networks, we might all benefit from a better understanding of information behavior at the inter-organizational level" (1997: 101). In theory, it is easy to surmise that networking should facilitate the "free" flow of information and the exchange of ideas between members of a professional community; however, in practice, such an assumption may be challenged by harsh political realities.

Another factor that further complicates the idea of productive information interchange in highly creative settings is that information sharing may take more unpredictable, serendipitous or "irrational" turns. The mere existence of interconnected parts that unpredictably interact in a community of practice setting will unavoidably mean that seemingly "irrelevant" information will be disseminated among its members. Furthermore, the practice of sharing seemingly irrelevant information may trigger events that eventually result in the recombination of disparate information sources. The sharing of outwardly "irrelevant information," such as the politics of rumor assessment or gossiping, may appear to be a superfluous (and unproductive) activity for innovation, but gossips may occasionally contribute to innovative and creative thinking. Consequently, the distinctions between useful and irrelevant information or between unproductive and productive knowledge are perhaps not as clear as theory would suggest. Hence, what initially appears to be an improper knowledge or information strategy may actually prove to be quite an appropriate strategy in hindsight. Understandings may also vary because of different cultural and professional orientations.

The theories discussed so far explicitly account for various categories of institutional archetypes, so initially, it seems that inter-organizational frameworks address diversity (multiplicity). For example, factors that may vary between different institutions are size, organizational cultures, working practices, and so forth. So what these models stress in reality is the various forms of cultures and institutions, not rivalry between cultures or tensions within a network. While institutional frameworks account for the multiplicity of cultures, for example, in the world of personal and organizational networks, the notion of the culture of multiplicity instead accounts for the "culture's way of life" (Cook and Yanow, 1993) and the manner in which various cultural elements co-exist and, from time to time, collide. From an outsider's perspective, some cultural expressions (e.g., organizational rituals) might be perceived as bizarre or odd because these expressions are not compatible with "interpretive schemes" and the outsider's understanding and prior experience (Brown and Duguid, 1991).

Moreover, the multiplicity of culture manifests itself not only *amid* different and alternative organizational structures (models) but also *within* the same organizational systems that compose our institutional landscape. So it is then possible to challenge the widespread assumption that innovation partnerships in networks merely signify "collisions" between institutional cultures and organizational archetypes (see Chapter 2). In fact, collisions occur in more organizational spaces and levels. In its place, we instead develop an alternative notion of "friction" that accounts for how interactions and interests can clash and essentially conflict within a seemingly unifying culture. Wasen (2005a), for example, notes that cultural multiplicity does not only imply that several cultures co-exist and, at times, clash; more so, from such tensions and clashes new cultural forms emerge, and cultures may become innovatively "amalgamated" (merged) within inter-organizational network settings and activities:

> These forms of inter-organizational collaboration are considered to present significant potential for mutual learning, innovation and development, as ideas, cultures and traditions are being 'amalgamated' . . . [among] people who, in most cases, have different professional, educational and national backgrounds . . . [and] a multitude of different and competing organizational interests, personal opinions and perceptions of reality might come together. Quite literally, they merge, or even conflict. In many cases, disagreements and misunderstandings might

be a natural result of such cultural differentiation . . . discrepancies in outlooks and perspectives, however, do not need to have a negative impact on inter-organizational cooperation. Cultural differentiation may equally promote the creative growth of new ideas and organisational innovations.

(Wasen, 2005a: 17–19)

Recognizing the value of social and cultural diversity, not least for innovation, change and creativity, Wasen further suggests that inter-organizational tensions and "open confrontation can be an effective and useful mode of conflict resolution in post-merger integration. . . . The individuals involved should not expect that all tensions and possible conflicts will or should be eliminated when organizations integrate activities . . . the tensions might be said to generate a powerful driving force, the problem of course being the proper balance between tension and agreement" (2005: 19–20). Another, more recent, account of intra-organizational tensions and the key role of balancing different interests is provided in an interesting study by Xianghong Hao (2008). She followed a development project in the automobile industry at Volvo Cars, where value-creating design conflicted with cost reduction pressures in a car model "facelift" project:

External pressures from different professions in the organization that represented different interests regarding the cost and quality dilemma make it increasingly difficult for the engineers to take risks in their construction work, since different professions have different views and different professional practices. Dynamic tensions and struggles are inevitable aspects of the system engineers' work. These tensions may stimulate and guide the discovery and the development process, as well as obstruct the establishment of a common ground for all parties. Learning how to accommodate and cope with these external forces in the interest of the project as a whole constitutes the core of the system development engineers' work.

(Hao, 2008: 52)

Tensions may emerge, for example, when organizational and cultural differences lead to different interpretations of overall strategies. An organization's culture is self-organizing, or "emerging"; thus, it is constantly evolving. Scholars have illustrated how managers exert great effort in attempting to control, and sometimes even manipulate, professional settings in workplaces in order to influence corporate culture, as well as how employees locally attempt to resist or become trapped in such "engineering of culture" (Kunda, 1992). Doz and Hamel (1998) argue that a company culture is difficult to steer in a certain direction and therefore difficult to "manage" in a traditional sense, largely because it is influenced by a large number of chaotically interrelated factors. Cultural variance and organizational variance have always existed between different institutional logics and will continue to exist as long as different organizational forms exist. The notion of the culture of multiplicity stresses the importance of allowing *for* social and cultural diversity. Depending on how systems and networks address differences (and tensions) within themselves, they may be more or less successful in promoting social and cultural diversity.

Thus far, the discussion has addressed strategic management and change processes that are limited to innovation partnerships in an inter-organizational setting. However, network partnerships may easily start to spread and "attract" additional links in nearby networks and in other domains, on either a large or a small scale. This is captured by the notions "networks in networks" and "partnerships in partnership." Yet the complexity of specific business strategies increases drastically when networks connect to new social ties in networks because, characteristically, a larger number of inherently unique (sometimes incompatible) "interest points" will exist between actors.

Various cultural values and organizational forms co-exist, and partners safeguard existing power relations and personal interests. The multiplicity of interests that are involved and enrolled can easily lead to problems in the "design" of commonly accepted strategies. Some actors may have incentives to protect market shares, but as we will see, one of the most powerful "protection mechanisms" is the protection of self-interests and career pay off (Knights and Murray, 1994; Preece *et al.*, 1999). Partnerships thus are often talked about in positive terms, as something good and fruitful, but in reality, partnerships are better understood as social dramas, and such collaborative events and situations may unfold in various messy, turbulent and unexpected ways.

As we noted in Chapter 1, there is a political element of organizational life that can both spur and inhibit developments and can thus be equally positive and negative in processes of change. Badham and Buchanan describe the situation as follows:

> Avoidance of political issues may result in tacit support for existing organizational power inequalities, may lead to project failure and to disappointment of the hopes and aspirations of those persuaded to become involved in the change process and benefit from it . . . and may weaken trust in the professionalism of the change driver, who conveys an image of political and organizational naivety.
>
> (1996: 2)

A particular problem with power-blind representations and apolitical perspectives that may stem from adopting an overly harmonious and homogeneous approach is that such perspectives essentially lack even tentative explanations for the emergence of contradictory, resisted and contested events and developments in mutual engagements and social partnerships.

The force of social friction and movement is not neutral in a social and organizational setting. Actors pursue and defend various interests in battles over power and influence in organizations. Thus, in the process of organizational change, interests compete and power positions sometimes conflict:

> In talking about 'interests' we are talking about predispositions embracing goals, values, desires, expectations, and other orientations and inclinations that lead a person to act in one way rather than another. In everyday life we tend to think of interests in a spatial way: as areas of concern what we wish to preserve or enlarge or as positions that we wish to protect or achieve. We live 'in' our interests, often see others as 'encroaching' on them, and readily engage in defenses or attacks designed to sustain or improve our position. The flow of politics is intimately connected with this way of positioning ourselves. . . . The tensions existing between the different interests . . . [make] work inherently 'political,' even before we take into account the existence and actions of other organizational members.
>
> (Morgan, 1997: 163)

Tensions between varying interests are inherent in network partnerships and organizations. Such tensions highlight the importance of addressing the political nature of social and cultural friction. However, power may both spur and/or inhibit processes of change and can thus be either positive or negative depending on the situation (Badham and Buchanan, 1996). Rather than observing a COP filled with unnecessary knowledge friction, power tensions and conflict, we may acknowledge that both tensions and friction may at times be productive forces that foster change, creativity and innovation.

The orientation toward different antagonistic states among network actors varies from situation to situation, producing a great variety of possible outcomes. Some individuals may be inclined to release frustrations and tensions that have accumulated during a period of time. A relatively peaceful period may be followed momentarily by a fairly rapid release (or partial undoing) of social tensions or a series of instant clashes among network partners. Such a situation can have a devastating effect on network relationships and can undermine established trust in innovative partnerships. The negative consequences of rapid releases of tensions may lead others to pursue a strategic choice to avoid direct massive conflicts while seeking other more ordered ways of addressing frustrations to maintain the partnership. From a political perspective, there is value in the ability to recognize tensions in time and to seek diplomatic (tactful) solutions that allow for the release of such tensions. The mechanisms of friction forces represent a gradual release of tensions that may be helpful for addressing contradictions and tensions in social situations. Friction typically allows for an extended interactional process that may lessen tensions while preventing direct collisions and clashes.

One may perhaps use the term "frictioning" vis-à-vis friction to emphasize the processual nature—a distinction that partly reflects prior usage of "managing versus management" and "organizing versus organization."

However, further complicating the situation, variation in the strength of bargaining positions among various actors and groups will often exist, and these positions are themselves continuously revised and reconstructed. With regard to social choice, some managers may not have the proper "tools" to properly use their influence in the social situations that we have discussed in this chapter. Social friction self-organizes in network environments; it is an emergent phenomenon whose workings cannot be completely planned in minute detail, predetermined or rationally controlled. We cannot be in complete control of socio-cultural friction. For example, social relationships containing friction may persist for long periods of time without being settled, and dissensions and tensions may eventually become destructive for all involved parties. Such situations suggest that the underlying (and invisible) historical developments in network partnerships may be more important than we may think. There might be underlying relational "scars" that not only impair social relationships but also constantly hinder and resist change. This phenomenon, of course, is not unique to organizational collaboration. Even between different countries and cultures, we may find underlying unresolved (and unhealed) historical events that remain in collective memory and cultural heritage and that still quietly function beneath the surface level through various forms of resistance and social antagonism. As many observers have noted, history is socially constructed. Memories, observations and interpretations are endowed with meaning, and accounts of historical events are themselves never value-free and objective. In network partnerships, there typically exists an interplay (and potential conflict) between different versions of historical reconstructions that reflects both present contextual conditions and future anticipations. Critically oriented approaches that recognize the role of power and negotiation mechanisms (e.g., Buchanan and Badham, 1999; Dawson, 1994; Knights and Murray, 1994; Preece *et al.*, 1999) provide useful analytical tools and multilayered analysis to better understand Janus-faced concepts, as well as the multiplicity and inherent contradictions in organizational life (see, e.g., the political process perspective on innovation and technological change in Chapter 1).

According to Badham and Buchanan, "A deliberate and principled failure to address the political dimensions of organizational change can be portrayed as unethical, if not unprofessional" (1996: iii). Political process studies highlight and amply show that power issues unavoidably manifest themselves in various forms in labor relations, perhaps most notably through the struggle and resistance among those organizational members whose powerbase and traditional dominance may be contested and sometimes even eroded by the introduction of new business practices, novel ideas and/or advanced technologies. In summary, it has been noted that (mis)trust, conflict and strategy are key factors that shape and reshape culture in network relations and partnerships. Many mainstream approaches in the networking paradigm (for important exceptions, see, e.g., Mol, 2000; Stark, 2009; Swan and Scarbrough, 2005) have still not attempted to incorporate any of the effects that such tensions and organizational clashes may have in collaborations and networking efforts that seek to harness innovation.

FROM CONCORD TO DISCORD

In some inter-organizational contexts in which work activities center on spurring path-breaking discoveries and radical innovation and taking risks, a more complex relational logic seems to emerge. The relational logic is more complex in the sense that several more or less co-existing dominating cultures rather than one dominating culture might exist. This multiplicity of cultures calls for new institutional arrangements that foster increased social inclusiveness and professional participation so that all actors become socially integrated. Cultural open-mindedness, trust and tolerance for increased variety are important traits for this type of complex network collaboration (set up to generate radical innovation). These networks typically comprise a large variety of actors and a muddle of relationships side by side. Docherty *et al.* (2006) stress the importance of inclusive participation and observe that:

> Given the growing complexity of the issues facing companies, the need to include all stakeholders actively in transformation processes makes participation more important as well as realigning it from traditional arenas . . . [still] the complexities of the changes across not only two stakeholders in one organization but across a multitude of organizations and stakeholders create challenges requiring developed forms for conducting action research.
>
> (2006: 233)

The complexity increases when more horizontal interlinking of multiple networks exists, i.e., complex networks of networks. More network collaborations are likely to be set up to be socially inclusive for an increased number of participants, but these collaborations may face new challenges on the way that need to be addressed.

Indeed, *network* and *networking* are perhaps two of the most prevalent concepts of our time, and these concepts are regularly used in different contexts and debates to describe, perhaps too many, features of contemporary business life. Despite some disapproval with mainstream cultural approaches to professional networking, many of these theoretical frameworks still provide a rich conceptual apparatus and usable explanations to further our understanding of the underlying mechanisms that make coordinated efforts and "acts of social bonding" possible in the first place. We have seen that culturally oriented traditions provide complementary explanations of key mechanisms that explain how actors unite and interlink in multiplex network partnerships. But we also noticed that partnership links cannot be taken for granted: social couplings are fragile, and thus, what seems to be a trustful relationship may quickly turn into a distrustful one, and what seems to be a valuable partnership may in reality prove to be a "fantasy" or fiction (e.g., a fake relationship without any substance).

What is perhaps the most salient feature in organizational studies on the cultural aspects of networking—and what distinguishes culturally oriented frameworks from other more structural-oriented network frameworks—is an appreciation that relationship building is not only a process of "linking" social "ties" but also a robust process of "coupling" ties that often make networks more long-lasting and forceful. These processes are key variables for understanding the emergence of durable social ties and couplings in innovation partnerships and networks.

In today's global and pluralistic societies, "net-working" individuals (with an emphasis on "net") symbolize quite different business values, professional backgrounds and personal passions. Consequently, it is reasonable to assume that increased variance in networks and networking will be a rule rather than an exception. In the best of worlds, divergence would be a norm, different orders would be allowed to overlap peacefully, and cultures would quietly co-exist. However good and tolerant such a pluralistic world may be, history has taught us the hard lesson that social and cultural variance allows for various social tensions. Indeed, the effects of such tensions in social relations can be quite far-reaching. In the organizational context, for example, earlier close ties in professional communities may suddenly be challenged because of certain events, networking partners who once had strong confidence in each other may promptly stop trusting each other because of certain human deeds, and actors who once shared the same business goal(s) and benefits of inclusion may suddenly stop believing in the benefits of networking. Because everything is constantly moving and changing, what is (or "seems") to be a coherent fact at one point in time may later prove to be quite unstable.

Traditional network-based concepts such as "shared values," "solid trust," "mutuality" and other more harmonious constructs in culture-centric management theories do not seem to account for clashes, network tensions and professional conflicts. It is important not only to stress how matters ought to be in ideal situations but also to reveal how matters are in real-life situations (e.g., non-ideal conditions). We are thus in a position to re-approach the thesis of homogeneity and instead to formulate a new thesis that stresses tensions and frictions rather than uniformity and harmony. Tensions, whether good or bad, emerge in most change processes, but they perhaps take the most extreme forms in antagonistic states of fracas. However, we focus on the productive forces that may spur innovation and change in organizations in an orderly fashion.

The two scholars, Gibson Burrell and Gareth Morgan (1979), have amply demonstrated that every dominating sub-paradigm in sociological theorizing has its own particular ontological assumptions about the world that affect the analysis of institutional life. Network frameworks are based on some core assumptions as well. In the seminal book *Images of Organization*, Morgan (1997) addresses various complementary metaphors for understanding organization and organizing. For example, Morgan (1997) uses the "brain metaphor" to shed light on certain key aspects of networking. Every approach is based on certain assumptions, and network theory is inspired by natural systems. This metaphor is one of many available "lenses," highlighting issues related to properties in complex systems such as learning, self-organization, communication and interconnectivity (the last of which draws on the observation how brain cells are connected to each other). Behind this conjecture is the elusive idea that a social network principally is an arena for human (social) communication. This idea is explicitly reflected in more recent work. Castells (2012), for example, notes that the networks of networks idea concerns how "humans create meaning by interacting with their natural and social environment, by networking their neural networks with the networks of nature and with social networks. This networking is operated by the act of communication" (2012: 5–6).

While the communication perspective is indeed essential for understanding the evolution of human interactions in networks, it represents a rather limited view of innovation partnerships. If networking is merely reduced to a communicative exercise, then there is a risk of overlooking social and material factors that may impede network building and other related organizational activities (e.g., cultural, political and social frictions inherent to institutional life). However, it is reasonable to assume that neither in a distributed biological network formation nor in a formal (mechanistic) organization are all such relationships equally distributed and that some network actors are more powerful and dominant than others.

Castells (2012), for example, treats power as the option or possibility among network actors to determine who is in and who is out, so to speak. Despite its rather "social deterministic" flavor, the notion of exclusion provides a lens to focus in on some of the underlying socio-political mechanisms that affect network building where different "building blocks," figuratively speaking, are put in place or possibly "maneuvered." Yet such a purposeful act and differentiating mechanism implies that the meaning of power in a network is ostensibly fused into a single conception that integrates discrimination ("influence") and "exclusion" into the overriding notion of "the power to exclude" (this reflects perhaps the analogy of a "club membership," which by definition is "exclusive"). Castells (2009) writes: "There is a fundamental form of exercising power that is common to all networks: exclusion from the network . . . there is one form of exclusion—thus, of power—that is pervasive in a world of networks: to include everything valuable in the global while excluding the devalued local" (2009: 50).

This assumed distinction between inclusion and exclusion in a network, however, is rather problematic because, first, it takes for granted that actors actually want to remain in a network and, second, it disregards the fact that there may be an exit strategy at play at the other side of the negotiation table. In this instance, it is more likely that power relationships are more equally distributed and that interactive networking involves negotiations over membership. For example, as Hagel and Brown (2005: 83) note, managers are gradually becoming increasingly more reliant on business partners "for key elements of business value, but all the effort of coordination with outsiders takes its toll. It requires time and money to get relevant information about them, negotiate terms, monitor their performance, and, if needs are not met, switch from one partner to another." This statement illustrates how the "exit strategy" dynamic may be played out.

The active choice to leave a partnership entails that the risk of being excluded no longer remains. But the idea of power of exclusion then loses its force. Exit strategies do not downplay the role of what is referred to as "a power to exclude" but rather suggest that power in networks is a rather multifarious and "slippery notion": network powers change over time and, perhaps even more important, are bound to limited periods of time because power is not everlasting. Network powers are also contextually embedded in historical and cultural circumstances and are dependent on (invisible) bonds of trust and more or less active participation.

Moreover, another power mechanism also exists in networks, which, broadly speaking, plays out at a more aggregate macro-level in institutional life, namely, the leverage and influence of one powerful network collective over other similarly powerful formations. This mechanism is perhaps more accurately captured in the phrase "networks of powers" (here, stressing the pluralistic impact of power—hence "powers"). From a "networks of powers" perspective, innovation activities are usually embedded in a multitude of settings where drawn boundaries are constantly redrawn, renegotiated and contested. Where the actual boundaries are sketched between various network collectives and formations is a matter that itself represents contested terrain. While boundaries may be difficult to tease out, earlier in the chapter we noted that the common distinction between "internal" and "external" processes in an organization's environment in fact is an equally tricky and restraining distinction. Yet if the idea of interrelatedness in networks is stressed too much, it may create a fictive illusion that boundaries are absent and that everything is fluidly networked and interconnected.

The problem is not that networking as such assumes a more or less harmonious state of collaboration, with the peaceful co-existence of different actors "sharing" a culture and mutual friendship. Indeed, this is one of the many feasible states or contexts for networked life. Rather, the problem here is that when such coherence and harmony is assumed, other important states, including important states that may account for other types of social dynamics (e.g., discordant and conflictual events and maybe even catastrophic and cataclysmic situations), automatically become excluded and discarded. However, such terminology has rarely been used in modern network theories. Thus, it is important to embrace a more comprehensive situational understanding of networking. In the final section, we therefore more closely explore the issue of tensions and network frictions, a topic that seems to have been largely overlooked in the mainstream literature on networks and innovation partnerships.

NETWORKS AND NETWORKING ARE NOT FRICTION FREE

In the Academy Award-winning movie *Cast Away* (2000), the systems engineer Chuck Nolan (Tom Hanks) embarks on a journey, but his plane encounters a fierce rainstorm, and he becomes stranded on an island. He is in a state of shock and distress after the devastating plane crash, but worse, he finds out that he is stranded on an uninhabited island that is enclosed by a massive coral reef, far from modern civilization. Hence, being completely alone and having only a few supplies, Chuck has to fight against the powerful unpredictable forces of nature. When the heavy rain stops falling, Chuck tries to create a fire by rubbing a stick against a piece of wood, just to create enough heat. But it does not work, and he cuts his hands and loses his temper. How will Chuck Nolan survive? Yet perseverance and determination eventually pays off: Chuck manages to start his first fire, and the rest is history!

The same mechanisms of movement, effect and interaction that generate heat apply to the modern means of transportation that we rely on. Consider, for a moment, how the wheels of a car (or bicycle) merely spin in the air if there is no ground beneath them. While the wheels are in motion, either the car or the bicycle remains still. But when the spinning wheels eventually meet the asphalt road's rugged, dry and hard surface, the wheels then begin to encounter some resistance. Fighting to overcome this resistance, the wheels turn, and now the transportation vehicle starts to smoothly accelerate down the road. Both these cases illustrate the workings of friction.

In an engineering study of friction and wear in industrial applications, Bittencourt (2012) defines physical friction as follows:

> Friction exists in all mechanisms to some extent. It can be defined as the tangential reaction force between two surfaces in contact. There are different types of friction, e.g., dry friction, viscous friction, lubricated friction, skin friction, internal friction. Friction is not a fundamental force but the result of complex interactions between contacting surfaces down to a nanoscale perspective. Due to its complex nature, it is difficult to describe it from physical principles.

(2012: 23)

The interest in friction management in robotics and other related engineering practices arises from the fact that if friction is properly understood, monitored and modeled, the likelihood of attaining greater stability, control, durability and overall performance for a system in motion will increase. *Tribology*, a specific branch of science, emerged in the 1930s to specifically address interacting surfaces in relative movement, and nano-tribology emerged in the 1980s. One of the basic tenets in this branch of science is that friction effects display nonlinear behavior, as first observed by Stribeck in 1902 (Besson, 2013). This book provides a fresh perspective to understanding the social frictions and creative tensions that, in and of themselves, provoke new ideas and novel interpretations that can yield unexpected results in organizational innovation.

Concepts such as network friction, organizational tension and polarization have not been used extensively in social science to discuss the emergent and multifarious characteristics of networks (e.g., the complex and messy processes underlying "partnerships in the making") or, for that matter, the possible routes that contribute to undermining and dissolving innovation partnerships. But an increasing number of scholars have begun to emphasize the role of heterogeneous rationalities, conflicting worldviews and epistemic cultures that underpin social, technological and organizational innovation (see, e.g., Hagel and Brown, 2005; Stark, 2009; Wasen, 2005a). Stark, for instance, uses the notion of friction to elaborate on entrepreneurship as creative recombinations and acts seeking to exploit uncertainty, and he "further regards recombinant processes as friction . . . [and describes] entrepreneurship as the organization of friction," where a key challenge in entrepreneurship is to develop and explore the capacities to keep manifold evaluative principles simultaneously in play (2009: 182). Here, friction focuses on organizational processes (overlies) where different principles of evaluation may conflict and where performance criteria may collide; thus, the quest for entrepreneurs is to seek to benefit from the resulting friction emerging from such multiplicity and ambiguity.

Network friction may include the rivalry of evaluative principles and overlaps in entrepreneurial activities, as described by Stark. But in the realm of innovation partnerships and inter-organizational networks, friction takes on a broader meaning and extends to all scales of organization and social networking. To this point, for example, few researchers have attempted to link organizational friction with friction in data, information and knowledge.

One of the first accounts of friction in science and technology studies is provided by Nowotny (1993). She notes that frictions emerge in acts that dissipate energy, which can be both functional and dysfunctional and have both stabilizing and destabilizing effects on interactions:

> In non-linear systems instabilities may occur which open up new pathways of development. Friction as a coupling mechanism is bounding

these instabilities at finite amplitudes. In social life, friction is implied in every form of interaction, yet too much friction may mean antagonism and violence that entails high costs. . . . To regulate friction in such a way that it acts to match energy with what it is to be used for in social life while incurring only gradual losses, rather than sudden and high ones and yet without preventing change and innovation from occurring, might be considered one of the hallmarks of the civilizing process. . . . Friction prevents the system from going completely berserk if that system becomes instable—as all non-linear systems inevitably do. In the play between the instability inherent in non-linear systems friction functions as a regulator. It enables the emergence of the new whenever instability reaches a point which no longer can be compensated with old means, while acting as stabilizer in preventing the system to fall apart completely.

(Nowotny, 1993: 41–2)

Håkansson and Waluszewski (2001) draw on Nowotny's distinction between stabilizing and destabilizing effects in networks and introduce a distinction between inertia and friction, where the former implies an unwillingness to engage in motion (or social change). The concept of network friction advances Nowotny's (1993) notion of friction by more explicitly stressing the social aspects that may generate friction. Social self-organization, a less regulated form of organization, is considered to promote bottom-up initiative, creativity and innovation (e.g., Wasen and Lodaya, 2012). However, in many instances, autonomy and self-organization owe their very existence to friction and instability, as social frictions and cultural clashes trigger transformations and modifications in systems, which, in turn, challenge stiffness and regulation. Indeed, any system in a mode of stagnation and stability also lacks a high degree of friction, which hampers self-organizational activities.

Classic actor–network theory (ANT) emphasizes the ordering mechanisms that eventually lead to stability in networks. ANT stresses that systems should be viewed as heterogeneous systems that are part of wider systems (biological, technological, social and natural environments) and thus not viewed as "closed" and homogenous systems. What caught scholars' imaginations was the appreciation of a social constructivist approach in ANT alongside the recognition of the key role of power, manipulation and negotiation in systems. What is the role of tension then? Mol (2000), for example, interestingly notes that this useful notion is absent in classic ANT. Mol summarizes and elaborates on the meanings and usefulness of classic ANT terms and shows how one of these notions, "association" (see, e.g., Latour, 1986), was used to describe the powerful mechanisms that explain how actors become tied and linked to networks:

> For a technology to succeed, it must somehow interest financers, builders, users. In order for a network to form, associations have to be

made . . . [but] the term 'association' cannot begin to cover all forms of relatedness. Further words are needed: collaboration, clash, addition, tension, exclusion, inclusion, etc. . . . different 'networks', simultaneously interdependent and in tension.

(Mol, 2000: 259)

While the notion of association refers to instances in which gaps are bridged in networks, this also implies that key differences are overcome. The notion of association thus reflects, more generally, a preoccupation with stability rather than radical change and uncertainty. In an elaboration on typical early ANT terms, Mol finds that some notions cannot capture the nature of relatedness to signify that some things also simultaneously can be in a state of tension. She writes: "These days most ANT researchers no longer unravel singular networks, but attend to co-existing ones in tension" (2000: 264). Clearly, network stability fails to recognize the inherent conflict in and between network actions, as well as the disorganizing properties that affect modern systems. What is relevant here is that Mol stresses the essential idea that we should understand networks pluralistically (i.e., the multiplicity of networks), and drawing on this idea, she writes that tensions will exist not only within a network but also between networks:

As soon as attention shifts to the co-existence of different realities (or logics, or modes of ordering) the question arises as to how these hang together . . . 'association' does not hint at the frictions that persist even after linkages have been made. It hides the fact that, more often than not, gaps are only partially bridged, while tensions endure.

(Mol, 2000: 264)

The types of enduring tensions discussed above, despite not being linked to cultural factors as such, seem to largely correspond to what we have discussed thus far. Leonard-Barton (1998) also shares an underlying concern for multiplicity in organizational innovation and uses the notion "core capabilities" to highlight the factors that, paradoxically, can both promote and obviate change and innovation. This paradox ironically exists because a company's strength can simultaneously be its weakness. Repressive mechanisms that may block innovative efforts represent the opposite mechanisms that underlie the idea of core capabilities; these mechanisms are captured by the notion of "core rigidities." Leonard-Barton (1998) elaborates on the idea of "creative abrasion," where management's task is to:

recognize the potential inherent in a portfolio of often conflicting signature skills. Some managers of innovative organizations select people because their ideas, biases, personalities, values and skills conflict—not in spite of their differences. Why? Because an effective guard against people's considering only a few problem-solving alternatives or, worse, framing problems so that they can be solved only with familiar solutions is to involve a variety of people, with their diverse signature skills, in the task. As different ideas rub against each other, sparks fly. However in a well-managed process, the sparks are creative, not personal . . . [and] emphasize that energy generated by the conflict can be channeled into creating rather than destroying, into synthesis rather than fragmentation.

(Leonard-Barton, 1998: 63)

The term "creative abrasion" is one of the most interesting terms discussed so far. It was originally coined by Gerald Hirshberg, a former director of Nissan Design International, and it emphasizes that disagreement and heterogeneity in organizational life create enormous productive opportunities for creativity and innovation. Although Leonard-Barton's (1998) detailed elaboration on the central role of "productive clashes" or "sparks" is interesting and very relevant here, it primarily concerns "intra-organizational" circumstances.

Creative abrasion is further elaborated on and extended to the realm of inter-organizational networks by Hagel and Brown (2005), who note that in key developments of flat panel display (FDP) technology in Japan, innovation and change:

Occurred not because the interactions between the companies were seamless but because the activity at the seams was challenging, stimulating and catalytic . . . by mixing it up with other organizations. Keep in mind, of course, that productive friction doesn't usually happen so naturally. It can't be relied on to carry the day. As we all know, when people with different backgrounds, experiences and skill sets engage with one another on problems, misunderstandings arise, arguments occur, and time is consumed before resolution and learning take place (if they do at all). Too often, in fact, the friction becomes dysfunctional.

(2005: 85)

Leonard-Barton (1998) notes that it is difficult to induce creative abrasions to unfold productively in a single organization; thus, integrating multiple actors from many organizations coming together for a joint cause must be even more challenging. The social drama of networking and innovation partnerships requires an examination of competing strategic objectives, opposing power bases and contradictory interests, as well as how these factors change over time. But how can we explore these types of tensions and frictions *in situ*, where the most interesting changes are not within a single organization but across institutions and within complex networks of networks? Multi-partner business networking is one possible context, but new forms of private-public partnerships provide another context for the social drama of partnerships. Innovation systems represent a challenging private-public arena for such horizontal interlinking of multiple networks (see, e.g., EU, 2011; Hofmaier, 2002), as well as a sphere of influence that specifically involves multifaceted relations between researchers and non-academics.

Activities that surround innovation systems and network clusters may involve conflicts and tensions in joint partnerships between practitioners and scholars in so-called "interactive research." This concept should not be confused with action research, which was used more frequently in the 1970s (the latter concept concerns intervention studies where scholars not only learn about the underlying dynamics of change and mutual participation in organizations but also are expected to influence the very processes of change; see Docherty *et al.*, 2006). Organizational development (OD) programs and OD specialists have employed various rational-linear models for the "effective" management of planned change. Although Buchanan and Boddy (1992) critique the utility of such models, they also note that processes promoting rationalistic models or tools play a symbolic function "in sustaining the 'myth of organizational rationality' and, by implication, sustaining the legitimacy of the change agent. Such linear models may have a poor relationship with the actual unfolding of organizational changes, while in practice playing a significant symbolic and legitimating function in scripting the ritual that the change agent is required and expected to follow to gain organizational acceptance" (1992: 24). Legitimacy for change can be both used and misused to promote private interests. However, legitimacy is a "slippery" concept, and it may first become valuable to the extent that it is recognized among workers in the organization. In Sweden and Norway in the 1970s, for example, OD specialists collaborated closely with trade unions and management in firms, but their legitimating function was jeopardized, as it was perceived to be intimidating as a political attempt and intervention to challenge existing power structures:

> [It] encourages people to question the existing situation and to reflect, and it entails change—all of which may be threatening to existing organizational norms, practice and structure . . . researchers saw their role as supporting primarily the weaker party (i.e., the employees) in the developments. The concept got a more pronounced political connotation. Not surprisingly, this conceptualization of action research met strong resistance among many managers. Thus 'action research' lost its legitimacy as a form of interactive research in industry . . . [as it sought to] shake the distribution of power and influence within the organization.
> (Docherty *et al.*, 2006: 230 and 234)

The situation and *zeitgeist* has changed since the 1970s, and many situations allow legitimacy to be recognized from the bottom up, so to speak, in more democratic (and less hierarchal) forms of organization. Docherty and colleagues observe that forms of intervention have changed since the 1970s.

In contemporary partnerships between scholars and practitioners, in contrast to earlier action research initiatives in the late 1970s, less attention is paid to the improvement of working conditions, and more attention is paid to issues concerning an actor's influence in developing competitive regional efforts and strengthening business positions. Such partnerships may even seek to connect business partners who traditionally had strongly opposed interests but who might share a common interest and vision to reinforce a local, regional or national competitive position. Docherty and colleagues (ibid.) note that the change process in such partnerships, in terms of the level of complexity involved, may increase dramatically when focused business interests intersect with more generic goals and societal interests, such as sustainable development and social needs. In the realm of programs that seek to promote technological and organizational innovation, Hofmaier (2008) addresses the role of academic-business partnerships in triple helix settings, but notes that:

> Experience shows that there are at least two perspectives which complicate the picture. The first complication is the fact that individual or collective actors in every sphere of the triple helix formation have different norms, aims, and rules, and they represent different knowledge cultures. In addition, there are different institutional frames. Working together includes crossing such borders. Within the same sphere, such differences are—at least for some—not a very big problem, but it can be a problem when collaborating across borders between spheres.
>
> (2008: 181–2)

The underlying motivating factors (or active forces) may also vary considerably between collaborators. Therefore, it would be reasonable to expect that various forms and categories of social "glue" appear in relationships (with a range of different properties). Related to this observation is the common interest in such approaches in what we may understand as the social "superglue" effect, the binding force between human actors. This effect may help actors work together and pull in the same direction in various developments and projects. Members who are involved in networking may be more or less strongly "glued" to each other. An inter-organizational cooperation effort may have partly succeeded to create shared images (visions) of the network's goals among its members (Targama and Wasen, 2012), and such visions may gain legitimacy and acceptance in the network over time (e.g., Hellgren and Stjernberg, 1987, 1995).

In business networks, the "social glue" is typically a catchy slogan or a commercial vision that becomes accepted within a managerial hierarchy, or even among peripheral stakeholders. Strategic communication methods may also be used to spread various "visions" to encourage network corporation. In many instances, corporate visions and other forms of "shared images" do not necessarily need to be associated with "idealistic motives," even if this may also be the case, but it may suffice for visions to have strong appeal to those workers who share an enthusiasm for some aspect of the business. However, as we have noted in previous sections, change processes mostly involve a mix of organizations and a multitude of networking actors.

One such instance of "multi-networking" occurs in diffusely linked private-public networks. Moreover, such multilevel networks may bridge gaps between regional, national and supra-national institutions (e.g., the EU or the UN). In the EU, for example, a future challenge is to create new partnerships with science and industry to promote enterprise, allowing new powerful spin-offs to emerge from innovation networks that cross boundaries between institutions at regional, national and supra-national levels in public-private cooperation. Small and medium-sized firms (SMEs) increasingly partner and work together with large multinational enterprises in shared projects and new innovative developments. By bridging some of the many barriers that often impede innovative actors from working together successfully, new partnerships can establish a powerful foundation for sustained innovation and capacity building.

But we also know that in the politics of change, practitioners regularly employ more or less refined "micro-management" tactics and top-down "power steering" tools. In some situations, managers may certainly attempt to maneuver and exacerbate (or mitigate) frictions in social networks (e.g., provoke tensions between rival partners or go ahead with plans despite strong opposition among partners) to influence change processes, promote certain business interests or simply protect their own position and existing power base. Although such attempts may seem "rational" and deliberate and may succeed at times, the problem with friction is that it is a "slippery" concept; it cannot be easily controlled or "managed" in the traditional sense.

Friction can be neither steered in a rational-linear manner nor used as a tool for interventionist policy command and control. Frictions can be the emergent, messy and unforeseeable forces of powerful opposition and multi-scale contradiction across cultural diversity and interrelatedness. Friction may emerge across all "new scales of organization" (Wasen, 2013: vii)—multi-scale coordination from "nano" and "micro" to "meso" and "macro." This perspective complements the "social network-level" and "community-level" explanations adopted in earlier network theory and further extends political process studies by highlighting "inter-organizational relations." As it unfolds, friction in social networks can be both detrimental and beneficial for innovation, change and creativity.

SUMMARY AND CONCLUSION

This chapter has presented an alternative approach that provides a more nuanced explanation of the cultural dynamics and social complexities that come to play in network situations. We have shown that network cultures are not stable "entities" in institutional life. Instead, cultures seemingly evolve in multiple contexts and different spaces. Organizational cultures usually "live their own lives" in fluid and diversified relationships where social arrangements and material circumstances constantly change. Based on a processual-relational understanding of work organization, cultural diversity is recurrently "co-produced" in the encounters and states of contradiction, which we call network frictions. In social contexts, frictions can be simultaneously productive and unproductive, positive and negative, flexible and inflexible, and so forth. However, social and cultural-cognitive frictions differ from traditional physical (or economic) frictions in that the latter can be quantitatively measured and modeled. Social frictions cannot be summarized by a number or given a fix value.

Such an emergent processual-contextual understanding of friction suggests that both desired and undesired states paradoxically co-exist and recognizes that a positive motion or force in some situations may be negative in other situations. Friction is not subject to linear cause and effect relationships but instead emerges unexpectedly, and any nonlinear mechanisms may bring about both intended and unintended consequences. No magic button that can be pushed or wheel that can be turned exists to regulate the degree and intensity of friction. This understanding of friction, however, calls for a re-appraisal of traditional management thinking, which often has inspired rational-linear (universalistic) models of managerial influence and organizational development. In such conventional sequential models, it is often assumed that (A) something is identified to be "missing" and hence needs to be "initiated" (e.g., change, innovation and creativity among staff members need to be "triggered" or "fostered" through intervention from management); (B) it then has to be properly exploited (i.e., often assuming further managerial "supervision,"); and (C) when set business objectives have been met (or have failed to be met), any initiatives may signal a managerial intervention to terminate what was initially triggered.

With the acknowledgement that no networking exists without frictions and tensions, an alternative perspective has emerged. Much can be gained from developing this approach further. Building on more recently used terms in management and sociological research, the notion of "network friction" has been elaborated on to highlight what network tensions are, how conflicts within networks may influence partnership collaboration and how frictions may be developed or settled. This notion of network friction complements the traditional "social network-level" and further extends the valuable focus of political process studies by highlighting change dynamics in both "intra-" and "inter-organizational" relationships.

In this chapter, we have explored the impetus of network friction, particularly its cognitive-cultural and socio-political circumstances that may either support or hinder innovation and change management. Thus far, we have observed that various schools of thought theorize innovation management and innovation networks rather differently, and the reader has been introduced to key concepts in the literature that explain the factors that facilitate and obstruct innovation and competitiveness. There have been attempts to search for common ground among network perspectives to present a synthesis that reconciles disparate viewpoints (Borgatti *et al.*, 2009). However, a drawback in the majority of popularized concepts in the management discourse is that they assume homogenous and harmonious network collaboration in which professionals are expected to share a common background, business terminology and professional culture, among other commonalities. In recent scholarship, the focus has shifted toward heterogeneous and multidisciplinary network arrangements. Drawing on the motto "unity in diversity" or *in varietate concordia*, this chapter has nuanced the assumption of homogeneity by reinstating the value of diversity in cultural arrangements and innovation networks.

4 Two Cases of Robots in Medical Science and Health Care

In this chapter, we will address two distinct application areas and industries for health robotics—medical science and regular health care services. We begin this chapter by addressing a daunting dilemma faced by pioneers when challenging established conventions. In this section, we will see what workplace innovation means in terms of neurosurgery and thoracic surgery. Specifically, we will explore some of the issues and problems in the early phase of R&D in robotic surgery. In the second part, we seek a more nuanced approach to understanding health technology and address some of the challenges and institutional constraints that researchers/surgeons typically face when they pursue groundbreaking, radical changes or incremental innovations in health robotics. Despite the focus on technology and its new powerful capabilities and support functionality, in this chapter we also underline some of the subtle processes in the policy arena and in regulatory practices, and the latter stress the magnitude of social networking. In particular, the case illustration highlights the social choices and professional issues that arise in surgical departments at teaching hospitals and in medical faculties in universities and illustrates how frictions (both positive and negative) emerge within and across heterogeneous actors in these two settings. At the end of the chapter, we conclude that the nature of work has been redefined in medicine and health care in light of recent changes and maintain that the current trend suggests that work will involve more, not less, workplace innovation in the future, as more and more physically monotonous tasks and routine jobs disappear in this robot era.

THE PIONEER'S INNOVATION DILEMMA: STATE OF THE ART THINKING (IN)COMPATIBLE WITH CONVENTIONAL CULTURES AND NORMS

Impressive developments in robotics technology proliferate in the health care domain. However, this raises questions such as: What characterizes change and innovation in the health care domain? What does it mean for professionals to pursue disruptive innovations in a rigidly (hierarchical) orchestrated workplace environment that is set up to coordinate complex (and often acute) life-saving interventions rather than long-term cutting-edge R&D? In the couple of interview extracts that will follow in this section, we will have an opportunity to look more into what the surgeons and scientists understand to be the core dynamics of innovation and what particular dilemmas and challenges the pioneers of today face when they challenge established conventions, cultural norms and modern outside-the-box thinking. One scientist explains that as a young university student, before choosing to embark upon a career in surgery, he was very much influenced by Frederik Grant Banting (1891–1941). Dr. Banting studied orthopedics at the Hospital for Sick Children in Toronto and was the medical scientist who first successfully used insulin on humans, an innovation which has since changed the lives of millions for the better. For this breakthrough research, he was awarded with the most prestigious award in the scientific community: the Nobel Prize. However, the path to innovation success was not a straight one, and the surgeon explained why:

> Banting was a doctor and went on to practice in Ontario. He was going to practice in orthopedics, but I think his practice wasn't that great, and he wasn't doing well, so he initially applied to do research in Toronto, and the people in Toronto initially turned him down. And then, the next year, he applied again, and well, the people in Toronto said, "Well, you can go up and work in the attic." They went up and did their experiments, and discovered insulin, which became pretty big of course.

This Nobel laureate in medicine faced opposition and social friction, and the members of the professional community did not initially enthusiastically believe in his ideas, but he came back and back again and eventually his persistence and perseverance was awarded. In 1923, at the age 32, Banting received the Nobel Prize together with Dr. Macleod, and Banting is still the youngest scholar in the field of Medicine/Physiology to have received a Nobel Prize. The surgeon goes on to highlight the challenges of being a pioneer and thinking outside-the-box by illustrating his point of the role of bottlenecks in the community, especially those individuals who review the research in its early stage and whose decision-making positions and powers can have decisive effects on the initiation of innovative projects and the dissemination of new pioneering knowledge. This is the very fragility of the review process, not just in science but in reviews of innovation projects in general, such as assessing grant proposals and setting priority scores, etc.

> If you look at the people who have won the Nobel Prize, I suspect most of them during their career were thought of as crazy; I mean that guy is "crazy," talking about some funny things. However, that might be because the human brain is based on past memory, right, and we can take dispersed data and make a concept or guess what might happen. [But] if we don't have the link, if you come along and say, "There is a

new element, and I don't have anything in my past memory that links to those elements," you might think I'm crazy because you told me something that I can't relate to in my brain. So many of those Nobel Prizes winners, I suspect, are people like that. They come up with a very unusual idea not based so much on the past, so people who review their grants or look at their manuscripts can't link it and therefore reject it.

Later, the discussion moved on to how other scientists evaluated Albert Einstein's pioneering work and as the surgeon noted: "Albert Einstein's 1905 papers, there were three submitted, were reviewed by Rutherford. So, perhaps, the only person in the world that could recognize their importance reviewed them. So if they had come to me, I'd most likely have just rejected them, 'What is this guy talking about,' right?" Einstein, a scientist who is regarded as one of the most innovative and creative scientists of all, was well before his time; while he represented pioneer spirit and innovativeness, this was not a guarantee that contemporaries would see the significance in his work. The surgeon noted that these issues are not unique to medicine and robotics surgery and that examples from other fields also suggest that gridlocks and social frictions may block inventors and pioneers in their genuine efforts to advance knowledge and transform their ideas into useful products for the betterment of society. Whether it was Ernest Rutherford that reviewed Einstein's work or if someone else in the scientific community did is not the key issue here, rather, what is important is that this example highlights the pioneer's innovation dilemma. As the surgeon noted: "To get beyond a paradigm, that is a true paradigm shift that is not based on previous data, is almost impossible because almost everything has to be linked to something, but a few people seem to jump well ahead of the pack."

The problem is that many good and useful ideas are wasted, just because some people are not in a position to comprehend their significance or meaning; innovations that could solve some of the most pertinent problems for humankind and create better treatments for patients so that they could survive more deadly diseases are ignored or, even worse, ridiculed. However, passive disinterest or active friction also has to do with how the wider professional community and institutional environment is arranged in terms of decision-making powers and regulatory mechanisms. Thus, in the next section, we will turn to the health care context to see how various stakeholders in the health care industry explore some of the challenges to innovation (including bottlenecks in medicine and science) and what types of stalemates and impasses can bring adverse effects on advancing innovation practices.

INNOVATION IN THE WORKPLACE

To pioneer new thinking in the operating room (OR) is one challenge, but robotics surgery also revolves on mundane activities beyond the workplace environment in universities and teaching hospitals. Professional networking in these external settings also involves various frictions, not least because professionals seeking to pursue innovative projects must be able to secure the necessary resources and funding, which means "crossing different worlds," as one surgeon put it. While he pointed out that there are many technical ideas coming out of the surgical community that are not being realized, this partly relates to the fact that surgeons do not always manage to find a viable application area for their idea that is, to use one of the informant's words, "compatible with the present value system." Furthermore, there are many physicians and surgeons who have great ideas but cannot translate these ideas into something more concrete because they lack the necessary technical, organizational or economical knowledge.

One of the surgeons summarized this situation, saying that there exist parallel worlds and mentalities, but it is not a given that the actors in each of these will engage each other's worlds. It often requires what he referred to as an "enthusiast" who can encourage workplace innovation. "Souls-of-fire" was another term used to describe these individuals, a term for people with a powerful determination and driving force who work both within and beyond communities of practice:

> An enthusiast is a good example of this. Anyone who has the idea must also have a really great motivation to find his counterpart. Sometimes there are even officials who will try to find this relationship. Our society tries to administer such contexts through specific authorities . . . who attempt to establish a relationship between the inventor and a "soul-of-fire" to bring in the technical and economic expertise to develop ideas and bring in venture capital and so on. There're inventor associations trying to establish this relationship. . . . They are certainly open to these things, they certainly get in lots of suggestions, but suddenly a proposal comes in, and they realize and say, "We haven't thought about it along such lines before, despite our knowledge."

Moreover, while the surgeon believed that innovations in the surgical setting and, in particular, within robotics surgery demanded the involvement and participation of enthusiasts or "souls-of-fire," he hastened to add that innovation may become vulnerable if it only depends on these individuals or professionals, and thus competition in the intellectual and political marketplace remains critical, and the challenge is for surgeons assuming the role of "souls-of-fire" to find acceptance outside their own clinics. Before, surgeons could go down to their basements and re-make their surgical instruments themselves, if they were handy enough. However, that is no longer a viable option, at least not in the high-tech part of surgery that includes robotics, as one surgeon noted:

> The difference was that maybe 50 or 60 years ago when a surgeon had an idea to improve an implement, how to enhance and bend an

instrument so that it [the ergonomic design] would fit better in the hand and cut better through the tissue, then maybe the surgeon would take the instrument and go down to his workshop at the hospital where they'd repair boilers and whatnot. You'd tell them, "Please do such and such in accordance with my specifications, and I want to try it later." Back then, it was much easier to interact, now the technological development is immensely more complex and complicated than just bending a handle a little differently or constructing a pair of scissors in a different way. We work in a much more complex world of innovation today. And that essentially necessitates more professional players on both sides.

What is it that distinguishes the end-users of robotics in surgery? What makes these end-users truly exceptional in comparison with the many other users across various domains in the health care industry is that they seek to pursue two complex domains of robotics simultaneously. The first domain they pursue is related to how surgical robotics are used in academia to advance scientific knowledge. Such activities, of course, are not privileged merely to publicly funded institutes (e.g., in various university settings) but are also pursued in private regimes and R&D departments (or major NGOs backing research). Here, however, we will largely restrict our discussion to the implications of robotics innovation in the public-sector, science-based medical research that is carried out at universities.

Professional surgeons are exceptionally competitive and some have dual professional identities; these surgeons are often the ones leading the development of new techniques and pushing technological advances in their field. Moreover, they are usually employed at a teaching hospital as a physician (e.g., within specialized surgical departments), where they carry out regular procedures. However, these surgeons typically also hold a university position, and as a professor, they might pursue research activities, network with colleagues in the scientific community and participate in partnerships with firms in the health technology industry, in addition to supervising doctoral students and undergraduates at the university's medical facility (surgical residents employed at teaching hospitals typically have one foot in both of these worlds, both employed as regular staff by the hospital and pursing a doctorate at the separate university). Thus, they combine dual missions within their persons: on the one hand, to meet the day-to-day need to educate new medical students and, on the other, to meet the pressing demand to service patients in the community. Our discussion onwards will be restricted to how innovative work is organized in public hospitals and, more specifically, in the larger teaching hospitals.

Early and informed assessment of new health technologies is an important concern in society, and as one practitioner remarked, once a health technology causes harm to patients, it is then already too late to prevent it from happening. Hence the cliché "better late than never" does not seem to apply to the life-saving and critical practice of surgery. Concerning medical jargon, physicians not only adopt a strange and strong terminology, but they also use a rather harsh and cold jargon to describe their mishaps at times, which seems to serve as a channel to vent their feelings and allow them to distance themselves from the duties and heavy responsibilities they face every day when a person's life is at stake and wrong decisions can have fatal outcomes. However, from within the sometimes distanced and peculiar professional jargon and stories that travel within the medical community, there are other understandings among those health administrators that look at the economics of innovation and development work. Those policymakers whose role it is to interact with health staff and apprise them of changes and technological innovations have added another twist to the jargon: within their community, there is apparently a saying that goes, "It is always too early to assess a health technology until it is too late!" as one of the practitioners said. How, then, can we make sense of this contradiction? Let us examine a few more extracts to obtain a more nuanced understanding of these stances within the medical community. This statement was shared during one of the interviews:

> Is the technology good or bad? Should we have it or not? There is no way to tell if it is going to be good or bad. Right now it is pointing in one direction, but we can't say how it will be when we are in a phase of developmental progress. There might be things that, on the one hand, speak against it, but on the other, there might be special circumstances that outweigh the benefits and so on . . . one change evolves into something else, and just because it's damn hard to assess it, one shouldn't lie down and cry but instead embrace this complexity and try to promote systems that still provide some kind of support to the decision-makers. However, we will never make super-rational decisions based on complete facts, there will always be pros and cons. Rather, there are parallel decisions going on at many fronts at once along with some elements of facts and rationality and with a big portion of professional interests, emotions and intuitions. And we cannot expect to get rid of the latter.

This practitioner works partly with trying to identify and assess early medical technologies entering the health care industry, which the community of surgeons, for example, believes may be of importance for the patients, and to identify developments for health care organizations upon which to embark. It is most likely the game-changing technologies that are most interesting from a decision-maker's point of view, as there are likely thousands of novelties and minor incremental innovations introduced on a global scale. One of the interviewed policy actors said that between 10 and 15 technologies were selected each year and reported to those in power (i.e., laymen), who are not experts by any means. However, the very act of selecting those technologies is a process of subtle influence and control as well, and the policymaker acknowledged that there was interest in swaying powerful actors and key decision-makers' decisions in preferable ways that benefit the common good. However, how does one determine what is best for the common good? As a head of departments at one of the surgical clinics said, there is lot at stake when funds are distributed or re-distributed between different areas and domains of the health system:

> First, it is such a complex process, and there are many myths circulating; for example, that treatments of cancers have expanded at the expense of other things. Others say that orthopedists have taken all the funding. The neurologists have pursued projects without getting permission first. So there are always many opinions about what's fair. However, what are the factual circumstances? One can only answer this question by looking at the specifics, what actually takes place in practice.

Indeed, health care is a very complex arena, including multiple stakeholders, and the various voices from the field represent the various actors who embody complementary viewpoints and who represent professional bodies, interest groups and public institutions. While medical staff and scientists represent the main core of the people involved in applying robotics in surgery, they also connect with executive people in the policymaking process. However, once again, there is also a group of doctors who have taken on the role of policymakers themselves, representing various professional or industry interests, addressing occupational concerns and working with educational issues, such as skills retention, etc. The latter looks at how one assures a young generation of doctors that they obtain a proper education concerning the new robotic technology. These different groups of surgeons enter into various partnerships where they share common professional interests. All of these sub-groups can certainly represent quite different views and understandings of what the problems are in the big picture. Last but not least, when systemic changes are induced in the health system, which require significant investments, medically trained health administrators, hospital directors and health care policymakers with PhDs get involved, and this group of actors is familiar with many of the subtle nuances and should not be underestimated, not least because they have tight liaisons with political partners, although they sometimes represent their own interests as well.

At the time of the study, practitioners at hospitals in Sweden could freely experiment with new health technologies and departments did not need to obtain any approval from a government agency. As one interviewee put it, "There is no legal landscape that one has to navigate through and no public authority needs to put their stamp onto it." However, several respondents stressed that there are both pros and cons to such a non-regulative approach. Introduction of new technologies into publicly funded hospitals is still a highly politically contested terrain. It is political in the sense that every four years citizens vote, and officials representing various political parties are elected to represent public interests in the local health bodies (i.e., county health board), but it is also political in that different specialties and professional groups compete over limited funding and investments. While the hospital board of directors balances different conflicting interests and deals with the issue of organizing early development work more fairly, it is still more or less, as one practitioner phrased it, a "post hoc decision." Although the county's deputy health director had initiated a reform to introduce formal guidelines and general principles for the implementation of new procedures (including new health technologies), the respondent stressed that, at the end of the day, what it comes down to is what those in power give priority to, which depends on individual health actors' bargaining power, political will and broader economic circumstances (not least when budgets cuts ravage county health boards). Unfortunately, it is not always those with the best arguments to pursue a new technological development in their medical field who win.

The very processes that precede decision making and that guide allotting of funding to technological projects and investments in hospitals are shaped and influenced in conceived settings, what Goffman (1959) refers to as being the "back-stage" of social life. In this context, various stakeholders, both those for and against pursuing new developments, shape the decision-making processes and make way for the emergence of the various frictions in this process. However, one of the respondents claimed that such processes were a part of the rules of the game. Providing various stakeholders with relevant and adequate information on advances in robotic and other surgical innovations was a challenging task, as one interviewee explained, not least because:

> It's really difficult to find a receiver for all this information. Who is actually the decision-maker? That will depend quite a lot on the type of technology being considered. Many times politicians [in local county health boards and members of parliament] don't have a clue about what is actually going on, that is the rule rather than the exception I'd say, they find out about developments first when budgets show a deficit, when costs swell. And they fight about the money the county will have to cut [from the health budgets] and restructurings. However, what happens below the surface remains pretty much hidden, and if one then tries to explain what is happening that will just make them feel unsafe. They'll say, "That's interesting and we understand how much is happening in genome technology, but what is our role in this, and how can we influence it?" They don't always have the necessary means and methods. And the individual experts [i.e., surgeons], they work with their technology and don't care about anything else. They don't see all the other things that are going on. They're just set for fights on budgets. As long as they mess around in their isolated organizational units, I'd presume it is fine to change working methods. However, when developments

require major investments, then you'll have to go up a few levels in the hierarchy and run riot a bit.

Having this in mind, for robotics in health care in particular and new treatment options in general, it was clear that several departments were not able to embark on their desired new roads, and that they also faced opposition from local peers and powerful interests groups. Additionally, when local health bodies faced the reality of the latest round of state budget cuts, which hit the local health organizations pretty hard, this limited their opportunities to sponsor radical and groundbreaking innovation. Hence, financing would have to come from sources other than the public health budget. How did the practitioners that succeeded in acquiring robotics manage to secure the necessary funding initially? They had to network and create new partnerships with like-minded entrepreneurs, as well as with donors, private research foundations and wealthy individuals, who had the basic financial strength to support such pioneering work. As one of the surgeons recalls, one of the pioneers in his area of expertise hired a team of skilled surgeons to begin to translate his professional desire to reduce the learning curve in laparoscopic surgery (so called key-hole surgery), and for which robotic surgery was a promising path of development, but pursuing robotics first became an option only because he received a "lot of money from a donor and wanted to build a program in something new and innovative . . . he can sort of be considered the main driving force behind robotics taking off because he started doing them, and he was able to market that very effectively." Clearly, professionals network and influence others, and surgeons regularly go to academic conferences not only to present and discuss recent research findings but also to get a feeling of what is happening in the field and to network and build relationships for future research collaborations.

"IT'S A NEW WAY OF WORKING"—SITUATING ROBOTIC SUPPORT SYSTEMS

We will embark upon the rest of our discussion by departing from the nexus between academic settings (universities) and teaching hospitals, and turn to institutional environments where we will find most end-users and pioneers in surgical robotics. In the early phase of robotics surgery, there were still doubts raised in the professional setting and in the international community of academic surgeons as to the degree of technological change. There seemed to be many questions still to be answered as to if and how the new technological systems and organizational arrangements would benefit the surgical procedures and if the patient outcomes would improve or not. While one of the interviewed surgeons who pursued innovative work in minimally invasive developments said that his interest in robotics in the beginning was "more intellectual, so to speak," he mentioned that he had been networking with a fellow surgeon who, just like himself, also happened to be a professor at a medical facility at a university. At that facility, there was a laboratory environment specifically set up for robotics, which was not interlinked to regular activities at the public teaching hospital. Informal networking and other more informal contacts in the professional surgical community, with members that pursued early work in robotics, eventually resulted in a research visit to a foreign institute. Here, the cardiac surgeon not only partook in a scientific partnership as a visiting scholar but, through his networking, also had an opportunity to test the robotic system in a con-trolled "laboratory setting," as he referred to the development site. As this happened during the early phase of developmental robotics, several aca-demically oriented surgeons stressed how important it was that the interna-tional research community allowed critical assessments and weighted pros and cons, as well as evidence data, before this radically new technology was implemented into regular procedures (i.e., what was referred to as being in production).

One physician, working in the field of neurosurgery, had experiences of different robotic systems, and maintained that while some of the sys-tems brought about advantages, they also meant that surgeons would lose something. He mentioned procedures in which there is no need for touch (e.g., surgical cases where surgeons remove malignant tumors), but has-tened to add: "However, if you do vascular surgery, where you are touch-ing microstructures, the sense of touch is paramount and the way I tell the residents the way to think about that is to try to imagine having really thick gloves on while trying to do microsurgery, it becomes very difficult because the forces are in play, and it becomes complicated. So if you look for micro-dissection . . . that's very difficult to do without touch. Not impos-sible, but you are losing something." Inferred from the quote, if surgeons lose the sense of touch, what do they gain instead? One of the practitioners, a trained technician in thoracic surgery, said he believed that robotics tech-nology is superior to humans in some respects:

I don't think we are so precise. A robot is more exact. Sure a robot is susceptible but not as susceptible as our arms. We'd be tired after five minutes keeping a [surgical] instrument fixed in the same position. However, a robot can stand like that as long as you've plugged in the external power supply, but a human would never be able stand that long. We get tired after an hour standing there [in the OR], passing instruments and standing concentrating. A robot would never lose its concentration as long as the person who controls the robot does not [lose it]. A machine rarely gets tired until something breaks. [With the robot] you maintain the position exactly where you want but wouldn't be able to hold an instrument like that, and I most likely wouldn't be able to do it more than five minutes, you'd get all the tension, but a robot does not feel any tensions. As long as the robot functions; just look at industrial production and how it has increased the volume of cars being produced—bam, bam, bam [an expression to stress the pace of the work], either repair it [the robot] or replace it with a human who'd never be able to adopt the speed of the robot, one simply just can't.

Conventional rationales for robotics in industrial manufacturing include that robots primarily replace heavy, repetitive, dirty and dangerous work. While the benefits and drawbacks of robotics were being assessed, it seemed that many surgeons believed at least in the potential of robotics for the future. For example, several surgeons stressed the prospective states of robotics rather than the short-term benefits, and this was perhaps also because of their rather limited hands-on experience with robotic work, yet in one of the surgeon's words, he truly acknowledges the potential as such, "because robotic systems have been used in the industry for a long time and have been very helpful for them in some manufacturing processes and so on." One of the surgeons explained why robotics was particularly challenging, should it be embraced on a large scale: "You have to think in terms of robotic surgery, it's not a technology like a normal drug that targets a certain condition . . . it's more a technology that may spread to all types of surgical procedures. So it's really more about communication. In reality, it's a new way of working."

While the robot transcends some human limitations, the opposite also holds true. Interestingly, a surgeon explained this in the following way: "So, bringing together the machine and the human takes advantage of the two worlds. I still have to have an experienced surgeon to do the guessing, and the robot gives the precision and accuracy." He also added that:

> The main risk of any robot is uncontrolled motion or non-commanded motion. . . . That's why all medical robots are slaves to human beings, making us able to make good surgeons, a very good surgeon, or at least give that good surgeon an armory that would allow them to conduct the procedure much like a great master.

Another surgeon's testimonial was even stronger, and he remarked that "robotics is definitely a paradigm shift in surgery," which echoes many surgeons' viewpoints. He believed that some routine tasks could be readily handed over to robots, but that view entailed questioning basic assumptions of how surgery was conducted. In neurosurgery, this means considering using new types of designs for the OR, and he explained, "What if we did the entire surgery inside a magnet, then you just have to get rid of your assistant and the nurse. I would make sure to ask the questions, 'What does the assistant do, and what does the nurse do, and how can we replicate these roles in this new environment?'" However, a technical assistant had another view, and remarked that this is a natural development because in the OR professionals have already "become computerized":

Well, they use more and more images, and they need more and more computer technology to do the surgery. Robotics and images. And then you become more and more dependent upon engineers, mathematicians and physicists, and not to mention, this is just in the operating room, but just look at the computer department. We are completely dependent upon them. You talk about dependency, and today in this hospital, we have only electronic journals nowadays. We don't have paper journals anymore and that means that we are completely dependent [on the computers]. The whole hospital would be shut down if the computers did not work. And if you cannot read the journals, you cannot treat the patients.

This highlights that the new systemic dimension of health care is increasingly vulnerable, should core technologies malfunction. However, this extract not only suggests how much health care staff are dependent on technology *per se*, but this also illustrates how important organizational issues are for the health care industry. Clearly, health care staff are more dependent on other multi-professional groups and expertise in network settings. Indeed, this represents a radical change in modern health care organization, which has not traditionally included highly skilled mathematicians, physicist and engineers.

While health care workplaces are becoming increasingly heterogeneous in terms of additional occupational groups, there are still fears that humans will be made redundant because of new technologies. Traditional work roles begin to crumble as robots are included as work partners in the OR. While the robot assumes new roles that support the lead surgeon, other (human) assistants in the operation room may play a secondary role. One surgeon continued to explain that, while technology replaces functional tasks in the OR, he is not convinced about technology's substitution potential within the context of an OR: "I don't think we are going to reduce the number of people in health care. Robotic-assisted surgery, which is really image-assisted surgery, creates more data." All the data that is generated through new visualization systems, such as 3D, 4D and "5D" imaging technology, renders new domains of work and must be interpreted by human expertise. Therefore, the growth in data generated means that people will shift their time and effort to new domains because, as the surgeon explained:

Data creation requires people, and data analysis requires people, so you are not decreasing but rather in the pathway of increasing the number of people in healthcare. This is a little philosophical; we used to have a doctor, and the doctor was kind of getting a little busy, so he hired a nurse, and then they became quite busy, so we better get someone to organize everything, and call that person the administrator, and then they said we need a speech therapist and a rehab doctor and so on, and it has continued to grow. We could decrease it a bit [with robotic surgery], and then we are talking about these paradigm shifts, instead of taking the tumor out of the body we implant something inside the body, that would be a significant paradigm shift. Then, I don't need all the people in the operating room when implementing these things, and I actually don't need to be in an OR. I could be in a hybrid thing where I have the principles of a robot and the principles of an imaging space.

Clearly, this surgeon's narrative is suggesting powerful futures where he is no longer bound to the working context and that may render old work roles superfluous. This particular surgeon has a track record of pursing novel inventions in the field of robotics, and he continues to pursue innovative work. For example, he sees future socio-robotic rearrangements as representing major challenges and innovation work in the field of medical robotics, recombining ideas to figure out how to perform a procedure robotically in new ways beyond current modes of practice.

SUMMARY

This study on robotics for medical science and health services examined workplace innovation. It also explored how these innovations were situated in the policy arena and politico-regulatory landscape. A number of robotics surgeons (scientists employed at universities as well as in teaching hospitals) pursue groundbreaking innovations focused around state-of-the-art solutions, and they stress how vital it is for them to mobilize resources and acceptance beyond their own workplace environment. What distinguishes these individuals is that they shuttle between medical science (in their universities) and the day-to-day work of a surgical practice (at surgical departments in hospitals). In other words, they live in separate, yet interconnected, worlds and have to address the local expectations and cultural norms in each of the organizations.

The case illustrates particular theoretical issues with and applications of the models and concepts discussed and reviewed in the preceding chapters. Analyzing and interpreting this case study material in the theoretical framework of innovation networks, COP and social friction showed how practitioners participate in both formal networks and in informal interactions in research partnerships and communities of practice. Analyzing this case material from the theoretical framework of friction will highlight other dimensions. Because of the radical nature of technological change, contradictions and tensions unavoidably emerge in such heterogeneous settings, and this finding indicates that innovation processes are not friction free.

In the new landscape of robotics surgery technology—and because of underlying social forces that make the technological development possible—radical adjustments and incremental rearrangements translate into new types of workplaces where something is gained and something else is lost, according to the practitioners. Radical adjustments in the health care domain originate at times from pioneering accomplishments in the scientific field. However, radical change is far from being an uncomplicated matter, as it often challenges many of the commonly held assumptions in the health care community, such as how operating rooms should be designed, how staffing should be optimally organized, how resources should be politically allotted, etc. Thus, technological and organizational innovations are embedded in complex network settings that span professional, cultural and national boundaries. Academic medicine in the scientific community is not an isolated island, therefore scientists on the academic side of robotics surgery network on a regular basis with fellow scholars and seek to challenge present modes of thinking, overcome resistance and find better solutions, trying overall to translate these ideas into practical products in the health setting.

A final note on workplace innovation and bottom-up initiatives for change: while surgeons are occupied (and perhaps always have been) in developing and refining their tools and methods, we see that innovative work methods extend to other surgical staff, such as organizing and interpreting vast amounts of data. Considering the current growth in technologies that generate large amounts of visualization data, and because these data need to be interpreted by experts (at least as of today, no robot is capable of interpreting as well as a surgeon), it is suggested that such tasks (i.e., data analytics) will require more staff resources and perhaps even increased budgets. At the same time, new robotics technologies entail displacement of some surgical (physical) tasks, which suggests that less staff is needed in some areas of health care services. This duality allows for contradictory definitions and understandings of robots and their significance to professional systems in organizations. Despite technological advances, surgical practice is still very much a professional endeavor, and it still thrives on creative skills and analytical abilities. The case study also considered the various support roles, and practitioners stress that while they gain something new, they remain concerned that they may lose something else. In summary, as science is making new advances, and as new technological breakthroughs are introduced, the biggest challenge for surgical practitioners in a robot society entails carrying out more, not less, innovation work.

5   Robots in Eldercare

This case study draws on studies of robotics technological development in scientific settings. The study included on-site observation and interviews at three different robotics research labs housed in publicly funded academic institutions. Currently, some research groups pursue radical developments to address the social needs of a growing population of elderly consumers. From a business perspective, this group represents an increasingly financially capable customer base. Because people live longer and survive more deadly diseases, there is a rapidly growing demand and market for innovative and affordable solutions to meet the escalating needs of elderly people. For example, there is an increasing demand to enable the elderly to remain at home longer and manage basic activities themselves, such as their medications. This change could save society and the publicly funded health care system considerable resources and allow existing personnel resources to be redirected to where they are most needed. At the three academic institutions included in this study, robotics departments have taken this demographic challenge seriously and targeted this market segment, directing their R&D towards robotic assistants.

Our population is aging, as most are likely well aware, and current trends and demographic predictions have been interpreted as alarming for several reasons. As one scientist comments, "It reads somewhat as a horror story, and the big question is when our politicians actually will realize that a rather difficult challenge lies in front of us . . . just the pure economics of it. Our health care system will face real problems shortly [if this trend continues] so it's important to start thinking about what we can do about it." During an informal laboratory meeting, one scientist initiated a lively discussion and noted that the number of retired citizens is expected to increase by 50 percent over the next 50 years and that the number of people aged 85 years and older will increase drastically over the next ten years. People in this group, whether they remain at home or live in institutions (e.g., a retirement village), will require assistance and advanced care services. This scientist also mentions that in the U.S., the ratio is predicted to change from three to two working individuals per senior citizen in the future, which fuels speculation that the retirement age might increase from 65 to 75. Members of the academic robotic community also discussed recent estimates for Europe, which indicate that the number of people in the labor market will decrease by 20 percent.

Clearly, members of the scientific community are well aware of the public discourse. One research leader who was responsible for a robotics lab mentioned that he believes that the growth of the elderly until 2033 implies that "the number of 85-year-olds will more than double by that point in time with huge social consequences as well as health consequences." These are rough projections of the proportion of the elderly population and should be considered educated guesses, especially for predictions as far into the future as 2033. However, patients with chronic diseases already represent a challenge for health care providers. Of course, this group of citizens is not only affected by age but also changing lifestyle and food consumption patterns, which fuel the generation of chronic diseases. For dementia, there is no immediate prospect of a cure or relief for patients, and dementia is among the greatest challenges to the health care community because it is places a considerable burden on health care resources. Robotics in the care sector (r-Care) provides a practical example of increasing R&D to meet changing demographics at the beginning of the twenty-first century.

However, robotic technology is considered for eldercare organizations to assist staff in daily service provision. In care institutions, robots may alleviate increasing workloads, and there is hope that innovations may relieve stress and pressure among staff. A key challenge in an institutional landscape that was developed to provide *welfare services* is to provide affordable solutions and equitable services to the growing number of elderly, especially those who cannot care for themselves (e.g., dementia patients). Although some health care regimes increasingly rely on family members (or voluntary workers) to care for their relatives, others suggest exploring technological opportunities. There is disagreement about whether robots allow seniors to avoid eldercare institutions.

Many different rationales and motives exist for developing robots for the elderly. During the early development phase, robotics scientists from different university laboratories maintained that robots are needed because there will be more elderly people than younger people who are working and paying taxes. This position draws on the implicit argument that economic and demographic realities require fewer younger citizens to work (harder) to support a growing number of elderly so that the latter may continue to receive the pension checks to which they are entitled. One researcher noted that demographic changes will definitively impact society in more than one way, but "very few elderly people are accustomed to using IT, so it's very important to think about how we should be able to reach this group out there . . . [and] people don't always think rationally. . . ." For many interviewed scientists, developing robotics for the elderly requires finding technical fixes to practical daily problems. For example, a "robot shall help you to eat on your own, [it] rolls around on wheels, taking care of simple health care duties." This scientist also said that robots could include "video-conferencing equipment on wheels as it moves around in the physical space."

> We need to see how we can enable people to stay in their homes so that they don't need to be transferred to an elderly care institution. A challenge here is to explore how technology can be used to provide a good quality-of-life. What I mean is that seniors feel respected and autonomous. It is not essential that one has to be autonomous, but more important is the actual feeling of autonomy. One should feel that one controls . . . the daily routines. Although I really wished to sleep in early in the morning, then it shouldn't be that someone tells me that they will come by and visit me at 7 a.m. in the morning, referring to an empty spot in their otherwise very busy schedule. That's just unacceptable! And one should also be able to choose the food of one's liking and not be served sausages when one really would fancy a nice piece of lasagna. It's not tolerable that caregivers then respond, "Sorry, that's impossible."

Despite inexperience with field studies, many robotics engineers adopted preconceptions, drives and ideas of what robots could accomplish for the elderly. However, many also seemed to recognize their limitations, and several engineers noted that they lacked real-life experience in eldercare. This limitation explains why engineers increasingly include health specialists and other academics in later stages of their scientific partnerships and network projects.

MARKET-DRIVEN SCIENTIFIC PARTNERSHIPS

At one university, the scientific leader and professor (who was the head of the department) said that he was provided "a clean table and money." Long-term financial support allowed his group to establish a completely new robotics laboratory, which had not previously existed at the university. Home and eldercare robotics became a strategic area for one lab team to pursue. Engineering work can be basic or applied. In the former, research is conducted in an open-ended fashion, as in the basic sciences, and explores ideas freely and creatively without a market or application in mind. However, the robotics R&D team deviated from this basic research approach from the outset and chose to pursue a focused (applied) market-driven approach for their scientific development work. One participant explained as follows:

> We have to think more about product demands and we have to think about whether these kinds of robots have a future, what kind of

applications [actually exist] in real markets. We have to look more seriously at the market trends and then reorient our research and development in such a way that is in accordance to the expected market demands or forecasted market demands.

Initially, the eldercare robotics team faced some daunting challenges that needed to be addressed promptly. Pursuing market-oriented research at the university presupposed and necessitated that external actors and firms be included in R&D in various ways through formal partnerships or informal networking. A specific concern among external firms was that their development work involved "too much basic research." This critique was considered by one interviewee:

> You would just have to say that [robotics] technology is one thing among many kinds of things. The elevator and the phone make it possible to live upstairs, and look at the different things that are automated; all these [other] robots and what they could do. It's partly that there are no companies that think that this is a thing of tomorrow, it might be a thing of the day after tomorrow. For most companies that is not the case. Even companies like Nokia are hesitant about home robotics. In that sense, this is still a scenario that is evolving, and I think that only the Japanese truly believe that there will be home and care robots. Security robots are coming, though; robots that walk around and detect thieves and so on. However, robots that would be companions and have features such as being able to closely communicate with people are still in the laboratories.

Hesitation among external partners and their unwillingness to participate (i.e., to financially support this early development work in robotics) created dilemmas for the researchers. Such reluctance was partially fueled by uncertainty about predictions and the "true" future market demand for r-Care robots. It was unclear whether robotics would be a dominant path; other technologies or non-technical solutions could prove more attractive and cost-efficient. Another challenge was designing and producing affordable and appropriate products for a wide group of end-users. As one team member described:

> It's difficult to develop this kind of robot because it is more long-term [work]. But, then again, all the types of communication, communication chips, batteries, cameras, computers, and software are continuously getting better, faster and cheaper. So by the time when you can make an affordable robot, [that is] a robot in the right price category . . . well, there are of course different categories, you can even sell one for 10.000 €, but I would imagine that for the upper middle class and technology freaks to be able to buy one, it would need to cost less than 2.000 €.

However, if you could make a modular one [robot] and it could do something, and then you could add things on to it; cameras or some services such as delivering medicines. Medicine delivery would be a neat feature and it would come and give you the medicines. And you could pay extra for more things, and in the end people would end up paying perhaps 5.000 € and they would be happy, but they would not buy it immediately if it cost that much. I think we are getting into the phase where we are thinking about what the [sensible] commercial cost is for these kinds of things.

Because none of the engineers had worked at eldercare facilities, they approached practitioners. An engineer explained, "One way is to ask the people who are carrying out this work and see what is most useful to them. What they are doing currently is to help [the elderly] people moving around, going out shopping, picking up things and helping them to manage their daily business like banking and so forth. Well, they can do anything really." As eldercare robot capabilities and functions are advanced and refined, they require testing.

To design and construct robots to provide something "extra" and become powerful, functional and easy to use in home environments, researchers must determine what end-users actually think about artificial assistants. If robots are to be used in professional settings, it is also important to consider what professional staff members think is important. Although workplace characteristics at retirement villages, for example, were not initial concerns among engineers, as work progressed and more prototypes were developed, the engineers moved out of their laboratories into the real world. This particular situation is referred to as "robots in the wild" among scientists. As was noted above, some robotics engineers had only vague ideas about eldercare working environments and the types of tasks caregivers perform, that is, what work at an eldercare facility really entails. As one team member explained:

So, we went into the village just to look around and see; is a robot going to be able to do some of the things that we think it should be doing? The caregivers go out in the mornings and they give medicines to people in their apartments, in the cottages or at the side of the property. And immediately we recognized that robots were not going to be able to do that because they couldn't traverse the curves, you know they just didn't have the technology to do it. They could stay in a building but they couldn't go from a building to a building. The caregivers also give people their medicines at mealtimes because it suits the caregivers to do that. You know, these people would come to, even within range, to come to the dining room so that they could give their medicines to them. But if you take a camera into a dining room and you pretend to be a robot going to a person, you take a photograph on somebody sitting with their back to the sun, you are not going to be able to recognize their face and you won't be able to find them if you were the robot. So we learned some of those things.

Previously, scientists were largely left to their imaginations and private experiences. Without the opportunity to observe professionals in action and ask their opinions, robotics scientists were not able to appreciate all the complexities in the social system. Spending a considerable amount of time in an "unstructured environment" and learning from new experiences seems to be valuable for engineering innovation. One robotics group proactively engaged with the staff of a local retirement complex; however, one participant in the inter-disciplinary robotics partnership observed the following:

> There was much resistance and fear. Huge amounts of resistance and fear . . . the residents were very worried about the big brother thing, you know being watched and observed all the time, there was concern about "Now the robots taking care of us, so we are not going to see any humans." And they were also concerned about robots being their supervisors rather than their servants. So they wanted the robots to be their servants and they wanted the robot to look like a servant, not like a human. If we stripped all of the anthropomorphic features off the robot, then it became a machine that was doing things that they wanted it to do.

Concerns about robots replacing humans were also voiced in some robotics researcher narratives. For example, one scholar has adopted an ambivalent position. He would prefer a scenario where people (not robots) continue to care for elderly people. In his own words, "My personal view, however, is that it would maybe have been even better if we had more people [employed], it's just that we don't have the money for it. We have to support more elderly people and the people who are working for 'em, for the ratio of retired and working people is getting worse. [Ideally] we should get more money to pay for staff workers who are aiding disabled individuals but at the moment there are not enough citizens [to employ], and it's getting worse." Thus, this scientist argues that developing robots for the elderly "should supplement, provide something extra" rather than replace care.

At one robotics lab, a behavior scientist was invited to provide feedback on their prototype, and asked unconventional questions and speculated that the design of the prototypes could be essential to social acceptance of robots. According to one engineer, some group members were initially surprised to hear this. The engineers prioritized functionality and robustness rather than design and aesthetics. However, it became clear that robotics scientists needed to draw on complementary expertise to increase social acceptability. Because eldercare is as much about social, medical and psychological issues as about technologically robust solutions, these engineering teams

were increasingly forced to engage in cross-disciplinary creative partnerships with "non-engineers" (e.g., behavior scientists and health care staff)
to pursue this knowledge-intensive work and ensure successful adoption of
innovation. Other scientists contributed new knowledge that complemented
and extended the engineering team's knowledge base in new and unexpected
ways as they developed robotic helpers that could increase independence
and autonomy among the elderly.

TIMESAVING ROBOTIC HELPERS FOR INCREASED INDEPENDENCE AND AUTONOMY

Health scientists contributed complementary expertise to partnerships and
reminded the engineers that any workplace system is not as predictable as a
mechanical system in a robotics laboratory. In a workplace, staff workload
invariably depends on a range of contingencies and events beyond their control. As one health staff scientist explained, "If you are seeing twelve people
in one day and you go and knock on somebody's door and you find that she's
fallen and fractured her hip and you have to call an ambulance and everything
and she is your third person that you are seeing today and you have another
seven to see, you are going to be very late with the others, so it's unpredictable
dynamics. So there's a complexity that we have to put into the robot." Few
engineers or robotics developers understand the intricacies of the eldercare
context, which may include the politics of setting work schedules and division of labor among and across professional groups in an organization.

The distribution of medication is an essential routine and among the most
contested domains in an eldercare facility. In the health care sector, regular
reports suggest that legal and practical standards are breached and that the
entire dispensing process of medications is complex. At this eldercare complex, the management of medication occasionally relies on staff members
visiting each resident. However, individual visits are not always required.
Some workplace rearrangements allow staff members to adopt other routines to benefit their workplace situations. However, novel arrangements
and routines may lead to tension between caregivers and patients. This lesson was learned from inter-disciplinary work, and one health scientist suggested that engineers could never know such intricacies without engaging
with the actual workplace setting.

For example, one challenge was to understand the distribution of medications, which represents potentially contested terrain. From the caregiver
perspective, bringing the elderly to the dining room at fixed hours to receive
their medications is preferable (i.e., staff members would rather not spend
their time running around to each senior resident). Elderly people often have
diverging preferences; although it would suit the caregivers to dispense the
medications from a central location, the elderly would prefer to have their
meals at home, in their cottage or apartment. Interestingly, one researcher

noted that the robot could actually eliminate this potential conflict by dispensing medications on schedule in the senior's apartment. Modern eldercare facilities, like other complex service organizations, are arenas where different (and often conflicting) principles of customer orientation are juxtaposed. Although the elderly should influence service provisions, they are also subject to regulation and discipline. Such a juxtaposition of expectations creates inherent tensions and conflicts.

The health scientist contacted both the operational and strategic managers at the retirement complex to follow up on their earlier collaboration to test the robots and was curious to learn more about the organizational implications of eldercare robotics. According to the scientist, the following dialogue with the operational managers ensued:

> "What are these robots going to do, I don't understand?" But I [then] said, "You've seen what the robots have been doing" and they said, "Yeah, but I still don't get what these robots are going to be doing because I've got staff doing these things, why do I need the robots? And are you telling me that you want me to get rid of the staff so that I may have cheap robots doing these things, I don't believe that the robot can do it as well and as reliably as my staff. And I just don't understand, you know, what do you want these things to do? And why? Why do you want a robot pick up people falling, or even record people falling, you know?" But, then, on a more strategic level, people were saying, "Why not. We have to think about the future because robots have certain implications on our infrastructure, if we build a building that in the future has to contain these robots and provide wireless functionality. . . . We have to build these buildings that can contain robots. We have to think about these things, we have to think about our infrastructure, and things like broadband and Wi-Fi and docking stations for the robots and pathways for them to move around, and currently our buildings don't have any of that infrastructure, and financially we cannot afford to build new buildings and have to re-build them to put that infrastructure in."

When the health scientist who was part of the robotics R&D partnership actually took time to talk to the staff at the retirement village about their professional experiences, it became clear that some practitioners doubted the role of robots in their organization. The operational manager seemed hesitant if not opposed to adopting this new technology. However, eldercare organizations also employ managers at other levels and a gap exists between the operational and strategic functions in this eldercare institution. Although more strategic people in the organization could envision a robotic future, the operational people could not. A health scientist with professional experience in health care settings believed that such gaps emerge as innovations are adopted for complex health services for the following reasons:

[The operations people] are just so busy with what's in front of them every day. A doctor and a nurse are busy with the collapsed patient in front of them, that's their focus, that's what they're interested in, they don't care about the technology and the information that's lying in a computer. They are trying to reassess someone in front of them or they are operating on someone in front of them—the information is something that supports what they are doing, it's not that it's not key but it's that it's not their first step in what they are doing with their patients. Whereas on a much more strategic level people are thinking, "What does the future hold, how are we going to get to the future, how are we going to get much better at what we are doing in the future. And technology and innovation are the ways to go, so how are we going to leverage those things to achieve those things that we want to achieve."

The difficulties in daily practices that the robotics group at one university encountered stem from how work is organized and how tasks are completed, that is, the areas where the operational people are bogged down—daily practicalities and emergencies. Usability tests in actual working environments also revealed that practitioners use different terminologies (sometimes peculiar and specific professional jargon) and think differently. As one health scientist explained during the interview, they seem to "live in different worlds, and they think completely differently." None of these fieldwork experiences would have been possible in a controlled laboratory environment on the university campus. Indeed, by moving out of the laboratory and engaging with end-users on their own territory, robotics engineers and other scientists broadened their perspectives and gained new insights, especially those who were unfamiliar with eldercare contexts. One scientist seemed to develop an understanding of the challenges ahead and displayed sensitivity to nuance. Various professionals, the scientist noted,

use different language, you'll hear the strategic thinkers are talking about infrastructure and you can see that they understand the requirements for that infrastructure, when you are talking with somebody on the emergency department floor, you can see they are thinking about, "the computer is just too far away from me to get to it and I need to do what I need to do, you know I'm trying to sort this person out and I have to walk to the computer and I have to clean my hands before I touch the computer because I don't want to get an infection, and pick up infections and those sorts of things. . . . I can't Google something because I can't get onto the bloody Internet because you know the Explorer is too old and it's incompatible with the way the Internet is working now, and why is the hospital not getting us up-to-date Explorer at the very "least". In the meantime, the strategic people are thinking, well, you know I've got that amount of budget and I've got that amount of stuff to spend it on, and what strategic decisions am I going to make?

Well, you know, I need to spend money on the basic software that clinicians need to be able to communicate with one another about their patients and Internet Explorer can work."

Interacting with professionals was critical to identifying diverging approaches and understandings of technology. The challenge for the multidisciplinary robotics team was to determine what people were thinking so that they could address challenges in the workplace. Engineers build robust machines. They typically adopt standardized logic, restrict variation so that technology behaves predictably and sometimes have an implicit idea of an "ideal user." However, the challenge of social systems is that humans rarely behave or act predictably. Despite manuals and instructions, humans may use technologies in unexpected ways that make sense to them (but not always to the engineers). However, by engaging with professionals in real-life contexts, developers and engineers may start to appreciate the thinking and language of the practitioner. Learning jargon facilitates communication with non-technical people and allows training professionals to explain the use of the new technology in safe and sustainable ways.

STRENGTHENING ABILITIES AMONG THE ELDERLY AND OVERCOMING ROBOT DISABILITIES

The underlying assumption, which was often explicit (but sometimes implicit), reflected in the viewpoints of robotics developers in multidisciplinary partnerships and networks centered on the widespread conception in the robotics community that a better life for the elderly entailed new technical solutions that would produce more independent living. This sense of independence was discussed in terms of objective functional (technological) properties and sometimes in terms of increased social autonomy and individual freedom. Being able to go to the toilet without asking someone else for help, for example, was considered a functional challenge to be solved rather than a subjective experience or feeling. During a faculty gathering at one robotics department, a team member addressed the need to uphold a sense of individual dignity and provided some examples:

There are clearly needs in the marketplace to be satisfied, and where robotics is concerned the question is how we can build a home assistant that can help with cleaning and other duties. And, for people with dementia, help to remind them to take their medicines. Help the elderly wake up and get dressed in the morning. However, equally important are the more personal things, such as I should be able to go to the toilet without needing to ask anyone to help me with that. I think that's a key part of all this.

The robots were designed and constructed to accomplish more tasks, which seemed unambiguous to the robotics engineers. However, as soon as the issue of social needs and (possibly varying) preferences among the elderly were addressed, standardized parameters were no longer applicable, which led to ambiguity. It became obvious to developers, especially after conducting experiments with potential users, that different end-users have different preferences and needs. Indeed, this dimension of innovative work was first considered a "softer" issue that proved to be an equal, if not greater, challenge to address. The following interesting dialogue ensued during a group interview. The interviewee initially centered on the functional tasks but the discussion turned to varying user needs and preferences:

> Let's say that somebody [from the outside] is calling [an elderly resident] using a telephone. Well, you can run an elderly person's place without a telephone just using internal communication . . . Suppose if someone was to use any type of doorbell, then that person would always have to run and answer calls at the door. In that case, you would need more people for those duties. The [telephone] in one way is reducing the need for manpower. I would imagine that certain tasks could be left for robots [to do]. Giving medicines, bringing food, . . ., checking if everything is under control, and so on. One can imagine that certain kinds of routine things could be handled that way. Now, I know that most people in any kind of [eldercare] institution would rather have a person than a robot taking care of them. But then, of course, there are some people who do not want personal assistance. They want a robot instead of a person. [A colleague breaks in,] "They want to be independent, a robot does not really threaten their independence." [He responds:] Yes, in that case you'd have your personal robot. If the robot works well, that enhances your independence because you are not depending on a person.

Interestingly, the developers connect the need for independence to technology, which replaces routine and time-consuming tasks. Being less dependent on help from external actors (i.e., being more self-sufficient) includes employees of retirement complexes as well as friends or family members in a home environment. In other words, the engineers assumed that end-users might prefer a robot assistant to a human assistant. Robotic solutions for the elderly at first glance assume a preference for less reliance on human support. Human assistants and caregivers can have bad days at work or may be generally unpleasant towards the elderly they are supposed to serve. Thankfully, such behavior among staff members occurs only sporadically and is considered unacceptable and unethical when it occurs. Robots are not known for being offensive, aggressive, ill-tempered or for displaying bad manners.

INNOVATION ADOPTION: MEDICINES AND BLOOD PRESSURE MEASUREMENTS

One critical complicating factor is how to allow staff (or relatives) to verify that elderly patients took their medicines correctly if the management of medications were delegated to robots. The medication routines can be complex and tricky because some medicines should be taken on an empty stomach but others should be taken on a full stomach, etc. However, as research progresses through R&D partnerships and scientific work, complications must be addressed. One scientist explained as follows:

> We knew there was a gap where nobody knows what happens to medicines when patients take them home, nobody knows. There is no research, nothing done to tell us what people do with their medicines when they get home. We know they accept their prescription, we know they fill the prescription and take the medicines home, we know that they take most of the medicines most of the time correctly because they come back and get a repeated prescription. But we don't know how they modify the instructions to fit their lives, we don't know if they actually are taking all the medicines they say they are taking, and we don't know if they take them at the right time and under the right circumstances. . . . We do know that because some people get sick, they don't take all their medicines when they should take them or they don't take them at all.

Some elderly patients have visual impairments, which may result in taking the wrong medication at the wrong time. In retirement complexes, elderly people (or their relatives) can pay a caregiver to ensure that medications are taken properly. However, even professionals at the elderly care facility who provide these services face difficulties correctly administering all medications as increasing amounts of medications are distributed. The organizational choice is to assign pharmacists to manage, pack and provide safety precautions (such as so-called blister packs) for all medicines. However, one scientist noted, "You know that all your breakfast medicines are together. Then, they would sacrifice the ones that have to be taken on an empty stomach against those that have to be taken on a full stomach just to make sure that they get some of the medicines in there. So, it's a very blunt instrument." Additionally, blister packs are occasionally mixed up and one patient may take another patient's medications.

Robots are equipped to perform tasks beyond medication management, including blood pressure measurement, reminders and alarms, and video calls. In one robotics group, a medical person noted that it might be more convincing to have a robot providing instructions than "if it's just a silly little computer telling them. . . . Our hypothesis is that the robot will do, or encourage or produce an additional length of these [healthy] exercises."

Therefore, health practitioners tested how people respond to robotic helpers and whether robots could encourage people to exercise more, thus promoting health and well-being. That is, "to encourage these behaviors. You know, is this robot going to make this person sit on that bike for a longer time or not? You know, because if the robot is, then it might be beneficial to put these somewhere like in a retirement complex, or something of that nature, or a hospital to encourage people to do rehab or things like that."

Reoccurring ideas that emerged during the interviews were autonomy, independence and freedom. However, a contradiction also emerged. One the one hand, too much dependence on social support was seen as problematic and was an issue that needed to be solved. On the other hand, after the initial trials, it became apparent to many of the developers that too much independence might also be problematic if people become socially isolated and unhappy. There is no formula to striking this balance, and a trade-off exists between relying excessively on social assistance and completely losing social contact. Striking a balance between independence and dependence is not straightforward. It was recognized that this balance would most likely vary by cultural context and social situation. For the developers, independence and autonomy were less clear than they first appeared because of the realization that too little human interaction and contact could be problematic and fuel skepticism and resistance. One scientist rightfully acknowledged that some elderly people were already facing social isolation and misery in their home environments. The developers therefore looked for an adequate compromise, a "technical fix" that might somehow overcome the social isolation conundrum on the one hand while enabling independence and personal dignity on the other.

One solution that emerged during the process was to equip robots with monitors and Internet connections to allow the elderly to become more socially active and communicative should they wish to do so. Being socially active does not only mean participating in community activities at their convenience but also being able to use modern video-conferencing easily to maintain professional contact with medical staff as well as with close friends and family members (e.g., grandchildren). However, video conferencing is not universally useful for all elderly people, especially those with visual impairments. Although the monitor addition seemed to improve opportunities for engaging in social interactions at their discretion, another issue emerged: unreliable Wi-Fi. Therefore, the engineers pursued new "technical fixes." Without Internet connectivity, the new features were less functional. Technical challenges remain to be addressed, and although some technical problems are solved, new problems emerge.

Where is the development of robotic helpers heading? Clearly, some elderly continue to live active lives and might fancy a robot that could help them with shopping or other tasks. A consensus among the engineers and robotics scientists that robots are timesaving technologies emerged. As one scientist discussed, "Another major [robotics] market that is being explored within the professional services sector is shopping, helping people get more quality time. What can we do to help people with their groceries? During a typical visit to supermarket, a person spends approximately 17 percent of their time running around and this is perhaps a waste of time as it could be automated." However, this scientist remarked that new challenges emerge when robots are brought outside of laboratory contexts.

Infrastructure is relevant because physical surroundings are primarily designed and constructed to fit (average) human and social needs. Therefore, an increasing number of academics in the global robotics science community have pursued the development of robots that mimic humans in shape and kinematic structure (so-called humanoid robots). However, such a design is not unproblematic as one robotics scientist observed. It may also be increasingly difficult to modify existing infrastructure. He said, "If you start beginning to modify the environment, [installing] reflecting tapes or so, then the market is reduced by a factor of ten. A helping device in your home where you have to put up reflecting tape everywhere is not something doable, so the ultimate challenge is to make it work in natural environments." Many robotic scientists refer a natural state in contrast to their structured university laboratories. In the professional jargon of engineers, a home milieu or a workplace context is an "unstructured environment." This case study presented some obstacles and issues in both structured and unstructured environments that inter-disciplinary innovation and creative academic partnerships address to develop robots for the elderly.

SUMMARY

This case study presents firsthand accounts of key challenges and contradictions encountered by research and development teams during various stages of creating and testing eldercare robots, from the initial idea generation to providing care robots for end-users. These accounts reflect the underlying uncertainty and ambiguities that pervaded much of the early innovation work. The case of r-Care is enlightening because it illustrates how complex boundary-spanning innovations develop and where preconceptions, interests and value-systems among professional groups and institutional domains diverge. Although the multidisciplinary partnerships and hybrid R&D work suggested that different standpoints existed (and partly conflicted because scholars were rooted in different academic traditions), supportive and complementary expertise helped advance knowledge and innovation. Tensions were mitigated during prolonged, complex field-testing, and social frictions and negotiations were beneficial because they exposed contradictions, which in turn allowed scholars to identify new problems and accelerate their innovative work to tackle these challenges. Cross- and inter-disciplinary connections proved important to the development and adoption of innovation.

Contradictions are related to economic considerations, unclear market demands and practical issues in the deployment of care robots in real-life environments and elderly care institutions. Strategically and operationally oriented managers employed in a retirement complex, for example, provided different viewpoints.

In the institutional and scientific contexts, eldercare robots are not just strategic choices or paths to increased freedom and autonomy but fuel innovations to improve health and well-being. One future domain that developers envision is the robotic encouragement of exercise. Caring robots are thus part of a wider social discourse of "self-care" management (see, e.g., Wasen, 2013), i.e., new techno-organizational solutions that enable individuals to take greater responsibility in monitoring their health status and managing some medical routines (e.g., medications). However, this case study suggests that although many aspects of the autonomy narrative emphasize independence, self-care management does not inevitably entail "total autonomy" or the complete removal of social (inter)dependence. Rather, self-care needs produce complex reconfigurations among humans and robots. New forms of techno-social dependency implicitly assume reliance on technology, which must be robust and functional. Therefore, it is possible to view robot helpers and emerging self-care services as innovations that allow autonomy as well as interdependence. In other words, the forces of autonomy and interdependence are not mutually exclusive but paradoxically co-exist. Trends in self-care as well as demographic predictions imply a new and growing market for robots. We have noted that contradictions may spur the emergence of innovations and solutions. Scientists exert considerable influence on new enhancing technologies and seek to address varying social needs in a growing population of elderly people.

6 Robots in Services

Industrial robotic laborers are an important segment of modern factory automation systems, and we observe in the preceding chapters that these artificial laborers provide an array of advanced functionalities that transcend prior limitations to conduct hazardous, dirty and tedious tasks. Although robotic technology has predominantly been linked to industrial work since the early days of automation, the next sections will highlight significant developments in non-industrial work contexts. Robotics in services comprises an increasingly important share of the "robot economy" in which the ultimate goal not only is to delegate unsafe and monotonous tasks to workplace robots but also to pursue time-efficiency gains.

This chapter presents firsthand case study findings on the application of advanced robotics and networking in two settings in Sweden: academic and public libraries. Libraries have traditionally been viewed as old-fashioned (bureaucratic) institutional structures. Therefore, it may be surprising that these organizations are not passive recipients of new technologies. Libraries were among the first workplaces to aggressively introduce and use computer technology and the Internet in the 1990s to benefit their patrons. Indeed, today it would be quite difficult to imagine a modern library without computers, digital catalogues or Internet access to eBooks, etc. More than 30 years later, many libraries (particularly subsidiaries) still cannot afford costly robotic systems. A limited number of institutions, mainly larger public metropolitan libraries in Sweden, have started to employ robotic laborers in their workplaces. Evidence from the cases suggests that robotic-led economic developments are deeply embedded in wider professional networks and partnerships, which stretch across and beyond libraries. Strategic choices about the extent to which robots are permitted to handle books and other library materials must be made. Professionals in academic and public libraries have chosen a path of robot delegation in which an increasing number of time-consuming (manual) tasks are delegated to robotic laborers.

SERVICE ORGANIZATIONS IN TRANSITION: ROBOTICS IN SWEDISH LIBRARIES

Many large research libraries in Sweden have pursued mass digitization systems, which are considered strategic priorities. Digitization is a political subject and "decisions [at the top of the command chain] have been taken that we should invest in digitization. However, if we shall be able to do that and deliver services that scientists and others demand, then we have to maintain a rate of production and it all comes down to that." Recent investments in technological solutions imply that the strategic choices of major academic libraries exert a considerable influence on new infrastructure arrangements that have been adopted by the Swedish university system. Some staff members in libraries note nearly compulsory demands from top management to digitize collections. This trend, of course, is not unique to Sweden but is visible around the world.

Although automated approaches that involve acquiring and using state-of-the art robots are appropriate to mass digitization goals in Sweden, these robotic approaches have only recently been introduced into large research libraries, which instead have relied on manual digitization of books and printed materials. As one staff member explained, "In principle, at least, we could still stick to the [old] flatbed scanner or the Canon camera and continue to take pictures page by page [manually] but that would take ages. This robot does not just scan materials reasonably fast, it has also been equipped with software that can make the image processing rather efficient." In the previous method, subsequent image processing of the materials generated by digital cameras was a time intensive procedure. Robotic technology is also connected to a time and resource efficiency narrative that emphasizes the economic value of time and money. One staff member noted, "The robot works faster and partly replaces the human factor; it provides a qualitatively better image." The robotic system automatically turns pages and scans up to 3,118 pages per hour, according to the robot manufacturer. At the academic library, scanning speed averages 2,500 pages per hour through automated page turning.

The robot processes books 35.5 x 35.5 centimeters (13.98 x 13.98 inches), and these books can be up to 15 centimeters (5.91 inches) thick. For the book insert, there is no restriction of paper thickness, and according to the producer, the ScanRobot® handles acid spoiled sheets as well as curly sheets from the fourteenth century and onwards. According to the academic librarians, a key feature of the robotic system is its gentle treatment of books, omitting the need to interact with fragile, valuable old books. The scanned book is provided with an unique ID-number, which is used in the automation process. To ensure high quality, staff members typically manually verify that no pages are omitted (which may happen when two pages are stuck together), and a software feature assists in this process. Once content has been digitized, it is stored on a temporary external server, OCR treated (which makes the content of the book searchable) and converted into a PDF document. This PDF is uploaded to the local catalogue and is assigned a unique post in the nationwide book catalogue system, Libris, which is controlled by the influential Royal Library (hereafter, RL) in Stockholm.

The RL initiated and legitimized the entire digitization project wherein millions were invested to digitize their massive collections. The RL instigated a project in the early 2000s to use backscanner cameras (reverse scan cameras) to take pictures page-by-page. They even shot photos of the covers and spines of books; however, one librarian at the academic library noted they "had poor image resolution. The rest of us [at the academic libraries] who followed their work wondered, 'What the hell are they up to? They cannot go on like that,' and eventually they realized that themselves, it would most likely take them 5,000 years to digitize all collections at the RL with this method." The RL approach included the entire object, whereas local academic libraries were merely interested in digitizing content. One librarian summarizes, "[We] don't give a damn about the object as such." The only time that library staff shot the binders was if they contained vital information related to the content of the book that was worth the extra time and effort; they were not generally interested in photographing the covers or spines of books.

The scanning unit principally generates revenues through internal charge and providing on-demand services that other sub-divisions in the organization must pay for. Digitization so far is essentially a research-driven enterprise. Theoretically, academic libraries could expand their offerings and services to other external stakeholders and customers (e.g., other universities, institutes, governmental agencies, etc.). Although there may be a demand for such services, there has been no plan or attempt to commercialize on a large scale. Still, it is clear that the librarian unit is actively targeting a broader customer base to finance its costly investment in robotics. As one librarian explained, engaging with new academic customers and being able to offer them a useful service that may significantly benefit their work is a viable "way to fund our operations as well where they have to pay X/€ per page." Scholarly projects are attractive to the scanning service unit. Research projects (from scholars and research departments) represent a growing customer base that is usually sufficiently well funded to pay for a large quantity of digitized material.

One ongoing project in the scanning unit processes between 50 to 60 thousand pages of archived material for a customer (for a research project at the university). A librarian explained, here we work with "interesting and relevant [research] material that someone wants to be processed and which someone currently is working with, so [our services] will be beneficial immediately. The alternative would otherwise be to start digitizing the library's old collections section and to commence on letter 'A' [and go on until Z], but it would most likely take seven years before we processed something significant that some bastard actually would want to see." A tension exists between two logics or practices. On the one hand, mass digitization enables archiving (i.e., storing data for future generations). On the other hand, materials can be used immediately (i.e., exploiting data now). The unit staff members seem to appreciate the input they receive from customers not only because it provides meaning and satisfaction that their services are valuable, or that their work schedule has structure, but also because such customer input provides usable feedback on the relevance, quality and usability of digitized material and services. However, being able to meet market needs also pertains to pure economic circumstances. The unit is managed to prevent additional expenses. Cost containment is a strategic part of a lean management trend in institutional life, which neither public nor academic libraries are exempt from, and the management of the scanning unit must oversee their "production line" and "output" so that they do not incur losses and, ideally, generate revenues to cover their costs. As one librarian explained,

> Because of the equipment costs [initially] and it is a pure fact that it is also costly to have the production process going, so then one might speculate who would buy this kind of robot, and who is interested in digitizing bound books? It is libraries primarily, but [for them] it's not a huge commercial success because the procedure uses pricey hand-built machines. The fact that technology costs, that's why I refer to "production rate," because assume we have invested 1.5 million to acquire the equipment but only process 100 books per year. What then, would the cost per book equate to? Clearly, that cost would not be justifiable, hence it must "pay off" somehow. It's a good thing to be able to kill two birds with one stone by digitizing the material people want [i.e., meeting a demand] while also getting money for it. If we can alleviate some of the pressure, then it's a good thing in the library.

Alleviate here has a double meaning, which refers to the potential for easing the financial burden of the organization by generating additional revenues to cover the initial investment and other expenses. This procedure is less labor-intensive and time-consuming, which also lessens the financial burden on the institution from employing people to conduct this work; in fact, automation produces larger outputs. As one staff member noted, "The idea is often to rationalize, they measure this and that, to statistically single out where resources are needed. Occasionally, we have seen some hard times, but we have been quite fortunate not to sack people, issues have been solved by temporarily freezing recruitments and pursuing earlier retirement programs instead." It seems that economics matter in the management of academic libraries, but there is a tension between modernization objectives (e.g., to improve patron and citizen access to library services and solutions) and new public management regulation, which emphasizes cost containment and efficient work processes (e.g., a focus on the production rate).

SWEDISH ACADEMIC LIBRARY SERVICE PRODUCTION

What is the organizational rationale to change the division of work and introduce robotic technology into the library environment, specifically into the digital reproduction unit? One staff member saw this as a strategic choice: "You do it for the same reasons [in other settings where robotics is used], to reduce the production cost per unit." However, this staff member hastened to add that the library unit must still justify its usage. Furthermore, "It's also a satisfaction to those who work with it, that you can get a nice flow going that works and which required as little human effort as possible, and where you get as much out of it as possible." The arc scanner has a similar functionality as advanced photocopiers, which does not require each page to be fed into the copying machine.

> We have to take all that which the robot cannot manage to handle. In exceptional cases we go back to other methods, and because this only happens in exceptional circumstances, the risk of being exposed to repetitive strain injuries is not so great. So the two processes we run are the robot and arc scanner. We are currently digitizing all the doctoral theses at the university, for them we have extra copies in a warehouse so we take them apart and just feed them into the arc scanner. It is the least harmful method for the body, you just take a stack of paper and put it into the scanner and then you just get into a state of rest in a comfy chair and wait until it has been processed, the only thing you need to do is keep your eyes on the screen and see that the nothing odd happens and that nothing gets stuck in the scanner.

The unit has the advantage that they have retained the old technology, which allows them to switch to manual scanning. One complicating factor in the work process, however, is the variety of books that exist. As one member reflected, digitization very much hinges on the nature and quality of the products being processed: "It'd be a huge difference if we were situated at the Art Museum, and we had to digitize 5,000 watercolor illustrations . . . it's much tougher for them to automate their art work."

Except doctoral theses, the digital services unit prioritizes the collection of classical books in their native languages, which is part of a nationwide campaign across Swedish libraries. Concerns have been raised that multiple libraries are engaged in ad hoc work to digitize materials, which may lead to duplication of digital collections. Plans to pursue nationwide coordination are believed to rationalize digitization but also seek to circumvent duplication of effort and costs. Paradoxically, historically autonomous research libraries are simultaneously being pushed to become more dependent on external stakeholders, and there is a risk that these research libraries will eventually lose influence over their resources. It is difficult to determine whether their autonomy and sphere of influence has been diluted by rapid institutional shifts. However, the findings suggest that radical changes in work organization in the digital context produce contradictory consequences.

A national network has been established to coordinate an appropriate division of labor among libraries. The official library, the RL, and the National library of Sweden (in professional terminology abbreviated to KB in Swedish) are situated in the center of Stockholm, the capital of Sweden. As one librarian noted, because of its special role, "The RL is an autonomous institution, it doesn't have any other institutions to address, they don't have a university to take into consideration." However, the RL stresses networking with local academic libraries and sees "benefits in jointly collaborating on how to achieve efficient operations of a scanning robot." It is no overstatement to surmise that the RL become the spider in the net of the national library partnership, but it was somewhat surprising that the lead coordinator was an economist and not a librarian. Perhaps this choice reflected that the planned purchase represented a huge investment for each member, which required managerial and financial expertise. Indeed, the growing prevalence of partnerships and networks is part of a broader trend in the public institutional landscape through which these institutions incorporate business models into publicly funded fields.

This network partnership was established to include half a dozen major academic libraries in Sweden. Members of the partnership were involved in a joint effort to pursue robotics given the digitalization trend, and meet regularly and travel to other European libraries to observe how different systems function. Based on these experiences and collaborations, members were able to initiate developments that eventually enabled robots to be adopted within each organization. Not surprisingly, the RL had much to say in the negotiations, and the entire robotics project was originally an initiative of the coordinating library in Stockholm.

During the acquisition of multiple robotic systems, the pros and cons were weighed and each member had their say, which perhaps is a distinct trait of Scandinavian consensus culture. These specific criteria were later presented to the producers. (At that time, at least five major firms competed; however, the second round of negotiations identified the three top candidates from Sweden, Norway and Austria. The firms under consideration produced various scanning robots.) One specific criterion was a technical feature that allowed materials to be scanned without opening the books more than approximately 60 degrees. Another feature required robots that could cope with dust (indeed, dust does accumulate in books).

The former procedural requirements (in technical terms, the aperture angle) excluded some potential robots, especially those that opened books 180 degrees. From a written statement (a memorandum dated June 1st, 2010), it is evident that the members of the joint Swedish partnership decided to acquire the ScanRobot® produced by the Austrian firm, Treventus. This robotic system meets the aperture angle requirement described above. Once the investment decision was made, it was communicated as a success story of several public, autonomous organizations joining forces strategically despite their difference. This was a major news story, and newspaper headlines stated that such a robot investment represented "a major business deal." Consequently, each member of partnership acquired and used Treventus robots. Indeed, it was a symbolic act that the first book robotically scanned at the RL was Maja Ekerlöf's seminal book, which was published in 1968, a digital end-product produced for the European Project "Fragen," which collects key texts from the second-generation women's movement in 29 countries.

As digital services have recently grown considerably, the RL encouraged and financed an innovative project that automates flows of information. As high-volume automated scanning is now in place, the challenge is to ensure that digitized solutions spread efficiently. The new organizational division allows more autonomous and directed work on this development: "What we're trying to achieve is to automate the entire flows [of digitization procedures] as far as possible. Ultimately, although there is always a manual step in the book scanning process that we cannot circumvent, where we want to go is to actually be able have as have as little human interference as possible." Such an innovation would entail digitization in which human interference is nearly absent, from early image processing and OCR (Optical Character Recognition) to later stages of the transfer of the digitized product for storage on information servers, and finally enabling automated entering of the new product into Libris (i.e., a national computerized catalogue system of available materials). The transfer of information between various computerized catalogue systems takes place during the late hours of the night. All these work steps are targets for automation. One librarian quite bluntly stated that the goal is that "we scan, into the system it goes [stresses this by snapping his fingers] and then it rolls off [by itself] and eventually it comes out at the other end." This sophisticated automation indicates a significant re-distribution of work and re-allocation of resources; however, because each library has its own catalogue system, humans must integrate this very long chain of steps. Those staff members employing and developing digital and programming skills gain influence as new software developments become dependent on these skills. As mentioned above, the mass digitization team belongs to the powerful DSU, and there exists complementary expertise to store the products (files) to automate the entire flow. This also signifies a shift from spending time on routine work cataloguing materials to more innovative work focusing on problem solving and social networking.

The academic library is digitizing all doctoral theses, which includes seven thousand documents, the first of which was produced in approximately 1900. Although new powerful technology enables the digitization of enormous amounts of conventional printed material, intricate socio-political matters still influence the reach and usage of digitized material. One staff member shared his frustration: "We suffer hugely because of the Copyright

Act." What the library is permitted to do (and not do) with the digitized material is controversial, and because of copyright compliance issues, it has chosen not to post several of digitized products online. Clearly, proponents of the Copyright Act represent a powerful, influential interest group that actively fights to uphold legal rights of original contributions, protect publishers and ownership of original and creative work. The balancing between maintaining ownership protection and allowing open access is contested in the academic world, and different lawyers at different academic libraries provide different interpretations of the law. To ensure compliance with copyright legislation, materials printed before 1880 are typically available online. The digital conservation of culturally significant works is relatively costly and new partnerships seek to coordinate their work given that they share a common vision and values. In the European Union, for example, more than 25 libraries are part of the eBooks on demand network through which literature published before 1900 is mass digitized. An ambition of this grand project is to preserve and disseminate European cultural heritage—a challenging and highly honorable goal indeed. Networking within European library institutions and beyond is critical for staff members to remain up to date:

> Somehow, we are constantly keeping track of what's happening out there in the world as far as technological developments are concerned to be prepared for what's happening. Had we, for example, omitted to see electronic resources coming and not developed the right skill set we would be facing a steep learning curve. Instead, we were early in purchasing electronic resources so this type of expertise is currently available in the organization. However, should we not have had anticipated this trend and being forced to start from scratch today and acquire new skill sets we would definitively had been in a much more problematic position, a really tough one. We live through such things regularly . . . [so] one must always realize that what is as common practice today may definitely not look the same next year because things happen.

For a professional working in a rapidly changing technological and institutional environment, trend spotting is central, which requires connecting with national and international partnerships and learning in informal library communities.

ROBOTS AS ARTIFICIAL AND SUPPORTIVE CO-WORKERS

As we observe the digitization process and the robot in action, it appears that scanning some books works like a charm. A special room has been devoted to the robot, and we see how the responsible librarian leans back in the office chair. The staff can sit in close proximity to the robot with their arms crossed while letting the robot perform most of the task. As one librarian put it, "From the first page and onwards, you don't have to do anything. It's not a story about tedious work anymore. Instead, I believe the problem is that you become [too much] relaxed and sit back in monotonous postures. I think the biggest problem is that because the robot goes on automatically, you must still be on guard and you then tend to tense up whilst sitting and starring at the robot . . . it's not that it will smash any of the books in half, but it occasionally stalls and that is a source of irritation, so there is an inherent tension built into the process." The staff member continued:

> You must load books into the robot in the right way, you have to tweak and fiddle a bit so that the book is mounted properly. The name suggests it is a robot but it is not a robot 100% because it is terribly difficult to scan a bound book [completely autonomously] without running into any trouble at all, right? It's almost impossible to do that because the books are so varied. However, it also means that you cannot afford to just leave the robot [working], you have to monitor it all the time, you have to be there and you have to watch and be attentive that nothing weird happens. For example, if it goes about and crushes a page of the book or anything like that. However, the pace of work is at least three times faster than the manual method on the scanner cradle. And you do not have those constant [repetitious] movements where you have to scroll and lift all the time.

Challenges remain in terms of addressing workplace needs and identifying solutions for the entire human-robot organization to function smoothly and efficiently, including new ergonomic workplace design, which includes elevated tables that provide a better working environment for the library staff. Replacing repetitive tasks is an ongoing concern in libraries and one practitioner also considered the more recent automation of the catalogue system to be a form of virtual robotization:

> [Robotization] appears and resembles how society is developing otherwise, so it is just to tag along, huh, it's completely inevitable. However, one can ask where it all ends with a library such as ours if digitization continues, eventually. Just think of Google that digitizes vast amounts of [book] material. The new materials that we acquire are essentially digitized and are delivered electronically too. So we find ourselves in an "identity crisis," what have we become, really? Certainly, we have books, but we have essentially become a "museum collection" more than anything else. Few [patrons] have a peek inside the books anymore because they are usually available electronically. So, have we just become a shelter were our student keep warm and a place where we provide them study rooms? If not, we may be situated anywhere really—the devil only

knows—and because we take care of about everything via monitors currently, so the question is what has happened to the library in all of this?

As noted, academic research libraries and the RL have been radically transformed in the wake of mass digitization and robotics. We have read professional accounts that illustrate how academic libraries pursued early developments in the area of automated mass digitization. We have also noted how robotized work has emerged to address the occupational perils of early mass digitization. Some professionals experience an identity crisis. Has the modern library become more of a broker of digitized content by adjusting its pace to the increased flow of information in society rather than remaining the calm and pleasant milieu of previous times where patrons could enjoy books and articles without stress? The shift to mass digitization occurred in the early 2000s, but primarily relied on manual efforts and did not initially include robotic installments. Interestingly, the same period of the early 2000s introduced robotics to the professional library context, albeit in a quite different form and arrangement to solve a practical dilemma in the organization. The robotic transition we have in mind occurred within the public (metropolitan) library context in Sweden, and we were able to follow this development for several years. We interviewed staff members at one public library that was the early mover in the library sector as the first library in Sweden to acquire two robotic systems to process some of its time-consuming and labor-intensive book logistics. During the course of a day, patrons would return books and other artifacts that amounted to more than a thousand kilograms, and the handling of such a quantity of books and media represented a strenuous and tedious physical task for professional librarians and library assistants. By employing new technology, staff members could delegate a large portion of such work to robots, which created more time for other tasks. Today, more than 25 libraries employ these robotic helpers in Sweden.

One experienced library assistant at a public library who had just turned 65 years old, the official retirement age in Sweden, reflected on the changes in the profession: "The robot becomes just like a human being." Similarly, another senior colleague remarked, "I see the robot as a work companion . . . a work companion that carries out tasks which we could and should do. The robot performs work that people otherwise would have to do." These two quotes represent a common theme in the empirical material, which suggests that robots can be viewed as artificial co-workers. Another librarian said, "To be sure, the robot carries out slave labor and work for us. It makes the work easier, the robot essentially relieves the strain on our bodies, but it is most crucial for the economy. . . . Robots are to be seen as robots and not humans, but are supplements to humans." Robots perform low status tasks (resembling slave-like jobs) at the library and relieve the heavy physical workload, which includes several thousands of kilograms (cf. pounds) of books per day. The robot either replaces human labor or complements the humans because of its work capabilities. Moreover, several library employees see that robots transcend them and their inherent (human) limitations: "The robots do what the humans do but manage to do things faster and are good at doing several things simultaneously. The [library return] robot is programmed and has no other sources of disruption but just goes on doing the same time over and over again. Once it receives information, then it carries out things at lightning speed. But at the same time it is sensitive if something faults on the way, he [the robot] doesn't have the capacity to think by himself but stops working . . . [but usually] it is outstanding compared to humans, actually. It has multitasking capacity." This interviewee emphasizes that robots multitask and quickly perform several tasks simultaneously that humans cannot.

A robot can instantly, physically receive a book from the patron, scan the book so it is deregistered from the database, physically deactivate the alarm tag, sort the book and replace it, provide the patron a receipt and communicates to the staff when the bin is full. By performing these steps quickly, the robot transcends human limitations. However, friction may emerge when robots cannot cope and humans must intervene to transcend the robot's limitations. Humans and robots transcend each other's limitations and together create a powerful workforce. One library technician observed, "The robots have taken on the strenuous and boring jobs . . . robots provide a pair of helping hands, they are customer-friendly and more enduring and consistent than humans." Yet, another interviewee found that the robot has certain restrictions in its functioning: "[Although] the robot performs the same movements monotonously over and over again, it has no intellect, no values, and no feelings whatsoever, and cannot become tired or fed up." However, she also noted, despite the fact that she was a junior employee in the organization, "This workplace is presently constructed so that the machine remains functional. And if the robot doesn't function, then the workplace is dysfunctional as well. We wouldn't be capable of dealing [manually] with all the books that patrons return."

Her colleague notes that this limitation applies to most advanced technologies, and this view of organizations "takes for granted that everything functions, but it's like that in most sectors." Several practitioners believed that timesaving technologies alleviated the strain on social systems because the robots perform a large part of the workload and thereby lessen the production pressure on the organization as whole, as articulated by one librarian: "The robot gets rid of tasks that meant that staff members would have to run back and forth to do. This is what machines are good at. It happens in society that machines conquest work domains and there is not much to do about it, the robots are usually more efficient. My experience is that people in general are not that aggravated about machines replacing tasks which are seen to be tough and rough." This voice represented another junior librarian, but others were also concerns that libraries might eventually be replaced by robots: "The robot becomes a competitor to humans. The robot takes away physical work from us, it would have corresponded to two full-time workers."

SUMMARY

The case study presented above examines the introduction of robotic laborers into service organizations, that is, academic and public libraries. The attempt has been to assess the strategic choices and rationales for service robotization in both academic and public libraries, and the case examples generate two main findings. First, service robots, unlike previous library technologies, are viewed as "co-workers" who now perform everyday tasks that their human counterparts previously performed. There have been positive effects of this transition from both customer and economic perspectives. However, some staff structures in libraries have become so reliant upon the high-volume service provision of their new robotic co-workers that when they stop being "operational" and "obedient," the entire workplace becomes dysfunctional. This, in turn, suggests a source of (inter)dependence, tight integration and potential vulnerability in modern socio-robotic work organizations (SRWO).

Second, the growth of robotics in modern libraries seems to produce and broaden cost-efficiency pressures in already heavily streamlined service organizations. Peculiar contradictory tendencies surface. On the one hand, service robotization relies heavily on innovation and more competitive human-robot partnerships, which implicitly assumes tighter collaboration and harmonious co-existence and (inter)dependence between humans and technology so that the total system operates smoothly and efficiently. On the other hand, justifying the significant investment costs of technological installments pushes management to pursue rationalization of staff structures. High-technology robots in library services increasingly replace and, to some extent, outcompete staff in the process of technological change.

Such radical workplace transformations evoke growing uneasiness among some staff members and may produce both physical and emotional stress. The possibility of diminishing professionalism and employment prospects may also produce social and psychological worries among staff members. Although robots liberate workers from strenuous and boring jobs, they eventually threaten their jobs. In other words, technological change creates new opportunities, but it takes away others. Such institutional and technological change is ambiguous, but this case demonstrates that contradictions can be a powerful source of radical change, creativity and innovation. There is a consensus among professionals that some jobs involving routine and low-skilled tasks are not likely to come back. Staff members explore novel opportunities and workplace innovations to extend the practice of automated laborers from the physical to the virtual realm of robotics, and by strategic choices, library staff actively redefine and renegotiate their professional identities and circumstances.

7   Robots in Agriculture

Most people would likely agree that it is vital to protect rural landscapes and might even take the supply of locally produced milk at affordable prices for granted. However, few people actually know how high quality fresh milk is currently being produced. Perhaps this lack of knowledge exists because many people have lost contact with rural life in the wake of the considerable urbanization that large cities have experienced during the last century, a shift that also means that farming as a profession has become increasingly underrated. Farmers are also increasingly exposed to milk price wars in the marketplace. Although consumer understandings of current farm complexities and market realities are incomplete, the products that dairy farmers produce are essential to modern lifestyles and food consumption habits.

Currently, robotics on the farm are radically transforming the social and organizational setting by reducing the role of manual labor and improving animal welfare while enabling higher yields in milk production. Robotic milking uses state-of-the-art technological systems that permit self-milking by dairy cows. An original case study explores over a decade of technological change and farming developments in the Swedish agricultural sector and identifies some challenges and constraints to innovation in the industry.

Many dairy farmers today struggle to survive: approximately ten percent of farmers have recently been forced to close their businesses (SVT, 2012a, 2012b). This topic is controversial, but the various public commentators in the national debate conclude that the dairy industry is in crisis, which is not unique to Sweden but seems to apply to most, if not all, developed countries. Dairy farmers are experiencing increasing international competition and financial strain stemming from rigid administrative policies on the one hand and calculating and aggressive milk supplier tactics on the other. From a dairy industry perspective, the Swedish sector experienced deregulation of the market in 1990. However, increasingly, influence and power are geographically dispersed and located at the top of the value chain.

Indeed, the lack of influence in negotiations over the pricing of milk products (prices per liter have steadily dropped) is perhaps a key explanation for difficulties in the dairy business during the twenty-first century. Despite the dangers of unpredictable milk prices (which are increasingly related to fluctuating milk demands in the global marketplace), there is also an inherent danger in utilizing large loans to finance expensive farm improvements (e.g., high-tech investments), which may risk surplus operating cash flow in farms. Fading profits are an enduring economic trend. However, local businesses must continue to invest if they want to move forward, and cutting-edge automated farming technologies are long-term investments that may potentially save labor and reduce the costs of feed and veterinary services. Maintaining a healthy and balanced budget and cash flow is vital for growing the herd. By investing in emerging robotic technology, farmers hope not only to improve the health and well-being of their cattle to improve fertility and ensure continuity of the herd but also to increase milk yields.

With his wife and children, one interviewed farmer currently operates a fourth-generation dairy farm in a beautifully situated farming district in central Sweden. The majority of the interviewed farmers had inherited their milk production businesses, but they have developed their businesses considerably by pursuing increased scale and technological capacity. Several younger farmers had their relatives living close to their business. During the interviews, older farmers willingly shared their stories and historical accounts from the early days of low-tech and pre-robotic farming. Most, if not all, dairy farms in the early 1900s in Sweden raised cows, pigs and other animals so the work environment was not as specialized or focused on high-yield production as it is today. Of course, these were different times. Farmers recalled that the introduction of bucket milking, which replaced hand milking, considerably reduced milking time. Bucket milking was a remarkable change in work methods, which, in turn, nearly doubled the number of cows that could be milked and dramatically increased milk production capacity. One dairy farmer recalls the following:

> My grandfather began to employ a bucket milking facility in 1946. They then had employees in the barn who did the work on a rotational basis, and they had extra replacement shifts. Sometimes they sat and milked by hand [out in the open on small footstools], especially if they were situated further away from the farm in the summer as they milked much smaller quantities back then.

Using a bucket milking machine takes approximately eight minutes, but milking by hand takes between 10 to 15 minutes. In 1946, farmers produced approximately 5 to 10 liters and 8 to 10 cows were out to pasture. The transition to new methods was not always painless or smooth. The conversion to robotic milking, or automatic milking systems (AMS), provides an example. Indeed, some older, retired farmers were suspicious and feared losing contact with the herd as farmer-animal interactions decreased. These farmers were initially wary, but the opposition among retired farmers decreased, and they gradually warmed to the idea of robotics. One farmer was eventually swayed when he observed that the robotic system allowed more time and attention to be devoted to calves and herd welfare. He said, "Indeed, we were a bit suspicious initially. However, you'd never believe that it was possible to have a machine to milk [the cows when they were hand milked either]. It was the same thought now with the robot. However, it worked too." At a farm operated by a father and son, the son admitted that the father was not keen on the robotic system. He thought it was a public stunt rather than anything substantial. Despite initial fears and concerns, no interviewed farmers wished to return to the previous methods.

The stories that retired dairy farmers shared highlight the feature that distinguishes dairy production today compared to previous times: new technology. Mechanization and automation provide functionality. Additionally, interviews reveal how competition in the industry has changed. The shift to new methods forced the cows to change their daily habits. Change may upset the cows, and the process of adjusting to a new way of milking can be slow. Friction and resistance can also occur. One farmer recalled that it took more than eight attempts to drive the cows to the waiting area and train them to use the robots.

Specialization in agriculture gained momentum in the 1950s, and the consolidation of small, family-operated farms into larger industrialized farms has been an ongoing concern. Perhaps fertilizer, new methods of processing grain, and improved plant breeding have most drastically changed agriculture. One farmer explains that increased competition and efficiency requirements produce additional pressures:

> Now you'll need to produce at least 80 liters of milk to pay for an hour of work for an employee. In the 1950s, it was less than 10 liters per cow . . . but we've seen yields being increased much more. In the 1950s about 4,000 liters was produced every year, today we produce 10,000 liters per cow and year [equivalent to 10.000 kilograms], this is where the efficiency gains have been realized in relation to the working hours needed. . . . You feel the pressure to increase the economic turnover and profits for every year that passes. The rising costs would get beyond one's control otherwise if one wouldn't be able to increase revenues.

On another farm, the average yield of the herd was approximately 10,000 kilograms annually. A consequence of external market pressures and smaller profit margins is that farmers actively seek new approaches and methods to manipulate variables and thereby optimize their milk production systems. Farmers provide the cows with much more food (energy and protein) for a 4,000-liter cow, which also involves optimized breeding of "better" animals (i.e., cows that produce more milk per year). On average, in automated robotic milking, a cow is milked approximately 2.6–2.7 times per day. Some cows are even milk three times a day, which increases milk production. In contrast, in the 1950s, for example, farmers usually milked the cows twice a day, early in the morning at approximately 4 a.m. and then later in the afternoon at approximately 5 p.m. (this "twice-a-day" milking routine is still practiced on many non-robotic farms). One farmer in a family milk business recalled how he helped hand milk the cows as a young boy: "I lived right here on the farm and then I got to hand milk, even here down by the road [i.e., out in the open]." He adds, "The labor force was not so expensive back then [in 1947] compared to now, we had 30 cows and an external employee, a farmhand servant [the previous title for a livestock caretaker] who helped out and who lived on the farm." Much has changed on dairy farms in one or two generations, and it would not be realistic to conduct conventional hand milking in an enterprise of approximately 300 cows (500 if one includes the calves). Usually, farmers who invested in expensive robotic technology strived to maintain a heard of at least 180 cows. Interestingly, several farmers have increased the number of robotic laborers on their farms since they commissioned their robots. Installing more than one robot not only generates economies of scale but also provides backup capacity to mitigate technological vulnerabilities.

In 2003, one farmer learned that there were approximately one hundred robotic dairy farms in Sweden. Today, there are over one thousand commercial robotic milk farmers in Sweden, but the total number of dairy farms has declined from approximately 10,000 to 5,200 over a period of ten years. Thus, there has been significant growth for robotic solutions in Sweden and a simultaneous drastic decrease of Swedish farmers as a whole.

Farmers have pursued automated solutions to alleviate some farm work. By seeking new ways to bolster milk volumes, local farmers are able to produce cheap milk in a more competitive manner. Although some farmers emphasize that robots are laborsaving devices, they also stress that it has become more difficult to recruit staff for two-shift milking:

> It's hard to hire people who will work 3–4 hours in the morning and then go home and then come back to do another 3–4 hours in the evening, then they'd practically have their entire day destroyed. Ideally [for the farmer], you'd start at 4 a.m. [in the morning] and milk until 6 to 7 p.m. and have off time in between. I'd say there is hardly anyone who would take part in such arrangements anymore . . . so it has become much more difficult for agricultural businesses to get hold of personnel, partly because the new types of work demand a different type of staff with technical skills rather than physical labor. In society, people would rather be working in media. In general, it's not a high status job.

Despite the increased prevalence of robotic milking and improved working conditions, farmers struggle to recruit employees because of inflexible working hours (i.e., tied up working). Uncomfortable working hours also increase the difficulty of recruiting new staff members, but the low job status also contributes. Uncomfortable working hours cannot easily be solved by holding fast to older methods of work. As a farmer noted, "If you don't have a robot then you'll need more personnel that work in fixed schedules."

Are these case study findings specific to the Swedish farming industry? Recent accounts from Australia suggest that similar institutional and socio-economic patterns emerge in developed nations and that networking is key to all the stakeholders involved. In Australia, robotic milking began later but has grown in popularity. Note the following:

> The rationale for the investment was driven by a strong commercial value proposition to enhance farm profitability and economic long-term viability of the operation. It is expected that the new robotic equipment will allow a significant increase in the number of cows milked per farm staff compared to the industry average. In addition, the new robotic rotary will reduce the need of costly after hour tasks. Labour cost is the second largest cost of producing milk in Australia. . . . It is widely recognised that technology has a vast role to play in helping Australia's farmers reduce the time spent on repetitive tasks, increasing the attraction and retention of employed labour in the industry and to provide and act on data to increase farm productivity to sustainable levels.
>
> (Dairy Research Foundation, 2013)

Unlike Sweden, Australia experiences extreme summer heat, which presents unique challenges for farmers, but many similarities are evident. The report mentions the robotic system described here, which is considered cutting-edge.

TEAMING WITH ROBOTIC TECHNOLOGY

The farmers noted that robots perform a person's job. In the milk production process, robots are paradoxically viewed as both machines and surrogate co-workers. The latter characterization suggests that the robot replaces traditional human labor in the milking process. This technology is an artificial surrogate worker in that they perform the heavy labor of milking and the same tasks as human workers. In fact, some of the farmers maintain that the robot performs equally well, if not better. The robotic system is equipped with multiple abilities and completes several tasks rapidly and simultaneously, from teat preparation to automatically washing the area around the cows (e.g., floor cleaning). Once the teats have been washed, the robotic arm ensures that the milk cups are appropriately attached. Towards the end of milking, the robot scatters a hygienic liquid to maintain high hygiene standards. The system is not only equipped with robotic arms but also uses an advanced supervision system (i.e., provides a pair of eyes) and vision capability that guides the robotic arm movements during teat acquisition (i.e., if the cow moves her body, the robotic arm automatically follows and smoothly adjusts). Many farmers consider the robot an artificial worker because the robotic arm moves comparably to a human arm. Farmers stress that although robots save labor and allow for flexible schedules, the idea that robots reduce the need for farmer-animal interactions is overstated. The welfare of the cows remains the top priority. However, working conditions have improved and work schedules have changed considerably:

> In the beginning, we had 60–70 tied cows and we then had to wake up earlier in the morning, one started working earlier and it also clearly took more working time per cow. Personally, I had no ailments of milking a tied up [non-robotic] milking system, but you'd never know for sure how you'd feel today after working like that [day in and day out]. The biggest gain is probably here.

This farmer notes that after the robot, he has fewer routine shifts and a more normal working schedule while the robots and staff perform routine work. Cows may choose to allow the robot to milk them at night. In other words, the robotic system permits self-milking by dairy cows.

The modern robotic milking facility is operational all day. One farmer explained, "The work goes on 24 hours a day . . . the whole system is up and running all hours of the day and the robots work all the time and the cows are milked during the night as well." The narratives that circulate among professionals indicate the robots act in both disturbing and appreciative ways, which highlights another contradiction. Automatic messaging functionality implies that the robotic system automatically sets off alarms regardless of the hour and transmits this information to the farmer via telephone. On the one hand, farmers not always appreciate this automatic functionality because it tends to deliver more messages than needed and farmers do not necessarily want to be troubled late at night by false alarms or trivial errors that can be addressed later. On the other hand, farmers truly appreciate the robot's watchfulness and messaging functionality when the entire production process halts because of technical errors, unwanted cow behavior, etc. For example, if the cow blocks the entrance to the robot, she also prevents other cows from being milked, which affects the well-being of the cows as well as milk output. As one farmer explained, "First one becomes bothered with all the alarms but then one appreciates the job it [the robot] actually carries out."

These alarms are both detested and cherished depending on the situation in which they appear (e.g., whether the farmer is at a remote location) as well as the type of dysfunction the robot identifies (e.g., a disruption of the entire production process). Understanding this duality is to see both negative and positive frictions throughout the workday that ultimately also "prevent some unexpected harmful or difficult situations." As one farmer explained, "All reductions in milking performance are unpleasant, if the robots are at a standstill too long, then less milk comes out in the next milking and it's not good for their udder health, it strains the animals and they risk incidents of getting udder infections in dairy cows if they remain unmilked." This serious problem may negatively affect future milk production.

INNOVATING TO ENDURE IN THE 21ST-CENTURY FARMING INDUSTRY

Some small, family-operated dairy businesses have challenged conventional thinking and sought innovative farm improvements to thrive despite low (and unpredictable) milk prices. As one farmer noted, milk prices were sometimes as unpredictable as the weather during the harvesting season. Robotics represents a radical technological innovation that provides some stability to the milking enterprise. Standardization and automation provides economic benefits to farming businesses engaged in milk production. There are also social and professional gains produced by the new human-robot organization. One farmer even noted that he and his family were able to vacation for a whole week. This particular farmer was among the first in Scandinavia to pursue multiple robotic laborers and have lengthy experience using high-tech tools in his local business. Although at least one person must be present at all times, the farm is managed with fewer employees. When the farmer was asked if he is able to leave for the day he responds, "For sure, you can get away for a day, and should an alarm go off then one solves the problem." The farmer can solve the problem when offsite because the robotics systems provides remote access to the management system from the office or home. Such remote access functionalities transcend prior limitations, and farmers are less bound to a physical location. Now, one person can manage the cows for the day. Moreover, this monitoring is compatible with smartphones and devices, a feature that this farmer seems to appreciate because he and his staff have gained additional flexibility and choices in their daily working routines. Farmers may even monitor live footage from the stall where the young and fragile calves are housed, which is a key part of managing this farm. The farmer now has two access options: camera footage or computer software. As one farmer explained as follows:

> You just login [remotely] from home using your own computer; that works amazingly well. No matter where I am, I can always access the robots and take charge of them, but it also depends on the type of alarm. If a cable has been detached, then the [remote] computer access won't fix the problem, but other types of alarms may be examined and resolved that way. It may be that one of the cows will get stuck in the booth, then I'll just release her as I assume power and control over the robot's functions. Speaking of technology, my son has just recently launched a new enterprise that works on supervision [at a distance]. See here [the interviewee picks up a smartphone from his pocket and

displays a live video stream]. I am able to observe exactly what happens [inside the building], it's transmitting live footage from the stalls, which provides extra assurance.

Previously, this farmer had to regularly travel back and forth from his home (approximately one kilometer away from the farm) to ensure that everything was in order at the yard, but now he can monitor the yard remotely from home or elsewhere. Although the farm is operated as a local business that employs several automated robots in its milk production facility, this farmer's son is drawing on this experience with robotics and farming to inspire innovations (i.e., a mobile application) developed by a new and growing technological business. By collaborating with specialists that provide focused expertise in application development for mobile devices, the firm connected to a new network that facilitates innovation and allows the design of tools that monitor and track events on the farm efficiently and systematically. This young entrepreneur has already reached out to a few local farms and provided workshops on utilizing the remote monitoring system. Indeed, because farmers feel like they must verify that gates are closed and that machines are functioning, there appears to be demand for this type of remote assistance. Performing all monitoring on-site would be considerably more time-intensive, but the mobile app saves farmers time and effort, which can be spent on other innovative work.

As we will see, robotic systems save time and allow farmers to spend more time analyzing data and optimizing by tweaking systems to increase milk volumes. In 2014, a major robotics producers launched a mobile app for its Lely Astronaut system® called "System" that farmers can download from the Internet. System provides monitoring and surveillance functionalities that alerts farmers when it is time to service or replace brushes and other essential parts to keep the system running (and to avoid unnecessary disruptions). This application is another example of technological and software-based innovations that complement robotic systems to provide functionalities that create different working environments and new forms of control. When a farmer wants to monitor an individual cow, he does not need to look up her information; the robot is programmed to close the gates when the cow enters a pen. This feature can save the farmer an hour or two each working day. As the farmer explains, "If the cow enters the stall it will call and deliver a voice message: 'Cow No. 146 is here.' If I'm going to treat the cow or I am just to look at the cow . . . the robot calls and tells me when the cow is available. It will not start milking the cow and I have ten minutes to come up here or the robot releases the cow." This farmer seems eager to use this feature to separate out cows for veterinary care, etc.

Farmers may assume manual control over the system. However, control is multifaceted and extends to data and information management, which, in turn, is heavily dependent on advanced sensory systems. These sensors generate considerable data, which the farmer can interpret and analyze. One farmer states, "We see everything. We see that they [the cows] don't eat properly, if they don't milk, that milk quality is bad, or if they've got mastitis [an inflammation]. One can even see if cows have a fever. You can monitor almost anything. You see everything . . . [the ability] to be able to see if something is wrong well in advance [is vital], otherwise it'd take quite some time before you'd noticed it yourself, but the robot senses it." Farmers report that the cows' teat conditions have generally improved and mastitis has decreased to a minimal number of cases. These data present an opportunity for farmers to save time (and money). Key figures to farm management are automatically calculated, which allows farmers to allocate more time to other important tasks.

Data analysis for which the farmers have no formal education signifies their enthusiasm and eagerness to engage professional challenges and identify new, sustainable ways forward to improve their odds of success in the unknown future of the dairy business. Some farmers have taken the unusual step of employing several robotic systems side-by-side to not only bolster production volumes but also manage frictions and hedge against sudden malfunctions. Social networking allows farmers to pursue new knowledge, partnerships to develop skills, and promising innovative solutions so that they can continue to update their farms in the robotic age.

EXPANDING NETWORKING RELATIONS TO PROSPER IN ROBOTIC MILKING

One farmer produces and delivers approximately 1,200,000 liters of milk each year. This farmer observed that documenting this output is "a must and without the [management of] data, it would be impossible to keep track of it all." Some data are also shared with the robotic milking community. Networking and data sharing, however, are not unproblematic. Occasionally, destabilizing regulatory tension and unexpected technical issues unfold while submitting data to officials and other stakeholders, such as veterinarians. In Sweden, farmers are required to upload data to a national livestock database. One farmer noted that much is at stake should the process fail: "It would be complete chaos in all of the National Board of Agriculture's computers, so I must get it right." In addition to the pressure to provide correct data, networking involves establishing social relationships with key members of the community, such as environmental and health officers in the local districts. These officials exert power and influence because they decide whether to pursue an issue. Such networking is sometimes straining for farmers and occasionally involves tense negotiations and conversations; however, maintaining cordial and productive relationships with external stakeholders is essential to ensure that farmers receive all the necessary permissions to operate their businesses. Farmers also engage with provincial governments to obtain permits for farm robots. Some farmers expressed frustration about the time-consuming administrative work. One farmer explained that even for the robots acquired, "you had to apply for a so-called 'pre-investigation decision' . . . we are such bureaucrats in Sweden. It's unbelievable. You must notify the provincial government about even the slightest little thing you do." This suggests that the adoption of robots entails new time-consuming activities. Note that decentralized partnerships and centralized bureaucratic regulations are not mutually exclusive (see, e.g., Wasen and Lodaya, 2012, who explore the term centralized decentralization). Even powerful dairy firms, perhaps the most influential bodies in the entire industry, must approve the installation and utilization of robots. This regulatory system maintains control and influence over the milk quality and safety regime, which defines abnormal milk, etc.

In the Swedish context, all the interviewed farmers are cognizant of events in the general dairy industry as well as in their specialized domain(s). Professionals increasingly network to share the knowledge and learn from experts and other members of the robotic milking community. Perhaps because of the less hierarchical culture of Scandinavia, various stakeholders gather and communicate informally, which allows them to establish collaborative networks. Networking suggests engagement beyond traditional professional boundaries to remain current and exchange knowledge and lessons about robotic milking systems.

Maintaining and operating such a complex system requires that farmers challenge themselves and seek ways to accelerate their learning. Following development while simultaneously operating a business is difficult and the professional working domain is rapidly changing. Therefore, farmers engage in networking to learn and draw on external expertise to guarantee the continued feasibility of their businesses. Interestingly, some farmers refer to scientific reports that they have heard about or read, such as scientific studies published by the Institute of Agricultural Engineering or the Swedish University of Agricultural Sciences (SLU) as well as technical reports published by professional associations and robotics producers. The Swedish company DeLaval, for example, is an R&D market leader in robotic milking systems, and there is a long tradition and commitment in the Swedish dairy industry to drive innovation in the field of automated milking and livestock robotics. The case study findings suggest that robotic milking not only involves novel work arrangements in farming but also engages knowledge networks that are embedded in wider inter-organizational support structures around local farmers and their complex work systems. The professional farmers indicate that they sometimes feel forced to participate in networking that is demanding and time-consuming, which was earned through timesaving technology. This finding contradicts the discourse of networking and points to a more directed process that is not friction-free.

SUMMARY

Robotics has clearly changed the work of twenty-first century farmers. Taking advantage of all the capabilities of robotic milking is challenging and complex. In a new organizational environment, changes are necessary, but, as we have seen, not all situations can be easily changed. New technological capabilities have presented farmers with strategic choices. By pursuing reconfigurations and organizational arrangements, professionals adjust the settings of their complex milk production systems to their economic favor as well as to the cows' welfare. Surprisingly, robots are seen as surrogate (artificial) co-workers as well as modern equipment. The latter suggest that robots are firmly linked with other forms of technology (e.g., computers, mobile devices, etc.). The former suggest that robots that have taken over the daily duties of modern dairy farming. However, socio-bio-robotic systems still need human intervention (and judgment) to ensure that all work flows smoothly and efficiently. Robots liberate farmers and staff to shift their focus from tough, dirty and repetitive physical work to computer-work, such as data analytics and other innovative tasks. Hence, the workplace environment has changed drastically in the wake of institutional and organizational adjustments along with new social interactions with robotic technology.

In light of recent institutional transformations, a new level of professional autonomy has been gained in farming. An implicit assumption is that such autonomy is beneficial for both farmers and animals. In the abandonment of the "twice-a-day" milking routine, cows are more autonomous as they freely walk into the robot to be milked automatically whenever they so wish (or rather as long as the programming of the robot allows them to do so). This voluntary milking concept works smoothly for the cows and they generally seem to appreciate the new rearrangement because it places less stress on them. All the interviewed farmers and staff also cherish autonomy and flexibility, which is largely possible because they have been relieved of heavy and difficult physical farming work. This case study has discussed how the farmer's job has radically changed from primarily physical and routine tasks on the farm to data analytics and social networking. Robots employ advanced sensors to generate a massive amount of information that can be input into innovative work and integrate herd management with farm management. Environmental thinking increasingly drives exciting new conceptual and material innovations to facilitate clean and sustainable solutions. Robotization in agriculture thus produces new types of work that rely on interpretative and diagnostic skills to understand complex arrays of data.

Moreover, due to the inherent system complexity of robotic milking, many farmers chose to engage in networking communities and partnership with experts in areas such as computer science, mechanical engineering, and biological sciences. Some farmers even pursue innovation and develop new solutions to create economic value. By gaining access to expertise, farmers also obtain useful and complementary inputs, which allow them to resolve emergencies promptly, service machinery more efficiently and adopt methods to better analyze the vast amount of complex data that the robotic sensors generate. This shift in work arrangements from two milking sessions to continuous milking is possible because of labor- and time-saving robotic technology (and support staff) that performs the remaining routine tasks and allows farmers to spend time on improvements to drive their milk businesses and to focus on cow well-being. Indeed, happy and health cows produce more milk.

However, several farmers note that although they now have access to more data than they have ever had, and even when robotic technology is enhancing in multiple and unexpected ways, they do not always manage to spend enough time on data analytics to maximize functionality. Some professionals only use a fraction of the data generated to improve system efficiency. This contradictory finding suggests that although robots alleviate work, they also create new duties and restrictions (e.g., new skill requirements). Although robots work efficiently and autonomously, the entire farmer-robot-cow system remains dependent on human labor and professional knowledge. Perhaps the greatest benefits of robotics are realized when laborsaving technology reconfigures work so that farmers can spend more time on data analytics to optimize milk production, i.e., to increase the milk yield per cow without compromising the welfare of cows. The farmers generally seem satisfied with robotic systems and many have expanded their facilities and have added artificial robotic laborers as their businesses grow to remain competitive and attract employment. Although the number of staff members employed in the agricultural industry has steadily decreased since the industrial revolution, robotics in farming suggests that new organizational arrangements may offer more attractive workplace environments and more stimulating work for future farmers and employees.

8   The Paradoxes of Friction Management

In this chapter, we re-examine some of the key issues addressed in earlier sections in light of the preceding presentations of robotic applications in five different sectors, particularly with regard to the changing nature of work and professional experiences of robotics technology. The author's analysis highlights that elements of social and cultural-cognitive friction are characteristic of innovation processes in this new landscape. Frictions are not merely limited to interactions with robotic laborers or "work partners"; power asymmetries, differences in professional interests and levels of network competence are also crucial sources of tension and conflict. This chapter develops a novel angle that seeks to clarify and specify the meaning of the earlier conceptualizations on "network friction" in Chapter 3. The author pleas for a theory of "friction management" and discusses how it might be applied in practice.

Because our focus within the book's theoretical discussion has been largely upon explicit social friction activities or cultural dimensions, the next two main sections will elaborate on and discuss the role of innovation friction culture, beginning with critically assessing "friction-free" perspectives in network theory, that is, perspectives that involve the art of using any form of organizational "lubricant" to reduce social frictions and make things run more smoothly and efficiently. This section is followed by a presentation of a theory of "friction management," which is much more strongly informed by critical management approaches. Thus, this chapter aims to contextualize, analyze and discuss the empirical case study findings by bringing to the fore the multiple accounts and narratives on the uses of robotics technology in different industries and sectors. It is argued that complex innovation processes are intrinsically embedded in network practices and partnerships and that technological change is surrounded by paradoxes, management myths and contradictions.

THE MYTH OF FRICTION-FREE NETWORKS

This chapter links micro issues with macro perspectives in the field of innovation management and suggests that frictions in local workplaces (e.g., COP arrangements) relate to broader economic and political trends in culture and society and vice versa. In linking professional dynamics and frictions to economic and socio-political outcomes, for example, the analysis highlights the important reciprocity between the micro- and macro-levels. Hackman (2003) argues that good explanations in contextualized social science research stand out in that they address patterns by which various elements at multiple levels of analysis interact, thus yielding a "robust understanding of social and organizational dynamics [that] requires attention to higher as well as lower levels of analysis" (2003: 905). The workplace level is the primary level of analysis. However, while organizational innovation is the main issue in many of these new robotic work practices, the case studies suggest that innovations extend beyond workplaces. In this chapter, the discussion alternates between three parallel yet interrelated levels of explanation: the meta-theoretical, socio-cultural and technological levels. The reciprocity among these levels can inform our analysis and yield fresh and unexpected conceptualizations.

For example, in order to map out the characteristics of robot work cultures, one needs to understand technological attributes and socio-cultural elements as well as, for example, collectively held beliefs that (re)surface in historical discourses. This relates back to the earlier meta-theoretical discussion and critique of the one-sided perception of social interactions in disembodied COP cultures, which neither accounts for tensions in partnerships nor interactions with technology. When robotic "work partners" and "co-workers" are introduced into work practices and behave in new partnerships—in contexts that traditional approaches refer to as communities of practice—their organizational processes and work content radically change. Tensions and frictions are not merely limited to robotic partners, however; differences in human expertise and professional knowledge as well as asymmetrical ranks of competence and power are also a source of tension and conflict that can be both positive and detrimental to partnerships and innovation processes. Thus, more generally, the book also addresses social and occupational concerns in such development, which is a very fluid phase of change wherein employees are anxious about and fear technological replacement. The author argues in this book that we need to delve more into the positive and negative tensions in robot work cultures in future studies, e.g., by addressing the social worries and fears among professionals regarding technological replacement. The book examines varying responses by members of professional associations, commonly referred to as "communities of practice," and various change dynamics, and their attempts to promote (or resist) increased reliance on robotic laborers in workplaces.

Machinery that was originally developed to accelerate the pace of work and control the work of employees may regularly become a tool of management power and control. While robots as "enabling technologies" are an integral part of novel organizational arrangements, professionals simultaneously modify robots to suit their individual work abilities and manipulate the robotic workforce to reclaim control and stay in command of the pace of innovation work. Workplace innovations involve the manner in which these actors approach adjusting and optimizing robotic technology to fulfill organizational goals and objectives as well as the manner in which they engage in political processes of managing, negotiating and maneuvering developments to fit their conflicting and diverging interests.

In Chapters 2 and 3, the intention was to determine the organizational circumstances and environmental conditions under which processes of innovation may best develop and flourish and possibly even be propelled and accelerated. For this purpose, we reviewed various theories on formal innovation networks and partnerships as well as informal networking in COP theory. We then contrasted a modified socio-political processual approach that acknowledges tensions and elements of cultural and epistemic multiplicity. What is contrasted in the theoretical approaches to dynamic networking interactions is the respective principal assumptions and key dimensions they each draw attention to regarding social tensions, power and processes of negotiation (or lack thereof). This conceptual comparison also notes what dimensions remain outside their line of vision (particularly with regard to mainstream network theory and prescriptive COP theory). It is argued that the socio-political processual approach, a tradition situated within critical management studies, as well as related work in critical sociology, encompasses the macro- and meso-level aspects in contrast to the original COP theory, which focuses on the individual practitioners and micro-level accounts.

In COP theory as well as other network theories, mainstream models adopt a harmony and unity perspective. From this perspective, innovation management, the author suggests, involves the art of using any form of "lubricant" to reduce negative frictions and make things run more smoothly and efficiently. Indeed, the very idea of friction-free interaction and innovation is found in trendy management formulas and casts an aura of power and legitimacy around business practices. In this idiom, the mainstream COP and network theory becomes an irresistible "lubricant theory," and it re-creates the notion of frictionless transactions in popularized management prescriptions (for treatments on the issue of management fashion, see, e.g., Abrahamson, 1996; Alvesson, 2012; Huczynski, 2012). Such harmonious and seductive notions should not be approved uncritically and taken at "par value." However, in a globally interconnected society and within multicultural workplaces, social dissonance and multiplicity are the norm rather than homogeneity and concord. Hence, understanding the dynamics of today's work cultures requires that we shift our focus from harmony and unity to productive tensions and social and cultural-cognitive frictions.

Indeed, pertinent to our inquiry and exploration of modern organizational innovations is the issue of friction management. By the term "friction management," we mean the "directing" of the multi-paradoxical forces of socio-cultural and cognitive characters that appear and flow in radical innovation, and the change processes that require coordination and adaptation. The goal is to combine and mobilize organizational resources to strategically increase innovation capacity, thus promoting the dynamic renewal of creative and counter-destructive friction.

FRICTION—THE MISSING DIMENSION IN INNOVATION MANAGEMENT

In the preceding discussions of change and innovation, we noted the various ways in which principal contradictions emerge between opposing elements, such as between symmetrical and asymmetrical tensions or between destabilizing and stabilizing or harmonizing and disharmonizing forces. In part, such tensions become visible when forces of creativity and discord clash with the stabilizing forces of conformity and challenge "business-as-usual" mentalities (cf. the "not-invented-here" syndrome; Leonard-Barton, 1998). Change management seeks to instigate transformation through strategic choices, social influence and participation but may often stand in conflict with pre-existing organizational routines and habitual actions that merely reproduce (and occasionally optimize) the exploitation of well-known production methods and old knowledge and knowing. This particular tension has been addressed in earlier work, such as in the seminal work of March (1991), who states that firms tend to enclose themselves to suboptimal routines and practices in their pursuit of exploitation, which simultaneously downplays exploration. Exploration occurs when enterprises break away from well-known, efficient and reliable paths to investigate unknown opportunities, such as innovative openings. While the distinction between exploration and exploitation and the division between continuity and change are classical themes in sociological theorizing and management thinking, the tension that we explore here is fundamentally captured in the conflicting forces between challenging the status quo and learning from mistakes (organizational innovation) versus exploiting well-known patterns and eliminating unusual errors (organizational manipulation).

The prior chapters have elaborated on the general notion of friction to explain contradictory tensions and variability in complex organizational events occurring in innovation partnerships and networks or in the micro-process of making sense of large amounts of ambiguous data to innovatively tweak work systems. For friction management, the intricate challenge lies perhaps in appreciating (and not discarding) contradiction and perplexing multi-paradoxical forces. The examples provided above suggest that elements of both sides of exploration and exploitation, or continuity and change, may embrace equally desirable states. The case illustrations in various ways suggest that the challenge for leadership and management is to pursue unfamiliar ways and unknown paths (innovation) whilst striving to minimize the negative effects on existing systems. Nevertheless, one of the ultimate goals of robotics is to exploit familiar ways to increase production volumes and to reduce production time (i.e., strive to achieve superior time efficiency). In other words, the management task or challenge is to integrate competing and often contradictory elements in new, yet sustainable and competitive arrangements, hence finding new ways of facilitating change that can mobilize transformation while also partly improving and retaining desirable qualities and practices as well as improving safety and reliability. No firm is an island, and we observed that practitioners rely heavily on external support structures and knowledge infrastructures.

Friction management clearly extends beyond mechanical and hierarchical workplace environments to include (in)formal networking and partnerships. Network junctures and multi-paradoxical forces typically evolve in several places or contexts simultaneously (and typically include multiple known and unknown actors, groups and alliances). Inter-organizational gaps may emerge between networking partners, and these gaps more generally reflect employee disinclination and distrust of managerial (and political) intervention. Therefore, engaging in seemingly borderless network collaborations can be rather problematic or at least challenging. Figuratively, social frictions may ensue in two (or more) fronts simultaneously. Typically, friction encounters in network contexts extend to complex multiple relationships between actors and groups in different settings.

Innovation partnerships in network collaborations are indeed multifarious and multidimensional arrangements that pursue groundbreaking developments and often entail competing interests, contradictory expectations and various "tensions" (see, e.g., Mol, 2000; Chapter 3) The powerful social frictions that emerge in partnerships may paradoxically both hinder and encourage accelerated innovation. The "inside" and "outside" of network arrangements are relevant, and power and influence may depend on the strategic choices of either including or excluding various partners in joint collaborations and innovation projects. As we have observed, socio-cultural frictions constantly and unexpectedly evolve and may take many different forms and expressions, depending on unique situational and historical circumstances. Indeed, the same outcome of friction processes may be experienced as beneficial among one group of actors but simultaneously viewed as negative and destructive among other actors (see Chapter 3, where it is demonstrated that social friction represents both a destructive and creative force). Hence, the social meanings surrounding friction are often inherently contested and highly ambiguous.

The conventional understanding of friction is that it results from physical interactions and/or the properties of materials. The very mechanism (powers) of friction may be part of an "engineered" process that is subject to influence, regulation and manipulation. In fact, most of us use the powers of friction daily without even realizing it. This use is often taken for granted—an "absent present." Without reflecting on this use of friction, we regularly rely on the "forces of friction" when we ride our bicycle (or car) to navigate through a crossing or drive down a hill, and friction also becomes helpful when we need to use the breaks to slow down. Certainly, we essentially take it for granted that physical friction is in our realm of control; if, however, we realized that it is not in our control, then it would most likely be too late to address this problem in any case. Thus, we are accustomed to the idea that the powers of friction work for us—at least most of the time, when we need them—or else we would be in serious trouble.

However, this preconception of being "in control" is deceiving us with regard to social frictions. In organizational settings, when pursuing creative work (e.g., complex innovative network partnerships), friction unfolds beyond the realm of command; hence, managers are rarely "in total control." Frictions emerge as a result of multidimensional, interrelated movements and interactions that evolve unpredictably in complex relationships that combine to include social, technological, political, cultural and organizational elements. Furthermore, friction is a general phenomenon that affects most, if not all, systems (e.g., social, political, biological, technological, bio-technological) that involve processes of transformation—in the sense that all these systems entail various forces and movements (as well as counter-movements). In most cases, network friction appears to be a spontaneously evolving mechanism within an environment or organizational setting that is in a state of constant "flux." While appreciating that social and organizational friction is an emergent phenomenon that cannot be entirely predicted, prearranged and "managed" to the same extent that physical friction can, this recognition does not prevent social actors (e.g., managers) from attempting to use their partial power bases to influence these frictions in some ways. Hence, at least to a limited degree, the principle of network friction can be theorized as human agency or as a form of collective action that seeks to influence movements in certain directions. By doing so, interventions may partially contribute to transforming existing organizational arrangements. It follows that a formal network's or informal community's *raison d'être* (reason for existence) is its ability to facilitate united innovativeness, primarily by mobilizing actors within the network itself and by engaging different nodes (e.g., local groups) where and when appropriate.

However, it is equally important to note that such social actions and interventions differ from the traditional conception of "command and conquer" in organizations. Such a top-down control mentality likely does not mitigate the pressure on creative activities and work settings involving change and innovation. As creativity and discovery can rarely, if ever, be commanded, innovations similarly cannot be forced to arise on command. Wasen and Lodaya, for example, explain as follows:

> Top-down command-and-control systems with tight specifications and rigid regulation tend to turn people into marionettes—expected to dance as the 'puppeteer' pulls the 'string.' However, in reality, this rarely happens, and even as much as it does, it is a highly inefficient utilization

of the real potential of human beings—one does not expect marionettes to be highly enterprising, innovative or productive. . . . While some degree of regulation is necessary and beneficial to any organization, overloading it with regulation can restrain the possibility of innovation and creativity. When practitioners are unable to follow managerial and political decisions because of lack of resources or personnel, the consequence may be a general 'disengagement' among knowledge workers.

(Wasen and Lodaya, 2012: 51–2)

One should not forget that the social frictions described in this book can considerably hinder and obstruct innovative practices. If a social system encounters excessive pressure, then tensions and resistance will most likely evolve in various forms and work against managerial attempts to spur innovation. In particular, opposition often emerges in organizational life when the status quo is being challenged by alternative routes and/or by new technological features. When change is looming, human resistance and institutional inertia often arise when something new challenges prevailing habits and ways of doing things. This possibility for failure also explains why many managerial attempts to promote organizational transformation often settle as failed "change management exercises," partly because they conflict with conventional organizational routines, established infrastructures and the politics of hierarchical arrangements (e.g., career paths and power structures). Furthermore, if critical frictions are being ignored or not handled properly, then such neglect may undermine the very organizational changes that are desired in the first place.

Related to this overall theme of interpretation is the observation that processes of innovation may paradoxically both hamper or block progress and facilitate and spur the acceleration of innovation as social (collective) actions unfold in network interactions and business partnerships. Many companies and public organizations engage in multidisciplinary networking efforts because of their need to acquire essential information and knowledge (Ebers, 1997; Ring, 1997). Simultaneously, multidisciplinary networks function as "gatekeepers" in protecting new knowledge opportunities and innovations as well as novel information from external (competing) organizations. Such enabling or resisting forces are, for example, situated in the politics of expert networking and the protection of essential information (and reluctance to share such information), and they involve professional participation and learning in communities of practice. As we noted in Chapter 2, another obvious benefit of cooperating in networks is that such settings offer the opportunity to share costs and business risks in the development of innovation. The case studies also suggest that innovative and state-of-the-art developments are very much dependent on economical parameters (see also, e.g., economic policymaking, technological assessments and regulatory statutes) and that the success of innovative work is related to the resources provided. There is not space to delve too deeply into the financial aspects here, but suffice it to say that economics matter, and without proper financial backing, it is very difficult to succeed in new technology; a lesson that also applies to innovation management in general.

An understanding of network frictions therefore offers important insights into the processes and complex challenges of "managing" innovation, suggesting that innovative opportunities typically arise when contradictions and ambiguity are embraced. Friction management provides a powerful lens for better understanding the logic of inherent tensions in innovation work and contemporary socio-technical transformation that are seemingly unfolding in robot society. Friction management will continue to play a critical role in managing radical transformation, which is increasingly situated in volatile markets and ever-changing global circumstances, and businesses are increasingly preoccupied with accelerating the pace of their pursuit of new innovations. By attaining a more informed understanding of the underlying mechanisms and various heterogeneous elements that arise in modern innovation processes and socio-robot work systems, practitioners can learn to cope with tensions and frictions. However, friction management cannot be captured in rational-linear models, because it primarily concerns how a variety of contradictions and paradoxical ambiguities are made meaningful. The successful management of change, technology, and innovation will call for an appreciation of diversity to productively cope with inconsistencies and paradoxes.

Thinking in dichotomies fails to account for cultural multiplicity and social variety in network contexts. In models of cultures in organizations, for example, the tendency to divide different groups in subcultures into "coherent wholes" reflects a more universal tendency in management science to describe things with respect to their opposites. The traditional way of thinking in dichotomies (e.g., warm vs. cold) has been criticized by Martin (1992), who argues that it leads to dangerous oversimplifications that distort social accounts and organizational events in a multiplex reality. Simplified oppositional (dualistic) thinking also appears to be a commonly held assumption of how physical friction works, i.e., the idea that two opposing poles (or surfaces) meet and rub against one another. This critique of black and white thinking, however, may lead us to suggest that viewing social friction as either a positive or negative encounter of opposite forces inevitably limits our understanding of real-life (multiplex) controversies and paradoxes. It is hoped this discussion can stimulate critical reflection among scholars and managers and can inspire the development of new perspectives to address the issue of contradictory forces and opposing logics. Although friction has been widely theorized in traditional sciences, such as physics and mechanical engineering, the topic has been largely overlooked in business, economics and management theory. Friction management has a central role in the functioning of organizations and networks and therefore deserves proper theoretical exploration and analysis.

Friction management is a key concept to consider because it may acceler-ate key advances, but it may also occasionally slow the pace of change and innovation. The previous chapters have touched on the links among social friction, cultural variance and innovation management strategies, particu-larly those chapters discussing the scholarly literature on innovation and change management. In the next section, we will discuss the role of science friction (not to be confused with "science fiction") in greater detail.

"SCIENCE FRICTION" AND THE PIONEER'S INNOVATION DILEMMA

The case studies address various network contexts in which tensions co-exist in various forms and constellations, but there does not appear to exist a single straightforward explanation as to why social arrangements differ. We have observed that networking is a politically contested terrain in educational hospitals and academic institutions and that political forces may either suppress or encourage diversity and variety. Case study findings on robotics surgery demonstrate how professionals navigate in multifaceted and politicized terrains, and one of the surgeons used the word "friction" to suggest the tensions created between different professional and organi-zational mentalities (e.g., between workplace environments in universities and teaching hospitals), and such situated activities exhibit the surgeon's/ scientist's changing role in the new political, economic and technologic landscape.

The pioneer's innovation dilemma (Chapter 4) highlights the challenges to being a pioneer and thinking outside the box. This is a case in point about the close relationship between cultural-cognitive forces (frictions) and the very fragility of the review process, not just in science but in reviews of innovation projects in general, such as assessing grant proposals and set-ting priority scores, etc. To understand the politics surrounding innovation management, it is essential to recognize that for something to be identified and accepted either as a breakthrough innovation or as a known fact, it must often fit within the professional community's paradigm. Thus, local professional communities and innovation networks are highly political and cultural arenas. These arenas are more or less tightly integrated in wider historico-cultural interrelationships in which a common form of adaptation and socialization unfolds and shapes the institutionalized habits of thinking, a powerful force that directs our reasoning in some ways but not in others.

The idea of collective understandings among practitioners in specific cul-tural and epistemic settings in which shared values, mutual reliance and social cohesion are developed and formed as part of a knowledge creation process is highlighted in various concepts, such as "local theories" (Elden 1983), "theories in use" (Argyris and Schön, 1974) and "local knowledge" (Geertz, 1983). In these perspectives, actors are regarded as creating their own theories (both individually and collectively), which in term regulate and shape their mutual encounters. For example, the concept "local theory" has been elaborated on in participative research contexts in discussing the process of establishing a novel exploratory understanding of local practices—that is, an understanding of "the way things are" in a particular local context (Elden, 1983). We interpret and make sense of events based on collectively shared beliefs that are (re)produced; as Geertz (1973: 5) explains, "Man is an animal suspended in webs of significance he himself has spun." One of the earliest accounts in the social sciences on like-minded groups of practitioners is provided by Ludwig Fleck (1896–1961), who defines a "scientific thought collective" as "a community of persons mutually exchanging ideas or maintaining intellectual interaction . . ." (1979: 39). Discussing the significance of Fleck's work, Giedymin notes as follows:

> An individual may belong to more than one thought-collective, but it is the latter that is the originator and carrier of knowledge, since knowledge is always social in its origin and character. . . . Fleck's epistemological views were the product of his participation in several thought-collectives (medical, philosophical, sociological) and hence thought-styles, a fact which according to his own theory explains, partly at least, most discoveries and innovations.
>
> (1986: 179, 181)

Scientists, similar to professionals in other occupations, form protected belief systems that heavily influence judgments among members in an epistemic community. Based on Fleck's observation, the production of scientific facts is deeply socially determined. Not only are knowledgeable experts restricted to pre-existing knowledge but administrative officials and employees at higher management levels are equally constrained by organizational cultures (Leonard-Barton, 1998).

However, we also know that disagreement is likely to emerge in any situation in which territorial borders are redrawn. Within communities of practice, various forms of power conflicts can emerge as a result of changes in and renegotiations of professional boundaries and spheres of influence and power. For example, when a clash emerges between the most skilled and highly esteemed scientific practitioners, alliances between various members may emerge to counter such professional battles. However, this development may in turn affect how work is organized and how labor is divided in scientific workplaces, thus generating political implications for professionals and organizations.

Conventional analyses of scientific communities and relationships tend to emphasize stabilizing "lock-in" mechanisms (a type of "glued-together" effect) in organizational life, but the contrasting perspective is that such factors may "trap" actors to think coherently in various ways. For example, avoiding "group think" means countering any paralyzing forces that may hamper innovative activities. In such instances, another powerful force is at play. We may entertain the idea of a counter-force that works against such "lock-in" mechanisms and that is likely to materialize in the breakdown of social relationships in formal organizations or informal communities. We shall understand such dynamic forms as "science friction," that is, powerful forces that can underpin breakthrough innovation, such as by spurring the introduction of a new ideas or a novel theoretical framework and thus threatening or challenging existing theories or relationships. This distinction is important because science friction represents a powerful force that may counteract any dominating (repressive) mode of organizing by either radically changing it or replacing it. Drawing on the understanding that networks consist of the coupling of ties that hold relationships together, science friction may be understood as a force that encourages change and development and that encourages un-coupling ("un-gluing"), a process in which powerful forces arise to challenge the status quo by partly disrupting or completely disorganizing conventional ways of doing things. From a processual-contextual perspective, science friction is an emergent phenomenon. It represents an ongoing and more or less erratic counter-force that causes the strength and firmness of usual ties (i.e., the "glue") to either weaken or dissipate. How science friction evolves over time is largely an empirical issue, and the question of whether it is commensurable with harmonious approaches is a question that the author leaves for future researchers to explore. Such questions clearly lie outside the scope of this book.

When interests conflict, tensions emerge. However, it is possible to draw a distinction between what we have referred to as "conflict of interests," tensions and social frictions. In science, for example, we observe this effect in academic controversies and polemics, arenas for intellectual battles in which a form of cognitive and linguistic friction unfolds. This friction may manifest as an intellectual confrontation and/or verbal altercation between two or more opposing perspectives or arguments. Many scientists would likely agree that such intellectual debates represent stimulating situations. "Intellectual battles" appreciate "creative abrasion" (Leonard-Barton, 1998; see also Chapter 3), and although such exchanges can be painful and/or passionate at times, they can also lead to the development of better arguments and new knowledge. Science frictions, whether positive or negative, are clearly associated with wider organizational and professional concerns. This point is important because it rejects the often implicit assumption that the creative recombination of scientific knowledge is somehow unrestrained from political and organizational forces and that human imagination and ingenuity are relatively unconstrained.

Contemporary science is situated in an institutional politico-economic environment in which secure core funding and "soft money" appear to steadily be in short supply, while short-term appointments appear to be more widely embraced in many developed and industrialized countries. While certain knowledge domains confront financial restrictions, new costly investments in exclusive, spectacular knowledge infrastructures are emerging, which means that priority setting in scientific communities becomes more politicized and contested. Moreover, recent technological developments have facilitated networking opportunities that were not previously possible, wherein networks and not organizations have become the primary operational units (Bartlett and Ghoshal, 1999; Boisot, 1998; Castells, 2000). Scientific networking is forced to emerge and span across (supra)national borders. What Ziman (1994) calls "post-academic steady state science" indicates a new organizational culture administered by politico-economic and business-minded objectives that has largely replaced the traditional ideology governed by the mere pursuit of advancing knowledge and knowing:

> The transition to 'steady state' science, makes new, more stringent, demands on every institution of the R&D system . . . individuals, research entities, academic departments and whole universities are expected to be more economically efficient, more scientifically excellent, and more socially beneficial. They are in public competition, across the nation, around the globe, to demonstrate that they can produce more and better with the same or less. . . . Much of what is said about science policy concentrates on the arrangements by which public funds are allocated downwards to various research areas and research organizations . . . [new organizational network arrangements which] force universities and other institutions to become much more entrepreneurial in spirit. . . . What may be equally significant for science and for society is an ever more radical transformation of the organizational culture of academic science, as between individual researchers, research entities, academic departments and faculties, and university central administrations.
>
> (Ziman, 1994: 138–40)

However, pressures to downsize, streamline and accelerate processes of knowledge discovery are parallel forces. Paradoxically, while external forces express a wish to accelerate scientific discovery, Ziman (1994) expresses the concern that the decreased freedom and increased external regulation of science alongside short-range thinking and decreasing funding may risk jeopardizing innovativeness. Elzinga (1985) defines the term "epistemic drift" as explaining the move from the internal criteria and reputation control used to evaluate scientific research to an emphasis on external criteria in the policy arena. Internal criteria assume a subsidiary role in regulatory policy-oriented decisions that tend to, for example, place greater emphasis on societal justification, the marketability of results, public relevance and socio-economic gains. All of these developments suggest that academic "thought collectives" (Fleck, 1979) are greatly affected by changes in society. Both business enterprises and science enterprises increasingly become the subjects of intensified forces of rationalization, standardization and competition over resources. The advent of new business models thus appear to increasingly influence scientific work and academic institutions and such reforms are likely to increase both positive and negative "science friction" (for more on new public management in science, see Elzinga, 2010, 2012).

There is a consensus in recent research that the business landscape is rapidly being redrawn. Clearly, changes in culture and society generate changes in the epistemology and practice of sciences; for example, researchers pursue new collaborative research in network arrangements. Such support communities or knowledge networks typically span different cultures and nations, including scientific domains and professions (e.g., cross-, trans- and multi-disciplinary projects) that may not only boost scientists' job satisfaction (certainly, it is stimulating to collaborate with international groups of researchers) but also accelerate their learning. R&D teams in the elderly care robotics domain clearly draw on one another's complementary disciplinary backgrounds to create innovation, and surgeons interact with technicians in multidisciplinary scientific networks.

Thus, how does cultural and social diversity translate into innovativeness in professional communities? Stark (2009: 179) notes, "Organizational diversity is most likely to yield its fullest evolutionary potential when different organizational principles coexist in an active rivalry within the firm." Amin and Roberts (2008: 361) note that in pluralistic professional communities, there is typically room for creative experimentation and discharge of resourceful energies, but such collaborations typically also involve "experts with substantial egos, high expectations, frequent turnover, rudimentary rules and procedures, tight deadlines, and considerable ambiguity and uncertainty." The authors further observe that "creativity in such collaborations thrives on the juxtaposition of variety. Novelty comes from fusing elements not connected before, drawing on heteronymous interactions and a degree of willingness to venture into uncharted territory . . . how variety and ambiguity are reconciled has a central bearing on whether the fruits of creative engagement can be harnessed in epistemic communities" (ibid.).

Today's R&D environment is increasingly dynamic and complex in that collaboration beyond traditional disciplinary boundaries is often required to address issues such as problem solving, innovation, and the development and exploitation of products and services in joint network settings that extend beyond conventional borders and contexts. In the European context, the EU has attended to the need to pursue a major cultural change in the sciences by encouraging scholars to access new innovative network partnerships, in which one of the future challenges is to extend beyond traditional domains of research and education and connect with partners in wider public services and address their various needs and demands. By engaging in such network partnerships, scientists may become directly involved in innovation work both locally and together with actors in the public sectors the jointly formulate and envision alternative futures that promote social justice and serve the common good. Hence, in its policy formulation, the EU presents the normative idea of embracing "service cultures" to acknowledge differentiated needs among different user groups:

> The current generation networks must evolve into service-enabled infrastructures that provide a platform for innovation by users. . . . The networks can be key drivers of public sector change, enabling service delivery and partnership. By aggregating smart users, the European networks can help drive innovation in public sector service provision, assist in reducing the costs of public service and improving the user satisfaction.
>
> (EU, 2011: 12–13)

By engaging in innovation partnerships, inter-organizational networks and informal communities of practice encounter the opportunity to involve knowledge workers in remote institutional locations and to use their expertise and input to find new innovative solutions. The book also addresses new issues and argues that these transformations in the landscape are interrelated to the broader global issue and practice of workplace innovation that emerges in different networks and partnership gatherings. Recognizing that no single firm or organization is an island, the theoretical discussion draws attention to the significance of creative tensions and multiplicity in network arrangements and professional partnerships that support the formation of organizational innovations.

The general theme that emerged in the preceding chapters emphasized that cultural multiplicity and professional variety may be necessary to stimulate and accelerate innovation because it implies frictions and creative tensions. An illustrative example is provided by Lester and Piore (2004: 54), who discuss the role of conceptual vagueness in early developments of cell phone technology, an innovation that largely resulted from a conversation between members of the radio and telephone industries based on two rather different professional communities: "Ambiguity is the critical resource that makes the conversation worth having, not the exchange of chunks of agreed-upon information. The cell phone emerged in the space created by the ambiguity about whether the product was a radio or a telephone; by playing with that ambiguity, the device became something that was different from either of them. . . . Novelty and originality lie in the space of ambiguity." However, as noted by Lester and Piore (2004), although there has been a steady drive for arrangements and marketplaces in which novelty and creativity can flourish, there is a key lesson to be learned with respect to innovation:

> On the central question of innovation, we argue that the lessons learned up to this point are, if not outright wrong, then seriously deficient. Those lessons emphasize the effectiveness of market forces in inducing innovation while essentially ignoring the interpretive processes that are the wellspring of creativity in the economy. The dominant approach

to innovation seeks to strengthen and extend the domain of market competition. But the interpretative perspective points in the opposite direction, toward the creation of sheltered spaces that can sustain public conversation among a diversity of economic actors who would be unable to interact in this way on their own. Unless a better balance is established in both management strategies and policy priorities, we face a real danger that the nation's innovative performance, so vital for its prosperity in the long run, will [decline].

(Lester and Piore, 2004: 170–1)

As this book demonstrates, various practices bring together "associative interpretations" (Targama and Wasen, 2012) in collective sensemaking events, which is crucial in organizational change because such events typically generate new ideas (i.e., via brainstorming) that need to be addressed (critically assessed) through processes of positive friction. Interpretations are key to innovation (Lester and Piore, 2004), and they allow actors to pursue radical and incremental novelties by seeing new additions or angles in their work that allow them to exploit new opportunities, recombinations and manipulations (for a detailed analysis on visual practices in science-based innovations and cultures of interpretation, see Styhre, 2010; Wasen and Brierley, 2013).

RECOMBINATION AND MANIPULATION FOR WORKPLACE INNOVATION

Because a rich variety of professional perspectives and interests exist within an epistemic community or a community of professionals and experts, hidden opportunities (and threats) can be detected and explored at an early stage. Although all of the interviewed respondents in the science, health care and elderly care sectors (see Chapters 4 and 5) worked in academic groups at universities, they represented very different subfields and distinct professional cultures within the broader field of robotics, ranging from academic disciplines such as engineering and mechatronics ("hard robotics") to computer science and health informatics ("soft robotics"). Behind the most recent technological advances and developments of powerful robotic laborers, we find an armada of various professional groups and networks: programmers, system developers, mechanical engineers, technicians, accountants, entrepreneurs, administrators, policy makers, and business managers, among others.

One of the more interesting concepts is "lead-user innovation," and research into this stream analyzes how idea generation in the lead users' processes represents a significant source of innovation to shaping relevant concepts, not the least because these actors (i.e., lead users) tend to experience needs for a given solution earlier than the conventional share of the population in the targeted domain for products or services (Urban and von Hippel, 1988; von Hippel, 1986). As we can see from the case illustrations in Chapters 4 to 7, many groundbreaking organizational changes require workplace innovations. Focus is placed on innovative activities that developed standardized functionality, software recombination and other forms of value generation activities. Thus, professionals from many workplaces that use robots were preoccupied with various workplace innovations (e.g., experimentation and creative work), which also typically involved technological changes in the workplace environment (on the role of user-driven innovation in the creation of new products and services in the cultural and creative industries, see Hawkins and Vickery, 2008).

It does not appear that we have become slaves under robot taskmasters; rather, the contrary is true, and we have been freed from heavy, repetitive and dangerous jobs. Barrett (1977: 222), however, notes that there are dangers looming in the wake of technological change, arguing that we tend to confuse freedom with our "will to power and our frenzied manipulation of objects." Indeed, the manipulation of objects (both physical and digital) seems to be moving workplace innovation forward, and such creative work as enabling software tweaking have become the central elements of present working cultures. This illustrates how technological objects are sophisticatedly calculated (in this case, by the robot's programmers) and how manipulated outcomes are skillfully embedded and seemingly integrated within the robot's infrastructure such that it appears to give robots a potent capacity for "agency" and the power of initiative.

While robots often bring about dramatic efficiency gains and quality improvements, this book demonstrates that robotics technology today is neither "innovative" nor "creative." Robots at present are not "innovators" in the sense we attribute to human activity. Innovation (as well as efficient robotic processes) is heavily dependent on human involvement and their calculative reconfigurations (e.g., tweaking of robotic software). It would not be controversial to state that in order for an advanced robot to run smoothly and reliably, it requires preventive repairs and proactive care. However, the case studies presented in this book suggest that robotics technology and its various sub-processes are so complex, multifaceted and complicated that they bring about unintended effects, not the least because robots are parts of more complex systems (both social and technological). While this book demonstrates how robotic innovations represent crucial support systems (e.g., by alleviating or "liberating" organizational members from difficult and repetitive work or taking over routine labor-intensive and time-consuming tasks), workplace innovations have no definitive "end-point" and are usually modified and adjusted on a continuous basis.

Modern high-tech workplaces in institutional life are confronted with conflicting organizational logics, and there exist plenty of paradoxes and contradictory expectations. The management of change and innovation has taught us that, occasionally, institutional practices and logics radically transform and that such transformation may challenge assumptions, power relations and inequalities that are often taken for granted. An organizational and economical outcome of radical transformations may constitute what was previously regarded as two contradictory factors in the division of labor but that, because of certain developments, suddenly ceases to be viewed as conflicting or opposing forces. This chapter shows that such a reassessment must occur in innovative recombinations in which novel technological arrangements emerge and extend beyond conventional understandings and accepted practices. Organizations and their members are also inclined to pursue acts of manipulation and calculation to seek out the best possible economic worth and to obtain the best possible results within the given limits of current socio-robotic production systems.

We have seen how social systems innovatively use and reconfigure new digitally enhanced processes in institutional life. Librarians employ mass digitization and robotization by creatively integrating conventional "physical robotics" with automation laborers in the virtual realm. While farmers have access to huge amounts of data their robots provide, many of them are able to recombine these data into useful discoveries and innovations when they engage with partners in a network. However, these workplace innovations also suggest the use of sophisticated and deliberate "manipulation" (manipulation is here to be understood as a systemic property because robotics is heavily embodied in and integrated with data analytics in the overall farm management). In practice, such innovations entail creative tweaking to optimize milk production in order to increase yields. Innovative work in the realm of robotic workplaces, the author argues, demands access to technological (robotic) support functionalities just as much as access to social support systems (e.g., network expertise in formal partnerships and informal communities of practice). More importantly, the analysis of the empirical material suggests that social and technological (robotic) systems transcend each other's limitations in the interaction between professionals and robots. There are opportunities among practitioners to initiate innovative work so that such limitations can be exceeded (e.g., through optimization), and such innovations render new production systems that are both more powerful and more competitive.

While the case studies provide a number of solid examples of how robotics represents socio-political attempts to modernize and "humanize" workplace settings, they also show how technology is tactically employed and under human control, influence and participation. Related to such social choices is another stream of technological development known as "enabling technology," but much remains to be explored in that area in terms of robot-human or robot-animal system integration and bionic confluence under the label "enabling technology." In sum, in an era promoting new hybrid technological advancements and entwinements between man and machine—of biological, bionic and digital reconfigurations—the skill and capacity for creative interpretation, manipulation and recombination is the new currency.

ROBOTIZED SUPPORTIVE FUNCTIONALITY

Social science disciplines, such as management, anthropology and sociology, theorize meaning creation and draw attention to how shared understanding is created in organizational life. Working cultures are made up of (inter) subjective meanings and collectively shared beliefs that are continuously created and re-created in workplace systems through daily social interactions and ongoing sensemaking events among people across and beyond occupational communities. Indeed, work cultures often have distinctive traits, and a group of professionals may share unique rituals, artifacts and languages that differentiate the group from other groups (i.e., an "us versus them" mentality). In these working cultures, practitioners also ascribe values, benefits and functionalities to robotic laborers based on their social and cultural-cognitive representations. However, representations, per definition, are always selective and never provide a holistic image or understanding of a given phenomenon. In the case of employment of robotics technology in real-world cases, the representations clearly emphasize the calculative exploitation and manipulation of artificial labor. However, there is also a limit to how much robots can be pressured and exploited. Eventually, even they will "resist" such attempts and become dysfunctional. Representations are influential because they construct one type of social world to cherish certain values—in the case studies, standardized functionality, digital control, software manipulation and economic worth are emphasized—which excludes other social worlds.

In this book, the author now sees a development where professionals create new types of socio-cultural meanings as they talk about robots as "co-workers." In doing so, they stress the work roles of robots and their accommodating functions: robots work fast, efficiently, with high precision and with the ability to work non-stop 24/7, that is, all hours of the day every day. For example, milk farmers talked about how robots use telephone lines (another technological infrastructure and functionality delegated to the robot) to engage in "natural communication" by using an artificial voice, and robots regularly communicate by such means during any hour of the day. While carrying out several work tasks simultaneously, the robot may find that one of the cows got stuck in the cage by using it advanced sensory capabilities (akin to human sensory systems such as vision, hearing and smell). This has to be communicated to the farmer, so the robot autonomously calls the farmer. Based on the information provided, the farmer may need to get out of bed and go to the farm to solve the problem, that is, when the robot cannot solve the problem itself. Even though the robot's voice has been programmed by another person, the farmer talks about the voice as if it is an integral part of the robot. These robots are likely the most sophisticated, competent ("intelligent") and autonomous of all the different robots covered in Chapters 4, 5, 6 and 7. These robots are able to dynamically adjust and act (and react) to the sensory data that are generated from their intricate interactions with the biological system. These robots are genuine "workhorses" in that they work all hours of every day, and they transcend human limitations because they do not become tired, bored, stressed or overburdened by the repetitious and physically demanding work of milking cows day after day. These artificial laborers alleviate the workload of human workers by providing free time for their masters to spend more effort on meaningful tasks, such as learning new things, managing innovative work and reshaping arrangements of work by new technological means. Together, the new human-robot partnership appears to create a stronger and more powerful platform compared with prior manual work forms, as robotic functionality and social systems transcend some of the shortcomings of each of their elements.

Weiss and colleagues conducted a focus group study to explore people's perceptions and expectations on the future roles robots could suitably assume in working life (Weiss *et al.*, 2009). Interestingly, the participants in their focus group study believed that robots should be constructed for functional roles to perform given tasks, and this finding was linked with the social acceptance of robots in society. Weiss and colleagues argued that robots are less likely to be accepted if they are designed for social (non-functional) collaborations with human peers. The research presented in this book on people's day-to-day interactions with robotics technology in workplace environments supports this argument and similarly suggests that people stress the benefits of functionality. Organizations primarily emphasize work functionality more than social relationality toward robots. It is therefore not primarily the robot's communicative or social attributes that are of greatest importance in workplaces. This argument, however, contradicts some mainstream developments in social robotics that are based on the assumption that robots are more likely to be accepted if they look friendly (non-threatening), behave politely, and adopt social capabilities such as the ability to communicate in natural (human-like) language in human-robot interactions.

Robots can be understood to be supportive functional work systems, just as human co-workers sometimes provide alleviating support. The robot's superior functionality and ability to perform many tasks simultaneously are the distinguishing traits of artificial robot labor that can interact with social systems in new ways. As we noted in the introductory chapter and afterward, robots are not "innovators" but are essentially very central support functionalities. Several respondents mentioned that they now cannot envision their organization without robots. At the same time, they stressed that everything depends on well-functioning robotics technology. This suggests how much organizations are dependent on technology. In the robot economy, robotic laborers work non-stop, untiringly and efficiently. However, the implicit assumption is that robots are "robust" and "functional." When robotic laborers are "dysfunctional," however, it may be a great disaster in some work organizations. Innovation management in a robot society represents an organizational challenge as well as a social choice to pursue robotics technology.

SOCIO-ROBOT WORK ORGANIZATIONS (SRWO)

Modern workplaces are becoming increasingly concerned with socio-robot work organizations, and this dynamic is key to understanding the emerging powerful economic forces at play in robot society. This is a new organizational challenge that is redefining the nature of the economic worker, which in turn is disrupting traditional power relationships in workplace environments and beyond (e.g., in innovation networks and partnerships). To understand what is happening in the institutional landscape, we explore what a variety of new supportive functions among artificial robot co-workers offer to social systems at the micro-level of organization.

What supportive functions, then, do service robots provide to social systems (i.e., organizations)? We have empirically scrutinized the early developments of robotics enhancement in health care organizations and in robotics surgery, for example, where some very highly educated workers (e.g., surgeons) are affected by new functional roles and excel in new professional abilities using powerful new robotic capacities. It has been noted elsewhere that robotization extends to high-status professions, bringing about a paradigm shift in working life (Wasen, 2010).

The case of robotics in surgery suggests that technology in one sense "liberates" organizational members from tedious and routine tasks. It is certainly not an optimal (or sustainable) arrangement to have highly educated staff (e.g., surgical residents) stand in a stiff position and monotonously hold a bulky and heavy camera system manually for several hours in a row during a complicated surgical procedure. A robot could do this task and allow the surgical assistant to focus instead on other tasks (s)he was educated for (ibid.). Hence, new workplace arrangements may be seen as an opportunity to be relieved from unpleasant or horrible working conditions. Depending on the social considerations, these arrangements may create openings for professionals to redirect their efforts at work toward more stimulating innovative and discovery work. Professionals could therefore use their time and effort more efficiently in other domains of the health care organization.

Innovation is increasingly relying on "robotized support functionality" provided by both physical and virtual robot labor. As robots take over routine physical tasks, staff should direct their attention more to innovation and start asking for more varying, meaningful and developmental work. For example, surgeons could spend more time analyzing and interpreting the digital visualizations (e.g., 3D and 4D images) modern health technology makes possible or pursue creative work in developing new surgical implements or radical process innovations that could improve treatments and benefit patients (see the case study on robotics surgery in Chapter 4).

In a growing number of workplace environments, computerized as well as robotics technologies will continue, essentially, to interact directly with humans or replace them in some way or another (Wasen, 2005b), but there will also be instances where humans in some instances will leave the robots to autonomously carry out their work. This is the case in space robotics, where robots need certain autonomous capabilities because of the time delays. Of course, there will likely also be flexible arrangements in organizations, that is, compromises where humans and robots can alternate and work alongside each other in various work assemblages. This type of flexibility manifests itself in the case of milking robots, as farmers sometimes assume control of the robotic arm and manually guide its movements (a form of total supervision). However, the other extreme is that the farmer completely leaves the robots to work on their own and manage the milking of the cows (e.g., the delegation of milking tasks to robots during night hours).

In light of robotics technology becoming increasingly "intelligent" and providing additional functionality and supportive roles to professionals, several respondents noted that they see robotics technologies as surrogate "work partners" and "co-workers" in a number of workplaces. Therefore, it might not be farfetched to imagine a future state that envisages "robots as artificial surrogate work partners and workers" and where robots will play an increasingly important role in business operations and organizational life, perhaps similarly to the ways in which computer technologies were adopted and gradually disseminated into an increasing number of workplace environments in previous years (Wasen, 2010: 432).

The case studies presented in this book draw on empirical evidence and demonstrate that the present phase of robotization implies a shift to new forms of work and labor across industries. Robotization in industrial manufacturing was traditionally concerned with robotic systems designed primarily for standardized physical tasks, and this meant that manufacturing robots were isolated in large cages to prevent any risks of robots harming staff. There were also concerns about job displacement, and the workers affected and displaced by technology typically carried out low-status work at various factory sites. There is no reason to lament the loss of some unpleasant and dreadful work. We now see that the present stage of robotization challenges almost every industry. In the present phase of robotization, robots as "artificial workers" are gradually beginning to take on more qualified jobs, possibly even "highly qualified" routine work (not to be confused with what Perrow (1967) refers to as "non-standardized work"). Such a shift unavoidably challenges the bargaining position of high-status workers, for example, those employed to carry out discovery work (e.g., in science laboratories) and advanced problem-solving tasks that are susceptible to automation (e.g., in business analytics). Introducing and exploiting robotics solutions and automation systems in this domain could potentially have significant consequences for the rationales to reconfigure organizations and reshape the division of labor in the future, not just in science but in other domains as well. From this vantage point, and recognizing that knowledge is intrinsically tied to power and influence, the presence of robots significantly challenges professional structures and power relationships in working life.

In summary, the various developments and innovations accounted for in this book suggest that a new phase of robotization is up and running on a daily basis. This research shows that we already live in a robot society. There is an urgent need for pioneering research that takes seriously these radical changes that have and will continue to have social significance in the global economy. Therefore, in this book, we suggest creating a novel domain of knowledge and a specialized field of research that falls under the "socio-robotic work organizations" (SRWO) heading, that is, an academic discipline that addresses paradigm shifts brought about by the diffusion and employment of robotics technology in working life. In the next section, we will look more closely into the serious social and professional dilemmas regarding robotic replacement that may bring about social friction.

THREATS AND OPPORTUNITIES FACING PROFESSIONALS

In the previous chapters, we have explored a series of workplace cases in which robots work either by themselves (semi-autonomously) or beside humans. Robotization extends beyond individual workplace environments. Indeed, innovations (e.g., new robotic partnerships) can be highly competitive and disruptive because they may potentially redraw boundaries in an entire industry and thereby shift the balance of power and influence. While humans have traditionally represented labor in society, we now see a new class of powerful labor emerge, which we call *robot labor* and which has the ability to replace even human labor.

This general theme applies to most, if not all, robotic applications. The cases have covered agriculture robotics, which perhaps is one of the most technologically mature sectors in society—mature in the sense that it was in this sector that the major shifts in employment (re)arrangements and dramatic productivity gains first occurred during the last century. However, we have also observed a similar tendency in the science, health care and service sectors. The elderly care case remains a comparatively "embryonic" domain for robotics, as social, technological and organizational change tends to be more associated with improvements in communication and quality of life than with gains in productivity and time efficiency.

Indeed, there is a growing sense of worry and anxiety regarding the effects of "technological unemployment" among professionals when sophisticated robots enter the scene and the concern that they will eventually be outperformed and replaced by robotic technology. Even staff members in highly educated professional groups are no longer safe or protected from this possibility (Wasen, 2010). Meanwhile, professionals are struggling to unite conflicting views of the new robotics technology, attempting to grasp both the desirable and undesirable at the same time. Robotic technology is a double-edged sword. An ambivalent state thus arises because robots are not only "enabling technologies" but also "artificial robotic co-workers" that clearly improve working conditions (i.e., less physically taxing) and generate new forms of work.

The majority of professionals appreciate and experience great work satisfaction collaborating with "artificial robotic co-workers," although this development path may eventually threaten their jobs. In other words, professionals want to work alongside robots but also want to hold onto their jobs. In such a contradiction, it becomes increasingly difficult to navigate the present and adopt a future orientation. There is a fear of replacement, and future prospects are rather shocking, not only because of the risk of losing the jobs that professionals have but also because there is an underlying fear of losing professionals skills and expertise. Many of the traditional manufacturing jobs that were rationalized and replaced by automation technology in the midst of industrial robotics will most likely not return. Thus, an entire profession could become obsolete, and employees are concerned that the old professional networks and occupational support structures on which they have previously relied may eventually vanish or collapse.

Indeed, science and service robotics are part of the most rapidly changing, innovative and creative domains of the global marketplace, and they also symbolize new growing domains for robotics technology. To what extent revolutionary robotics technology makes it possible to accelerate innovation and increase the intensity of an already fast-paced competitive race remains an open issue. At this point, it is sufficient to conclude that a radical reconfiguration of business logics appears to be underway and appears to involve rather dramatic rearrangements of knowledge workers and robotic technologies.

Although new technological abilities are essential and often transcend human limitations, it is important to note that it is still the human (and socio-political and socio-cultural) element that facilitates innovation and not technology as such. None of the case illustrations suggest that robots themselves are capable of innovating; therefore, innovation still relies on human efforts and coordinated work. In health care robotics, for example, Wasen and Brierley observed that images generated from 3D cameras during surgical procedures require human treatment and "must be processed and endowed with purpose, as well as a relevance that is ordered, interpreted, and analysed by professional surgeons. While a robot has the ability to collect and store data, it cannot analyse, interpret or act on the raw data generated from 3D imaging systems. The surgical robot in this case is not an 'innovator' or a creative entity; it is a sophisticated tool" (2013: 46).

One of the lead surgeons in neurosurgery has observed that new advanced technologies generate enormous amounts of data and information, and he therefore anticipated that his hospital would employ more staff to perform analytic and interpretative work. This observation suggests that in the future, work in teaching hospitals will increasingly be intellectually oriented rather than concerned with manual dexterity and physical labor. This trend is also observed in the agricultural sector, where robotics technology collects, orders and disseminates vast amounts of data.

Many of the professionals interviewed for this research have spent several thousand hours at work performing overwhelmingly repetitive, routine and sometimes unsafe work on a daily basis in dangerous workplace environments. Not surprisingly, these individuals view powerful robotic laborers as their redeemers. The jobs of farmers or industrial workers have become much less physically taxing while also becoming more knowledge demanding and sometimes intellectually stressful. For farmers, appropriately timing the milking process as well as finding the proper balance of supplied food and nutrients is a complicated matter, not least because these processes vary from one cow to another. The solution resides in finding workplace innovation that allows for the appropriate programming of robots as farmers are pressured to seek to optimize their milk production.

Because of increasingly intensified competitive pressures in the marketplace, in order for a small business to survive, farmers strategically seek to generate as large a volume of produced milk as possible from each of the cows by employing and optimizing the actions among several robotic laborers (a similar dynamic is at play in the employment of advanced industrial robots, which also entails pre-programming and optimization "tactics"). Although automated milking robots are capable of making a series of powerful and informed decisions, such as deciding which cows should be allowed to be milked and in what quantities, how many times and during what hours of the day, all these decisions are open to negotiation and are thus influenced by socio-political forces such as the programming of parameters. Moreover, it is the individual farmer who must make sense (interpret and analyze) of all the data generated and to act on that data to be able to optimize and rationalize milk production. For example, farmers collaborate closely with networked technical expertise to design and optimize not only the functioning of robots but also robot-cow interactions. This situation becomes clear in all of the cases of robotic laborers presented in Chapters 4, 5, 6 and 7. In the realm of day-to-day networking activities, new ideas and opportunities are constantly created.

While robots are not "innovators," this view also suggests that, despite technology being involved in modern innovative activities to a higher degree than ever before, social interchanges as well as human creativity are still fundamental aspects of an organization's innovative capability. Indeed, the very notion of automation is misleading and deceiving because no system exists (at least today) that can manage and cope on its own for a long period of time without any intervention whatsoever. Perhaps the term semi-autonomous is preferable.

The research reported in this book supports the notion that robots assume the role of "artificial co-workers" (Wasen, 2013), persistent and tireless laborers that may take on some of the functional roles of human knowledge workers and tasks that are delegated to them by their human peers (e.g., data collection, information gathering, and lower-level decision making). With the steadily growing variety (and "hybridity") of robotic partners, a highly competitive "pact" among humans, robots and other high technologies (e.g., computers) evolves in modern workplaces. In fact, there is an emerging stream of research known as "human-robot interaction" (HRI). The research area of SRWO differs from the main direction within the HRI domain through its concept formation. We would like to broaden the theoretical research on HRI to include wider organizational and societal implications of robotics. We suggest that this research area is more relevant and suitable for economists, sociologists, psychologists and management scholars. In this research area, what perhaps makes the particular "truce" between robots and humans powerful is not the technology's new interactional or functional abilities *per se* but rather the wider (political) labor market implications, strategic choices in workplaces and, last but not least, social considerations that allow for the regulation of working conditions. In working life, a SRWO represents a human-friendly organization in the sense that it ultimately facilitates the fight against poor and unsafe working conditions and the development of fairer and more humane and decent conditions.

Furthermore, this broad view allows us to analyze the emerging "robot work culture" through a different pair of "lenses." Do we now see the dawn of an emerging robot work culture where robotics technology will represent a governing class of artificial economic labor that is increasingly difficult to compete with in carrying out routine tasks? Are we on the verge of entering a robot economy? This work culture entails viewing "robots as work partners" and highlights the role of productivity, the introduction of a spectrum of new work forms and the modernization of employment and working conditions. Moreover, in the second wave of robotics, a rising "robot work culture" embraces a different "work ethos," and this shift necessitates a redefinition and reevaluation of the conventional view of the labor force, skills and knowledge infrastructures. Several advances are moving in this direction. Although the partnership between humans and smart machines sometimes takes unexpected turns, they are steadily being incorporated into an increasing number of institutional structures. The first generation of "obedient" robots was largely regarded as "functional" components and "slaves" set to varying use primarily in industrial systems. However, in the second wave of robotics, smart robots were adopted in domains beyond industrial usage to include health care, services, agriculture and finance, among others. The new generations of robots increasingly make their own decisions, engage in new interactive forms of machine-to-machine coordination and robot-human collaboration, and are able to work and function semi-autonomously and more flexibly than before. Such new partnerships and working relationships make new hybrid and productive institutional arrangements possible and sometimes also enable novel sets of multidimensional and multifarious power bases. More importantly, robotization spans across an increasing number of socio-economic sectors in what we refer to as a "robot society."

SUMMARY AND CONCLUSION

In conclusion, friction appears to be an ordinary quality in any innovation system or organization—both a blocking force and an enabling force that works beyond any direct exerting of narrow power steering or unidirectional top-down control. Similarly but paradoxically, friction management unfolds as both a productive and destructive force in workplaces and network arrangements. By the term "friction management," we mean the "directing" of the multi-paradoxical forces of socio-cultural and cognitive characters that appear and flow in radical innovation, and the change processes that require coordination and adaptation. The goal is to combine and mobilize organizational resources to strategically increase innovation capacity, thus promoting the dynamic renewal of creative and counter-destructive friction.

This book is a product of a new school of scholarly thinking. Our research, surprisingly, not only shows that innovation processes are affected by the frictions and obstacles in their surroundings but also that innovations create frictions themselves—tensions, for example, are emerging through the paradoxes that workplaces face. The proliferation of robotic technology prompts the rise of new paradoxes and controversies and interacts with a multitude of socio-political forces. Indeed, advanced robotic systems produce large volumes of products and services in short amounts of time. Thus, they more flexibly and cheaply render equally good or even superior quality work. Surprisingly, several respondents not only see robots as machines but also talk about robots being their "co-workers" and "work partners." Hence, professionals who interact with robotics technology also stress that robots carry out work activities that humans previously performed, often in a better, faster and more consistent way. Together, the new human-robot partnership appears to create a stronger and more powerful platform compared with prior manual work forms, as robotic functionality and social systems transcend some of the shortcomings of each of their elements. Machine power is combined with the power of creative human thinking and collective intelligence in multifaceted networks.

However, because robotic work partners perform an increasing number of human tasks, they are essentially becoming actors or partners in the chain of networking as they gain new types of material agency and abilities, thus becoming productive elements in organizational processes. Thus, it is reasonable to assume that both sides—i.e., the human/social *and* the technological—must be considered in concert. Robots are hence seen both as functional entities and economic elements in organizations and are shaped by various interlinked professional and socio-political forces. In other words, an informed analysis needs to take into account how complex interactions between humans and robots contribute to shaping workplace arrangements as well as how these arrangements allow more efficient production regimes and innovation. By adopting open-mindedness and observing beyond taken-for-granted assumptions, a different view of the socio-political implications of technological advances can be adopted.

As technology becomes increasingly autonomous and "intelligent," inevitably there grows a kind of "magic power" around technology that fuels the creation of new seductive myths. However, it is argued that novel socio-robotic organizational arrangements generate new time-consuming activities, thus bringing into question the popularly held assumption or myth that robotic laborers inevitably and completely alleviate workers and/ or render professionals obsolete. Although robotic applications in society clearly diverge in many important ways, as the different case illustrations in this book demonstrate, there is one salient aspect that they all share in their innovative efforts: optimization with regard to *time efficiency* and *increased volume output* alongside *less human involvement in physical labor* and *increased human presence in analytical, creative and innovative work*. Socio-political arrangements clearly exploit emerging technological advances and infrastructures to generate change, which also reveals opportunities for innovative labor and future paths of development. The case studies and many additional examples of robotization indicate that the robotic workforce expands into nearly every economic sector, and all of these factors relate more generally to how robotics is used to sustain market competitiveness. In the final chapter, we will discuss the social and professional implications of robotic technology.

9 Conclusion

Implications for Innovative Workers and Their Place in Robot Society

The robotic applications we have underscored in this book, and the human creativity and organizational innovation processes making these developments possible, have so far been applied to a number of cases and workplace domains. The proliferation of robotization is not merely confined to the five sectors presented in the book, that is, agriculture, health care, medical science, services and elderly care. There are other sectors that apply robotics technology, e.g., banks and finance, energy, space and underwater exploration, mining, sports, clean tech, and many other industries and services. Because of this broad-spectrum prevalence and use of robotics technology, we maintain that we already live in a robot society that is continuously changing and developing. By the term "robot society," we mean a new work culture in society, where robotic technological applications are available in almost all sectors and industries. Society applies the growing body of robot labor to boring, repetitive, heavy and dangerous work in standardized ways, and this powerful labor form is an important economic factor.

The empirical parts of the book consider parallel technological trends, professional experiences and workplace events in several industries and sectors. However, despite the broad-spectrum use of robotics in society, emphasis is also placed on the local peculiarities and distinguishing traits that characterize robotization within and across work cultures and occupational communities. Clifford Geertz, a distinguished anthropologist who inspired several generations of ethnographic researchers around the world, maintained that cultures do not determine social events, behaviors, processes and institutions but that culture is rather to be understood as the context that makes all these phenomena understandable and meaningful.

Geertz specifically encouraged us to relate narratives and "thick descriptions" of peculiar micro-events to wider societal issues: "The aim is to draw large conclusions from small, but very densely textured facts; to support broad assertions about the role of culture in the construction of collective life by engaging them exactly with complex specifics" (Geertz, 1973: 28). The different case studies presented in this book have presented unique and detailed accounts of robotic laborers in agriculture, medical science, services, health care and elderly care. While studies of workplace innovation imply that the group of professionals becomes the focal level of analysis, any good explanation must engage with the topic on many levels, macro, meso and micro, because they depend on and influence each other. Therefore, this research has adopted cross-level analysis (see, e.g., Hackman, 2003; Preece *et al.*, 1999; Willmott, 1997).

While the various trials and opportunities facing these workplaces and institutions were often specific to the particular circumstances in the industry and sector, they also revealed more general categories of dilemmas and challenges facing all firms and public organizations seeking to use robotics technology in an optimal way. Thus, it is possible to derive more general themes on robotic use that are applicable to most, if not all, industries in robot society. Essentially, these themes relate to radical changes in working life and the economy, such as transformations in innovation strategies for new creative jobs and changing working cultures and labor markets.

The research findings not only account for complex economic activity and politico-managerial (inter)action at the micro-level of organization but also explain how robots "liberate" members of occupational groups from previous unpleasant workplace arrangements where they were more or less required to carry out dirty, hazardous, tedious and monotonous tasks. Moreover, instead of being tied up and preoccupied with difficult, routine and standardized physical tasks, staff members could spend more time on creative and developmental projects, expand work content and improve future ways of working and work conditions. This finding, however, challenges Rifkin's (2004) radical notion that technological progress inevitably results in "the end of work" and in a decline of the global labor force. However, we need to ask what types of work will be replaced, and one cannot draw broad generalizations here.

The author is somewhat of a "worried optimist" and believes that repetitive work is increasingly being replaced by emerging technologies in the future, but modern forms of work will also emerge and jobs will instead be created in, for example, creative industries (for more on innovation in creative industries, see Hawkins and Davis, 2012). Nevertheless, the author is worried that the transition period may be painful and difficult, especially for some occupational groups in society. The important thesis fleshed out here is that work is most likely going to change drastically in the future and that new types of creative work, along with new occupational categories and new work domains, will come forward. This will take time, and it is important to see what forms of frictions (positive and negative) will emerge. We consider Rifkin's contention "the end of work" to be a myth rather than reality.

However, the radical shifts described are certainly not unproblematic—and it is therefore not surprising that robotization is a controversial and lively topic of debate in the public square. It seems that the term "robotization" is often used interchangeably with the notion of technological replacement (and unemployment). The replacement of human labor has historically been a contested terrain that has evoked both fears and resistance. Changes in working life today are perhaps not as dramatic as they were back in the early Industrial Era, when some workers at industrial manufacturing plants were replaced by automated spinning frames, for example. Nevertheless, technological change in our times raises various concerns in organizational life, and dangers are linked to worries about mass unemployment. For organizational members, concerns of technological job replacement may bring about psychological costs, such as worry and stress related to the risks of unemployment. This is an underlying problem and concern in the midst of workplace restructuring, with changes tending to arrive under the label "modernization."

Competitive and obedient "robot servants," on the other hand, are not exposed to such sources of social stress and do not worry about their "economic lifetime" or that they might (often) be replaced by a newer and more proficient generation of robots. Moreover, robots usually do not cause any troubles and are immune to social tensions and workplace conflicts. Perhaps this makes them "attractive," in addition to their economic worth and superior staying power that allows them to work day and night, tirelessly and without any complaints about working conditions. The research findings suggest that novel arrangements in socio-robot work organizations (SRWO) alleviate staff and that new robot-based support functions may free up time for employees so that they can pursue more creative and meaningful jobs.

A WAY FORWARD? NOT EASY, BUT NOT IMPOSSIBLE

What types of innovative skills will be considered necessary for newly emerging professions and jobs that do not exist today? It is likely that these jobs will involve increasingly more advanced high-tech solutions, creative skills and knowledge-innovative capacities (e.g., manipulation and recombination abilities). This also has consequences for professionals and entire occupational groups, who will need to become more adaptable, to have a skills-base that is "renewable" and to be capable of keeping up their learning in step with the heightened pace of change in order to continually stay up to date and remain competitive in the labor market. Indeed, due to the present intensity of radical change, a top priority for tomorrow's policies and political interventions is to redefine and transform the skill and employment agenda. It is imperative to recognize the need for developing proactive strategies to address coming challenges in a timely and sustainable manner.

The capacity to keep up with rapid changes and to adapt to new innovative arrangements and technological requirements not only poses a key strategic challenge for modern business managers and industries, it also poses a perhaps equal challenge for political regulation and various policy-driven interventions. In many developed economies, both within and outside the European Union, it has become a main concern to advance skill levels so that the workforce will remain competitive and up to date. Indeed, the securing of new skills for future jobs has been a major focus and top priority not only for ensuring economic growth and stability but also for providing adequate financing of public services. Thus, democratically elected officials and representatives are desperately seeking new measures to address major looming crises and predicaments with regard to reduced prospects of ensuring jobs and future employment opportunities for a growing number of citizens.

Many of the traditional manufacturing jobs that were rationalized and replaced by automation technology in the midst of industrial robotics will most likely not return. Instead, the hopes of society are directed toward job creation and new employment opportunities in creative professions. Thus, job creation is primarily expected to occur in the service and culture sectors (e.g., arts, service design and design thinking) and in the emerging green sectors (e.g., clean-tech and environment). Robots and computers, at least today, are not in a position to outcompete humans in various forms of "creative work" (aesthetic productivity), and this creative sphere of life is still privileged for human activity (not to say that digitization does not support creative work). It is therefore reasonable to assume that cultural work and educational programs that promote critical understanding and these creative skill sets at universities and faculties of art will become increasingly important in a society that thrives on creativity and innovation.

Innovation is central to curbing unemployment and boosting new jobs. High hopes are placed on innovation, and measures supporting innovative enterprises are believed to be the right path to meet potentially devastating developments with alarming social and economic costs for society. Innovation can be a new product, service, pioneering idea, knowledge or conceptual solution, but regardless of its manifestation, its primary purpose is to provide changing improvements for humanity and nature. Given scarce resources, the challenge is to intelligently create economic value for sustainable development.

In summary, all these workplace studies have contributed to suggesting the concepts presented in this monograph and have also served to anchor those concepts concretely in real-world robotics. Drawing on original case study materials, this book highlights a wide range of areas in which robotized goods and service production are productively used in society. Although some institutional domains are already intensely robotized, other areas are only beginning to witness the advent of robotic interventions. As computers were dispersed and used in an increasingly growing number of workplaces and businesses in prior decades, robot technologies are now similarly being aggressively embraced in the economy and productively used in a growing amount of sectors. There exist plenty other application areas for robotics besides the case studies that have been presented in this book. Industrial manufacturing, finance, journalism, space, underwater, construction, energy, raw materials, peacekeeping, surveillance, gambling, and household services are examples of other sectors and domains of society in which robots are being used. Overall, what we summarize in the notion of a "robot society" in this book fundamentally suggests a robot era in both business and society.

Bibliography

Abrahamson, E. (1996) 'Management fashion.' *Academy of Management Review*, 21(1): 254–285.

Abramowitz, M. (1956) 'Resources and output trends in the United States since 1870.' *The American Economic Review*, 46 (May): 5–23.

Adler, P. S. and Heckscher, C. (2006) 'Towards collaborative community,' in C. Heckscher and P. S. Adler (eds.) *The Firm as a Collaborative Community: Reconstructing Trust in the Knowledge Economy*. Oxford: Oxford University Press, pp. 11–105.

Alvesson, M. (2012) *Understanding Organizational Culture*. London: Sage.

Amin, A. and Roberts, J. (2008) 'Knowing in action: Beyond communities of practice.' *Research Policy*, 37: 353–369.

Andriopoulos, C. and Dawson, P. (2009) *Managing Change, Creativity & Innovation*. London: Sage.

Argyris, C. and Schön, D. A. (1974) *Theory in Practice: Increasing Professional Effectiveness*. San Francisco: Jossey-Bass.

Attewell, P. and Domina, T. (2011) 'Educational imposters and fake degrees.' *Research in Social Stratification and Mobility*, 29(1): 57–69.

Axelsson, B. (2010) 'Business relationships and networks: Reflections on the IMP tradition.' *IMP Journal*, 4(1): 3–30.

Axelsson, B. and Agndal, H. (2012) *Professional Marketing: The Business Market as Network*. Lund: Studentlitteratur.

Badham, R. and Buchanan, D.(1996) Power assisted steering: The new princes of socio-technical change. Leicester Business School, Occasional Paper 33, March.

Barnes, J. A. (1954) 'Class and committees in a Norwegian island parish.' *Human Relations*, 7(1): 39–58.

Barnes, J. A. (1979) 'Network analysis: Orienting notion, rigorous technique, or substantive field of study?' in P. W. Holland and S. Leinhardt (eds.) *Perspectives on Social Network Analysis*. New York: Academic, pp. 403–423.

Barrett, M., Oborn, E., Orlikowski, W. J., and Yates, J. A. (2011) 'Reconfiguring boundary relations: Robotic innovations in pharmacy work.' *Organization Science*, 23(5): 1448–1466.

Barrett, W. (1977) *The Illusion of Technique*. London: William Kimber.

Bartlett, C. A. and Ghoshal, S. (1998) *Managing Across Borders: The Transnational Solution*. Boston: Harvard Business School Press.

Bartlett, C. A. and Ghoshal, S. (1999) *The Individualized Corporation*. London: William Heinemann.

Berger, P. L. and Luckmann, T. (1966) *The Social Construction of Reality: A Treatise in the Sociology of Knowledge*. New York: Anchor Books.

Berggren, C., Bergek, A., Bengtsson, L., Hobday, M., and Söderlund, J. (eds.) (2011) *Knowledge Integration and Innovation: Critical Challenges Facing International Technology-Based Firms*. Oxford: Oxford University Press.

Bessant, J., Lamming, R., Noke, H., and Philips, W. (2005) 'Managing innovation beyond the steady state.' *Technovation*, 25(12): 1366–1376.

Bessant, J. and Phillips, W. (2013) 'Innovation management and dynamic capability,' in C. Harland, G. Nassimbeni, and E. Schneller (eds.) *The Sage Handbook of Strategic Supply Management: Relationships, Chains, Networks and Sectors*. London: Sage, pp. 353–371

Bessant, J. and Tidd, J. (2007) *Innovation and Entrepreneurship*. Chichester: John Wiley.

Besson, U. (2013) 'Historical scientific models and theories as resources for learning and teaching: The case of friction.' *Science & Education*, 22(5): 1001–1042.

Biemans, W. G. (1992) *Managing Innovation Within Networks*. London: Routledge.

Bijker, W. E. and Law, J. (1992) *Shaping Society/Building Society: Studies in Sociotechnical Change*. Cambridge, MA: MIT Press.

Bittencourt, A. C. (2012) 'On modeling and diagnosis of friction and wear in industrial robots.' *Linköping Studies in Science and Technology no. 1516*. Linköping: Linköping University.

Boisot, M. H. (1998) *Knowledge Assets: Securing Competitive Advantage in the Information Economy*. Oxford: Oxford University Press.

Boisot, M. H., Nordberg, M., Yami, S., and Nicquevert, B. (eds.) (2011) *Collisions and Collaborations: The Organization of Learning in the Atlas Experiment at the LHC*. Oxford: Oxford University Press.

Borgatti, S. P. and Foster, P. C. (2003) 'The network paradigm in organizational research. A review and typology.' *Journal of Management*, 29(6): 991–1013.

Borgatti, S. P., Mehra, A., Brass, D., and Labianca, G. (2009) 'Network analysis in the social sciences.' *Science*, 323(5916): 892–895.

Bourelos, E., Magnusson, M., and McKelvey, M. (2012) 'Investigating the complexity facing academic entrepreneurs in science and engineering: The complementarities of research performance, networks and support structures in commercialization.' *Cambridge Journal of Economics*, 36(3): 751–780.

Brass, D. J., Galaskiewicz, J., Greve, H. R., and Tsai, W. (2004) 'Taking stock of networks and organizations: A multilevel perspective.' *Academy of Management Journal*, 47(6): 795–817.

Brettel, M. and Cleven, N. J. (2011) 'Innovation culture, collaboration with external partners and NPD performance.' *Creativity and Innovation Management*, 20(4): 253–272.

Brown, J. and Duguid, P. (1991) 'Organizational learning and communities-of-practice: Toward a unified view of working, learning and innovation.' *Organization Science*, 2(1): 40–57.

Buchanan, D. and Badham, R. (1999) *Power, Politics, and Organizational Change: Winning the Turf Game*. London: Sage.

Buchanan, D. and Boddy, D. (1992) *The Expertise of the Change Agent: Public Performance and Backstage Activity*. London: Prentice-Hall International.

Burns, T. E. and Stalker, G. M. (1961) *The Management of Innovation*. London: Tavistock Publications.

Burrell, G. and Morgan, G. (1979) *Sociological Paradigms and Organizational Analysis*. London: Heinemann.

Carneiro, A. (2000) 'How does knowledge management influence innovation and competitiveness?' *Journal of Knowledge Management*, 4(2): 87–98.

Castells, M. (2000) *The Rise of the Network Society—Information Age Vol. 1*. 2nd ed. Oxford: Blackwell Publishers.

Castells, M. (2009) *Communication Power*. Oxford: Oxford University Press.

Castells, M. (2012) *Networks of Outrage and Hope: Social Movements in the Internet Age*. Cambridge: Polity Press.

Chetty, S. and Agndal, H. (2008) 'Role of inter-organizational networks and interpersonal networks in an industrial district.' *Regional Studies*, 42(2): 175–187.

Christensen, C. M. (1997) *The Innovator's Dilemma: When New Technologies Cause Great Firms to Fail*. Boston: Harvard Business Press.

Christensen, C. M. (2003) *The Innovator's Solution: Creating and Sustaining Successful Growth*. Boston: Harvard Business Press.

Clark, C. (2013) 'Robot amongst the herd.' *Diary Research Foundation Newsletter*, Faculty of Veterinary Science, University of Sydney, December 2013, 5(3), pp. 6–7.Coccia, M. (2006) 'Measuring intensity of technological change: The seismic approach.' *Technological Forecasting and Social Change*, 72(2): 117–144.

Cook, K. S., and Emerson, R. M. (1978) 'Non-exchange relationships in networks.' *American Sociological Review*, May–June: 130–135.

Cook, K. S. and Gillmore, M. R. (1984) 'Power, dependence, and coalitions,' in E. J. Lawler (ed.) *Advances in Group Processes*. Greenwich: JAI Press, pp. 27–59.

Cook, K. S. and Rice, E. (2001) 'Exchange and power: Issues of structure and agency.' In J. Turner (ed.), *Handbook of Sociological Theory*. New York: Kluwer Academic Publishers, pp. 699–721.

Cook, S. D. and Yanow, D. (1993) 'Culture and organizational learning.' *Journal of Management Inquiry*, 2(4): 373–390.

D'Aveni, R. A. (1994) *Hypercompetition: Managing the Dynamics of Strategic Maneuvering*. New York: The Free Press.

Davenport, H. T. and Prusak, L. (1997) *Information Ecology: Mastering the Information and Knowledge Environment: Why Technology Is Not Enough for Success in the Information Age*. New York: Oxford University Press.

Dairy Research Foundation (2013) 'Newsletter' University of Sidney, *Faculty of Veterinary Science*, December 2013, 5(3): 1–24.

Dawson, P. (1994) *Organizational Change: A Processual Approach*. London: Paul Chapman Publishing.

Dawson, P. (1996) *Technology and Quality: Change in the Workplace*. London: Thompson Business Press.

Day, K., and Kerr, P. (2012) 'The potential of telehealth for 'business as usual' in outpatient clinics.' *Journal of Telemedicine and Telecare*, 18 (3): 138–141.

Dirks, K. T., Lewicki, R. J., and Zaheer, A. (2009) 'Repairing Relationships Within and Between Organizations: Building a Conceptual Foundation.' *Academy of Management Review*, 34(1): 68–84.

Dewar, R. D. and Dutton, J. E. (1986) 'The adoption of radical and incremental innovations: An empirical analysis.' *Management Science*, 32: 1422–1433.

Docherty, P., Ljung, A., and Stjernberg, T. (2006) 'The changing practice of action research,' in J. Löwstedt and T. Stjernberg (eds.) *Producing Management Knowledge: Research as Practice*. London: Routledge, pp. 221–236.

Douglas, M. (1987) *How Institutions Think*. London: Routledge & Paul Kegan.

Doz, Y. L. and Hamel, G. (1998) *Alliance Advantage: The Art of Creating Value Through Partnering*. Boston: Harvard Business School Press.

Drucker, P. (1985) *Innovation and Entrepreneurship: Practice and Principles*. New York: Harper & Row.

Easley, D. and Kleinberg, J. (2010) *Networks, Crowds, and Markets: Reasoning About a Highly Connected World*. Cambridge: Cambridge University Press.

Easton, G. (1992) 'Industrial networks: A review,' in B. Axelsson and G. Easton (eds.) *Industrial Networks: A New View of Reality*. London: The Dryden Press, pp. 1–27.

Easton, G. and Håkansson, H. (1996) 'Markets as networks: Editorial introduction.' *International Journal of Research in Marketing*, 13(5): 407–413.

Ebers, M. (1997) *The Formation of Inter-Organizational Networks*. Oxford: Oxford University Press.

Elden, M. (1983) 'Democratization and participative research in developing local theory.' *Journal of Occupational Behaviour*, 4(1): 21–33.

Elzinga, A. (1985) 'Research, bureaucracy, and the drift of epistemic criteria,' in B. Wittrock and A. Elzinga (eds.) *The University Research System*. Lund: Research on Higher Education Program, pp. 191–220.

Elzinga, A. (2010) 'New public management, science policy and the orchestration of university research—Academic science the loser.' *The Journal for Transdisciplinary Research in Southern Africa*, 6(2): 307–332.

Elzinga, A. (2012) 'Features of the current science policy regime: Viewed in historical perspective.' *Science and Public Policy*, 39: 416–428.

Engeström, Y. (1999) 'Innovative Learning in Work Teams: Analyzing Cycles of Knowledge Creation in Practice. ' In Y. Engeström, R. Miettinen, and R-L. Punamäki (eds) *Perspectives on Activity Theory*. Cambridge: Cambridge University Press, pp. 377–404.

Engeström, Y. (2007) 'From communities of practice to mycorrhizae,' in J. Huges, N. Jewson, and L. Unwin (eds.) *Communities of Practice: Critical Perspectives*. London: Routledge, 41–54.

EU (2011) *Knowledge Without Borders: GÉANT 2020 as the European Communications Commons*. Brussels: European Commission, Information Society and Media.

Fleck, J. (1991) 'Information-integration and industry—A digest of the development of information-integration beyond CIM.' *PICT Policy Research Papers*. London: ESRC.

Fleck, J., Webster, J., and Williams, R. (1989) 'The dynamics of IT implementation: A reassessment of paradigms and trajectories of development.' *PICT Working Paper Series No 14*. Edinburgh: University of Edinburgh.

Fleck, L. (1979) *Genesis and Development of a Scientific Fact*. Translated by F. Bradley and T. J. Trenn. Edited by T. J. Trenn and R. Merton. 'Foreword' by Thomas S. Kuhn. Chicago: The University of Chicago Press.

Foucault, M. (1980) *Power/Knowledge*. Brighton: Harvester Press.

Foucault, M. (1982) 'The subject and power.' In H. L. Dreyfus and R. Rabinov (eds.) *Michel Foucault: Beyond Structuralism and Hermeneutics*. Brighton: Harvester Press, pp. 208–226.

Fox, S. (2000) 'Communities of practice, Foucault and actor-network theory.' *Journal of Management Studies*, 37(6): 853–867.

Freeman, L. C. (2004) *The Development of Social Analysis: A Study in the Sociology of Science*. Vancouver: Empirical Press.

Fukuyama, F. (1999) *The Great Disruption: Human Nature and the Reconstitution of Social Order*. London: Profile Books.

Galison, P. (1997) *Image and Logic: A Material Culture of Microphysics*. Chicago: University of Chicago Press.

Geertz, C. (1973) *The Interpretation of Cultures*. New York: Basic Books.

Geertz, C. (1983) *Local Knowledge. Further Essays in Interpretive Anthropology*. New York: Basic Books.

Gherardi, S., Nicolini, D., and Odella, F. (1998) 'Towards a social understanding of how people learn in organizations.' *Management Learning*, 29(3): 273–298.

Giedymin, J. (1986) 'Polish philosophy in the inter-war period and Ludwik Fleck's theory of thought-styles and thought-collectives,' in R. S. Cohen and T. Schnelle (eds.) *Cognition and Fact: Materials on Ludwik Fleck*. Dordrecht: Springer, pp. 179–215.

Goffman, E. (1959) *The Presentation of Self in Everyday Life*. London: Penguin Books.

Granovetter, M. (1973) 'The strength of weak ties.' *American Journal of Sociology*, 78(6): 1360–1380.

Gulati, R., Nohria, N., and Zaheer, A. (2000) 'Strategic networks.' *Strategic Management Journal*, 21: 203–215.

Gustavsen, B. (1990) *Vägen till Bättre Arbetsliv: Strategier och Arbetsformer i ett Utvecklingsarbete*. Stockholm: Arbetslivscentrum.

Gustavsen, B. and Hofmaier, B. (1997) *Nätverk som Utvecklingsstrategi*. Stockholm: SNS Förlag.

Gustavsen, B., Hofmaier, B., Ekman Philips, M., and Wikman, A. (1996) *Concept-Driven Development and the Organization of the Process of Change: An Evaluation of the Swedish Working Life Fund*. Philadelphia: John Benjamins Publishing.

Habermas, J. (1987) *The Theory of Communicative Action. Vol. 2, Lifeworld and System: A Critique of Functionalist Reason*. Boston: Beacon Press.

Hackman, R. (2003) 'Learning more by crossing levels: Evidence from airplanes, hospitals, and orchestras.' *Journal of Organizational Behavior*, 24: 905–922.

Hagel, J. and Brown, J.S. (2005) 'Productive friction: How difficult business partnerships can accelerate innovation.' *Harvard Business Review*, 83(2): 82–91.

Håkansson, H. (1987) 'Product development in networks,' in H. Håkansson (ed.) *Industrial Technological Development. A Network Approach*. London: Croom Helm, pp. 84–127.

Håkansson, H. (1989) *Corporate Technological Behavior: Cooperation and Networks*. London: Routledge.

Håkansson, H., Frost, D., Gadde, L-E., Snehota, I., and Waluszewski, A. (2009) *Business in Networks*. New York: Wiley & Sons Ltd.

Håkansson, H. and Johanson, J. (1994) 'A model of industrial networks,' in J. Johanson (ed.) *Internationalization, Relationships and Networks*. Stockholm: Almqvist & Wiksell International, pp. 153–158.

Håkansson, H. and Snehota, I.J. (eds.) (1995) *Developing Relationships in Business Networks*. London: Routledge.

Håkansson, H. and Snehota, I.J. (2000) 'The IMP perspective: Assets and liabilities of business relationships,' in J. Sheth and Parvatiyar (eds.) *Handbook of Relationship Marketing*. London: Sage, pp. 69–94.

Håkansson, H. and Waluszewski, A. (2001) 'Co-evolution in technological development: The role of friction.' *Synergia*, May–August: 171–190.

Håkansson, H. and Waluszewski, A. (2002) *Managing Technological Development. IKEA, the Environment and Technology*. London: Routledge.

Hamel, G. and Prahalad, C.K. (1994) *Competing for the Future: Breakthrough Strategies for Seizing Control of Your Industry and Creating the Markets of Tomorrow*. Boston: Harvard Business School Press.

Hao, X. (2008) *Coping With Complexity: A Study of a Yearly Facelift Car Project at Volvo Car Corporation*. Gothenburg: BAS Publishing House.

Harryson, S.J. (2001) *Managing Know-Who Based Companies: A Multi-Networked Approach to Knowledge and Innovation Management*. Cornwall: Edward Elgar Publishing.

Hatch, M-J. (2011). *Organization Theory: Modern, Symbolic and Postmodern Perspectives*. Oxford: Oxford University Press.

Hawkins, R. and Davis, C.H. (2012) 'Innovation and experience goods: A critical appraisal of a missing dimension in innovation theory.' *Prometheus*, 30(3): 235–259.

Hawkins, R. and Vickery, G. (2008) *Re-Making the Movies: Digital Content and the Evolution of the Film and Video Industries*. Paris: OECD.

Hellgren, B. and Stjernberg, T. (1987) 'Networks: An analytical tool for understanding complex decision processes.' *International Studies of Management & Organization*, 17(1): 88–102.

Hellgren, B. and Stjernberg, T. (1995) 'Design and implementation in major investments—A project network approach.' *Scandinavian Journal of Management*, 11(4): 377–394.

Herreld, J.B. (1998) 'Building smarter, faster organizations,' in D. Tapscott, A. Lowy, and D. Ticoll (eds.) *Blueprint to the Digital Economy: Creating Wealth in the Era of E-Business*. New York: McGraw-Hill, pp. 60–76.

Hippel, E. von (1986) 'Lead users: A source of novel product concepts.' *Management Science*, 32(7): 791–805.

Hofmaier, B. (2002) 'Building arenas for collaborative development in a Swedish context,' in B. Nyhan (ed.) *Taking Steps Towards the Knowledge Society: Reflections on the Process of Knowledge Development*. Luxembourg: Office for Official Publications of the European Communities, pp. 55–62.

Hofmaier, B. (2008) 'Diffusion of technological and organizational innovation as a process of social construction,' in K.G. Hammarlund and T. Nilsson (eds.) *Technology in Time, Space and Mind: Aspects of Technology Transfer and Diffusion*. Halmstad: Halmstad University, pp. 178–202.

Hoholm, T. and Olsen, P-I. (2012) 'The contrary forces of innovation: A conceptual model for studying networked innovation processes.' *Industrial Marketing Management*, 41(2): 344–356.

Huczynski, A. (2012) *Management Gurus*. New York: Routledge.

Jamie, K. (2013) 'New technologies in British pharmacy practice,' in K. Wasen (ed.) *Emerging Health Technology: Relocation of Innovative Knowledge and Expertise*. Berlin and Heidelberg: Springer-Verlag, pp. 53–74.

Jarillo, J.C. (1988) 'On strategic networks.' *Strategic Management Journal*, 9(1): 31–41.

Johanson, J. (1995) 'Marknadsnätverkens uppväxtår och framtid.' *MTC Kontakten*, Jubileumstidskrift, 1995: 7–9.

Johanson, J., Håkansson, H., and Anderson, J. C. (1994) 'Dyadic business relationships within a business network context.' *Journal of Marketing*, 58: 1–15.

Johanson, J. and Mattsson, L-G. (1993) 'The markets-as-networks tradition in Sweden,' in G. Laurent, G. Lilien, and B. Pras (eds.) *Research Traditions in Marketing*. London: Kluwer Academic Publishers, pp. 321–342.

Kafouros, M., Wang, C., and Lodorfos, G. (2009) 'The impact of R&D strategy and firm size in the returns to innovation.' *International Journal of Entrepreneurship and Small Business*, 8(4): 550–566.

Klein, J.T. (2010) 'A taxonomy of interdisciplinarity,' in R. Frodeman, J.T. Klein, and C. Mitcham (eds.) *Oxford Handbook of Interdisciplinarity*. Oxford: Oxford University Press, pp. 15–30.

Knights, D. and Murray, F. (1994) *Managers Divided: Organisational Politics and Information Technology Management*. Chichester: Wiley.

Kunda, G. (1992) *Engineering Culture*. Philadelphia: Temple University Press.

Latour, B. (1986) 'The powers of association,' in J. Law (ed.) *Power, Action and Belief: A New Sociology of Knowledge?* London: Routledge, pp. 264–280.

Lave, J. and Wenger, E. (1991) *Situated Learning: Legitimate Peripheral Participation*. Cambridge: Cambridge University Press.

Leonard-Barton, D. (1998) *Wellsprings of Knowledge: Building and Sustaining the Source of Innovation*. Boston: Harvard Business School Press.

Lester, R. K. and Piore, M. J. (2004) *Innovation—The Missing Dimension*. Cambridge, MA: Harvard University Press.

Lipparini, A. and Sobrero, M. (1997) 'Coordinating multiform innovative process: Entrepreneur as catalyst in small-firm networks,' in M. Ebers (ed.) *The*

Formation of Interorganizational Networks. Oxford: Oxford University Press, pp. 199–219.

Lindholm, S. (1990) *Kunskap: Från Fragment till Helhetssyn.* Stockholm: Allmänna förlaget.

Lomi, A. and Grandi, A. (1997) 'The network structure of inter-firm relationships in southern Italian mechanical industry,' in M. Ebers (ed.) *The Formation of Inter-Organizational Networks.* Oxford: Oxford University Press, pp. 95–110.

Lundgren, A. and Snehota, I. (1998) 'Ekonomisk organisation som nätverk,' in B. Czarniawska (ed.) *Organisationsteori på svenska.* Malmö: Liber Ekonomi, pp. 9–21.

Löwstedt, J. (1985) 'Contingencies or cognitions? Two paths for research on organization and technology.' *Scandinavian Journal of Management,* 1(3): 207–225.

Lütz, S. (1997) 'Learning through intermediaries: The case of inter-firm research collaborations,' in M. Ebers (ed.) *The Formation of Inter-Organizational Networks.* Oxford: Oxford University Press, pp. 146–173.

MacDuffie, J.E. (2011) 'Inter-organizational trust and the dynamics of distrust.' *Journal of International Business Studies,* 42: 35–47.

MacKenzie, D. and Wajcman, J. (eds.) (1985) *The Social Shaping of Technology: How the Refrigerator Got Its Hum.* Milton Keynes: Open University Press.

March, J.G. (1991) 'Exploration and exploitation in organizational learning.' *Organization Science,* 2: 71–87.

Marshall, A. (1919) *Industry and Trade.* London: Macmillan.

Martin, J. (1992) *Cultures in Organizations: Three Perspectives.* Oxford: Oxford University Press.

Miller, H.T. and Fox, C.J. (2001) 'The epistemic community.' *Administration & Society,* 32(6): 668–685.

Mol, A. (2000) 'Actor-network theory: Sensitive terms and enduring tension.' *Kölner Zeitschrift für Soziologie und Sozialpsychologie,* 50(1): 253–269.

Morgan, G. (1997) *Images of Organization.* Thousand Oaks: Sage Publications.

Mulhern, F.J. (1999) 'Customer profitability analysis: Measurement, concentration, and research directions.' *Journal of Interactive Marketing,* 13(1): 25–40.

Murphy, W.J. (1998) 'Making intranets obsolete: Extending the enterprise to partners, suppliers, and customers,' in D. Tapscott, A. Lowy, and D. Ticoll (eds.) *Blueprint to the Digital Economy: Creating Wealth in the Era of E-Business.* New York: McGraw-Hill, pp. 260–282.

Nohria, N. and Eccles, R.G. (1993) *Networks and Organizations: Structure, Form, and Actions.* Boston: Harvard Business School Press.

Nonaka, I. and Takeuchi, H. (1995) *The Knowledge-Creating Company: How Japanese Companies Create the Dynamics of Innovation.* New York: Oxford University Press.

Norton, B. and Smith, C. (1997) *Understanding the Virtual Organization.* New York: Barrons.

Nowotny, H. (1993) 'Re-discovering friction: All that is solid does not melt in air,' in N. Åkerman (ed.) *The Necessity of Friction.* New York: Physica-Verlag, pp. 31–60.

Oborn, E. and Dawson, S. (2010) 'Knowledge and practice in multidisciplinary teams: Struggle, accommodation and privilege.' *Human Relations,* 63(12): 1835–1858.

Orr, J.E. (1996) *Talking About Machines: An Ethnography of a Modern Job.* Ithaca: Cornell University Press.

O'Sullivan, D. and Dooley, L. (2008) *Applying Innovation.* London: Sage Publications.

Ouchi, W. G. (1980) 'Markets, bureaucracies, and clans.' *Administrative Science Quarterly*, 25(1): 129–141.

Péres-Bustamante, G. (1999) 'Knowledge management in agile innovative organizations.' *Journal of Knowledge Management*, 3(1): 6–17.

Perrow, C. (1967) 'A framework for the comparative analysis of organizations.' *American Sociological Review*, 32: 194–208.

Piore, M. and Sabel, C. F. (1984) *The Second Industrial Divide*. New York: Basic Books.

Powell, W. W. (1990) 'Neither market nor hierarchy: Network forms of organization.' *Research in Organizational Behavior*, 12: 295–336.

Powell, W. W., Koput, K. W., and Smith-Doerr, L. (1996) 'Interorganizational collaboration and the locus of innovation: Networks for learning in biotechnology.' *Administrative Science Quarterly*, 41: 116–145.

Powell, W. W. and Smith-Doerr, L. (1994) 'Networks and economic life,' in N. Smelse and R. Swedberg (eds.) *The Handbook of Economic Sociology*. Chichester: Princeton University Press, pp. 368–402.

Prahalad, C. K. and Hamel, G. (1990) 'The core competence of the corporation.' *Harvard Business Review*, 68(3): 79–91.

Preece, D. (1995) *Organizations and Technical Change: Strategy, Objectives and Involvement*. London: Routledge.

Preece, D., McLoughlin, I., and Dawson, P. (eds.) (2000) *Technology, Organizations and Innovation: Critical Perspectives on Business and Management, Vols. I–IV*. London: Routledge.

Preece, D., Steven, G., and Steven, V. (1999) *Work, Change and Competition: Managing for Bass*. London: Routledge.

Provan, K. G., Fish, A., and Sydow, J. (2007) 'Interorganizational networks at the network level: A review of the empirical literature on whole networks.' *Journal of Management*, 33: 479–517.

Rice, M. P., O'Connor, G. C., Peters, L., and Morone, J. (1998) Managing Discontinuous Innovation. *Research Technology Management*, 41(3): 52–58.

Rifkin, J. (2004) *The End of Work: The Decline of the Global Labor Force and the Dawn of the Post-Market Era*. 2nd ed. New York: Jeremy P. Tarcher/Penguin.

Ring, S. P. (1997) 'Process facilitating reliance on trust in inter-organizational networks,' in M. Ebers (ed.) *The Formation of Inter-Organizational Networks*. Oxford: Oxford University Press, pp. 113–145.

Rogers, E. (1995) *Diffusion of Innovations*, 4th edn. New York: The Free Press.

Sager, M., Bragesjö, F., and Elzinga, A. (2013) 'A framework for future studies of personalised medicine: Affordance, travelling, and governance of expertise,' in K. Wasen (ed.) *Emerging Health Technology: Relocation of Innovative Visual Knowledge and Expertise*. Berlin and Heidelberg: Springer-Verlag, pp. 101–124.

Savage, C. M. (1996) *5th Generation Management: Co-Creating Through Virtual Enterprising, Dynamic Teaming, and Knowledge Networking*. Boston: Butterworth-Heinemann.

Schumpeter, J. A. (1934/1968) *The Theory of Economic Development*. Cambridge, MA: Harvard University Press.

Seppänen, R. (2014) 'Who trusts who? The role of individual and organizational level in determining the nature of inter-organizational trust.' *International Journal of Knowledge-Based Organizations*, 4(1): 17–37.

Simmel, G. (1971) *Georg Simmel: On Individuality and Social Forms*. Chicago: University of Chicago Press.

Simmel, G. (1903/2002) 'The metropolis and mental life,' in G. Bridge and S. Watson (eds.) *The Blackwell City Reader*. Oxford: Wiley-Blackwell, pp. 11–19.

Skyrme, J. D. (1999) *Knowledge Networking: Creating the Collaborative Enterprise*. Oxford: Butterworth-Heinemann.

Solow, R. M. (1957) 'Technical change and the aggregate production function.' *Review of Economics and Statistics*, 39 (August): 312–320.

Spek, R. and Spijkervet, A. (1997) 'Knowledge management: Dealing intelligently with knowledge,' in J. Liebowitz and L. C. Wilcox (eds.) *Knowledge Management and Its Integrative Elements*. New York: CRC Press, pp. 31–59.

Stark, D. (2009) *The Sense of Dissonance: Accounts of Worth in Economic Life.* Princeton: Princeton University Press.

Styhre, A. (2010) *Visual Culture in Organizations*. New York: Taylor & Francis.

Swan, J. and Scarbrough, H. (2005) 'The politics of networked innovation.' *Human Relations*, 58(7): 913–943.

Swanson E. B. and Ramiller, N. C. (2004) 'Innovating mindfully with information technology.' *MIS Quarterly*, 28(4): 553–583.

SVT (2012a) 'Bönderna ger upp.' News article (in Swedish), 'Farmers surrender.' www.svt.se/nyheter/regionalt/mittnytt/nu-toms-ladugarden.htm (accessed February 15, 2014).

SVT (2012b) 'Fast i skuldfällan.' News article (in Swedish), 'Stuck in the loan trap.' www.svt.se/nyheter/regionalt/mittnytt/fast-i-skuldfallan.htm (accessed February 15, 2014).

Targama, A. and Wasen, K. (2012) 'Mutual intelligibility and organizational sensemaking: Theorising in action,' in K. Wasen (ed.) *Knowledge Production in Mergers and Acquisitions*. 2nd ed. Gothenburg: BAS Publishing House, pp. 99–126.

Teece, D. and Pisano, G. (1994) 'The dynamic capabilities of firms: An introduction.' *Industrial and Corporate Change*, 3(3): 537–556.

Thorelli, H. B. (1986) 'Networks: Between markets and hierarchies.' *Strategic Management Journal*, 7(1): 37–51.

Tidd, J. (1997) 'Complexity, networks and learning: Integrative themes for research on innovation management.' *International Journal of Innovation Management*, 1(1): 1–22.

Tidd, J., Bessant, J., and Pavitt, K. (2009) *Managing Innovation: Integrating Technological, Market, and Organizational Change*. 4th ed. Chichester: John Wiley & Sons.

Tomkins, C. (2001) 'Interdependencies, trust and information in relationships, alliances and networks.' *Accounting, Organizations and Society*, 26(2): 161–191.

Tönnies, F. (1955/1987) *Community and Association* [Gemeinschaft und Gesellschaft]. London: Routledge & Kegan Paul.

Tsoukas, H. (1996) 'The firm as a distributed knowledge system: A constructionist approach.' *Strategic Management Journal*, 17: 11–25.

Urban, G. L. and von Hippel, E. (1988) 'Lead user analyses for the development of new industrial products.' *Management Science*, 34(5): 569–582.

Vahlne, J-E., Johanson, J., and Andersson, U. (1998) 'Organic acquisition in the internationalization process of the business firm.' *Management International Review*, 37(2): 67–84.

Van de Ven, A. H. (1986) 'Central problems in the management of innovation.' *Management Science*, 32(5): 590–607.

Vedin, B. (1994) *Management of Change and Innovation*. Dartmouth: Aldershot.

Vedin, B-A. (2007) 'What future conceptual and social innovations?' *Journal of Future Studies*, 12(2): 91–100.

Vedin, B-A. (2014) 'Adding to the innovation taxonomy.' *International Journal of Business and Social Research*, 4(2): 50–55.

Wajcman, J. (2008) 'Life in the fast lane? Towards a sociology of technology and time.' *The British Journal of Sociology*, 59(1): 59–77.

Wang, C. and Kafouros, M. I. (2009) 'What factors determine innovation in merging economies? Evidence from China.' *International Business Review*, 18(6): 606–616.

Wareing, M. (2014) 'Using student lived experience to test the theoretical basis of work-based learning.' *International Journal of Practice-Based Learning in Health and Social Care*, 2(1): 35–50.

Wasen, K. (ed.) (2005a) *Knowledge Production in Mergers and Takeovers*. Gothenburg: BAS Publishing House.

Wasen, K. (2005b) 'Person-friendly robot interaction. Social, psychological and technological issues in health care work.' *In Proceedings of the 14th IEEE RO-MAN*, August 13–15, Nashville, TN, USA, pp. 643–648.

Wasen, K. (2010) 'Replacement of highly educated surgical assistants by robot technology in working life: Paradigm shift in the service sector.' *International Journal of Service Robotics*, 2(4): 431–438.

Wasen, K. (2013) 'Introduction,' in K. Wasen (ed.) *Emerging Health Technology: Relocation of Innovative Knowledge and Expertise*. Berlin and Heidelberg: Springer-Verlag, pp. 1–20.

Wasen, K. and Brierley, M. (2013) 'The visual touch regime: Real-time 3D image-guided robotic surgery and 4D and "5D" scientific visualisation at work,' in K. Wasen (ed.) *Emerging Health Technology: Relocation of Innovative Knowledge and Expertise*. Berlin and Heidelberg: Springer-Verlag, pp. 21–51.

Wasen, K. and Lodaya, A. (2012) 'Innovative knowledge networks for creativity and subsidiarity: Managing organisational renewal in health care,' in K. Wasen (ed.) *Knowledge Production in Mergers and Acquisitions*. 2nd ed. Gothenburg: BAS Publishing House, pp. 35–70.

Watts, D. J. (2004) 'The "new" science of networks.' *Annual Review of Sociology*, 30: 243–270.

Weber, M. (1952/1968) *Economy and Society: An Outline of Interpretive Sociology*. New York: Bedminster.

Weiss, A., Wurhofer, D., Lankes, M., and Tscheligi, M. (2009) 'Autonomous vs. tele-operated: How people perceive human-robot collaborations with HRP-2. *In Proceedings of the 4th ACM/IEEE International Conference on Human-Robot Interaction*, March 11–13, La Jolla, CA, USA, pp. 257–258.

Weiss, A., Wurhofer, D., Lankes, M., and Tscheligi, M. (2011) 'Looking forward to a "robotic society"?' *International Journal of Social Robotics*, 3(2): 111–123.

Wenger, E. (1998) *Communities of Practice: Learning, Meaning, and Identity*. Cambridge: Cambridge University Press.

Wenger, E. and Snyder, W. M. (2000) 'Communities of practice: The organizational frontier.' *Harvard Business Review*, 78(1): 129–146.

Westelius, A. (2000) 'Virtuell kontakt och kunskapsspridning – mot ökad demokrati? Om intranäts roll i spridning av kunskap och kontaktskapande inom organisationer.' *IMIT 2000:112*. Stockholm: IMIT.

Wikström, S. and Normann, R. (1994) *Knowledge and Value*. London: Routledge.

Willmott, H. (1997) 'Rethinking management and managerial work: Capitalism, control, and subjectivity.' *Human Relations*, 50(11): 1329–1359.

Ziman, J. (1994) *Prometheus Bound: Science in a Dynamic Steady State*. Cambridge: Cambridge University Press.

Ziman, J. (1996) ' "Postacademic science": Constructing knowledge with networks and norms.' *Science Studies*, 9(1): 67–80.

Zuboff, S. (1988) *In the Age of the Smart Machine*. New York: Basic Books.

Index

For Product Safety Concerns and Information please contact our EU
representative GPSR@taylorandfrancis.com
Taylor & Francis Verlag GmbH, Kaufingerstraße 24, 80331 München, Germany